WARLORDS
OF THE
ANCIENT AMERICAS
CENTRAL AMERICA

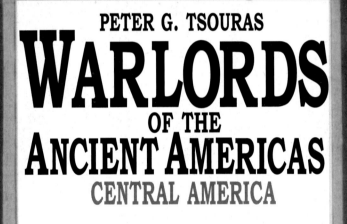

PETER G. TSOURAS

WARLORDS
OF THE
ANCIENT AMERICAS
CENTRAL AMERICA

The battlefield is the place:
Where one toasts the divine liquor in war,
Where are stained red the divine eagles,
Where the jaguars howl,
Where all kinds of precious stones rain from
    ornaments
Where wave headdresses rich with fine plumes,
Where princes are smashed to bits.

                  — *Aztec poem*

ARMS AND
ARMOUR

Overleaf: Part of the mural on the west wall
of the Upper Temple of the Jaguars, Chichén Itzá;
watercolour copy by Adela C. Breton

DEDICATION

When Odysseus wanted to commune with the spirits of the dead, he poured a blood offering into a pit to summon their shades from Hades. That was myth. Scott and Stuart Gentling have surpassed him in reality. As their brushes touched canvas, a magical vision breathed life back into a vanished civilisation of a mighty and terrible splendour. Nezahualcoyotl, the Poet King of Texcoco, rightly described such art as a 'tribute of beauty', and a long-dead Náhuatl poet unknowingly spoke of them in this poem:

> 'The artist: a Toltec, disciple, resourceful, diverse, restless.
> The true artist, capable, well trained, expert;
> he converses with his heart, finds things with his mind.
> The true artist draws from his heart; he works with delight;
> does things calmly, with feeling; works like a Toltec;
> invents things, works skilfully, creates; he arranges things;
> adorns them; reconciles them.'

This book is happily dedicated to Scott and Stuart Gentling, the 'Toltec' brothers from Fort Worth, Texas.

ACKNOWLEDGEMENTS

For exerpts from published material, I wish to gratefully acknowledge the following:

Bernal Díaz del Castillo, *The Discovery and Conquest of New Spain*, published in 1956 by Farrar, Straus & Giroux.

Nigel Davies, *The Aztecs: A History*, copyright 1973 by Nigel Davies. First published in 1973 by Macmillan, London Ltd. First published 1980 by the University of Oklahoma Press, Publishing Division of the University, Norman.

Fray Diego Durán, *The Aztecs: The History of the Indies of New Spain*, translated by Doris Heyden, translation copyright 1964 by the Orion Press, Inc., renewed 1992 by Viking Penguin; used by permission of Viking Penguin, division of Penguin Books, USA Inc.

Frances Gillmor, *The Flute of the Smoking Mirror: Nezahualcoyotl Poet King of the Aztecs*, published in 1965 by the University of Arizona Press.

Fray Bernardino de Sahagún, *The Florentine Codex: General History of the Things of New Spain, Book 12: The Conquest of Mexico*, published in 1979 by the University of Utah Press and the School of American Research.

Arms and Armour Press
A CASSELL IMPRINT
Wellington House, 125 Strand, London WC2R 0BB

Distributed in the USA by Sterling
Publishing Co. Inc., 387 Park Avenue South, New York, NY 10016-8810.

© Peter G. Tsouras, 1996
All rights reserved. No part of this book may be reproduced or transmitted in any form or by any means electronic or mechanical including photocopying recording or any information storage and retrieval system without permission in writing from the Publisher.

British Library Cataloguing-in-Publication Data: a catalogue record for this book is available from the British Library

ISBN 1-85409-237-5

Designed and edited by DAG Publications Ltd. Designed by David Gibbons; layout by

Anthony A. Evans; edited by Gerald Napier; printed and bound in Great Britain.

CONTENTS

PREFACE

The history of the Old World resounds with the deeds of men of war — conquerors and warlords, the founders and breakers of empires. The history of the original inhabitants of the New World, especially Mesoamerica, does not — but not for the lack of such men. These histories in English consistently emphasise either the culture and history in general or the Spanish Conquest. Native Americans, under the tramp of whose feet worlds trembled, are submerged in the broader histories or are secondary characters in the story of the Spanish Conquest. Biographies are almost nonexistent, except, of course, that of Cortés, and the two splendid histories of Nezahualcoyotl and Motecuhzoma I by Frances Gillmor in the early 1960s. Almost nothing has been written in which these Native American conquerors and warlords are centre stage.

Warlords of the Ancient Americas is a history of these men. The story stretches from Tikal of 378 AD to the death of the last Mexica emperor in 1525. In the 1147 intervening years, war scoured as bloody a course as it did anywhere else on this planet. And as elsewhere, civilisation was pushed along new paths, both destructive and creative. These men were the agents of great change and compelling individuals in their own rights. The reader of Mesoamerican history is constantly reminded of parallels with their counterparts of the Old World. In the histories of which we are familiar, the year 378 AD is recognised for the defeat of the Roman Army and the death of the Roman Emperor Valens at the Battle of Adrianople, a pivot of history. History also pivoted in that same year as the warlord of Tikal in Guatemala employed the techniques and cult of the new Venus-Tlaloc warfare now called Star Wars, to conquer the neighbouring kingdom of Uaxactún and kill its king. He set a fire in the Maya lands that would burn for four hundred years and then travel north to scorch the central Mexican source of the cult, the great city of Teotihuacán.

The Tepanec king, Tezozomoc, is often referred to as the Mexican Machiavelli; Nezahualcoyotl relived many of the episodes in the life of King David of Israel; and the Mexica emperor, Ahuítzotl is likened to Alexander the Great. Had the New World discovered the Old, perhaps we might have heard of Machiavelli, the Italian Tezozomoc! Then there is the blood-soaked Tlacaélel, the Mexica Cihuacoatl or Snake Woman, the warrior-priest genius, who is utterly unique in the annals of world history, the man who conceived and fathered the imperial idea that sustained the growth of the Mexica empire. If a match were to be found in the Old World surely it would have to include at least the First Emperor of China and Cromwell and many in between. Cuitláhuac, the ninth emperor or tlatoani of the Mexica, inflicted the greatest single defeat on European arms in the entire conquest of the Americas when he drove Cortés and his combined Spanish and native army out of Tenochtitlan in 1520, killing over 1,200 Spaniards and 4,000-5,000 Indian allies.

The most prominent place in this book is taken by the Mexica tlatoani. They are commonly referred to as Aztecs, a name they never called themselves. Aztec means 'Man of Aztlan', and refers to the people that undertook the great migration that led to the founding of the Tenochtitlan and Tlatelolco, twin settlements of the Mexica on islands in Lake Texcoco. Most sources use the term 'Aztecs' where Mexica would be more precise. I have retained 'Aztec' in those cases where I have quoted these sources and have risked a bit of confusion on the part of the reader rather than tamper with the original source. In every other case I use the 'Mexica'; it is what they called themselves and was the source of the name of modern Mexico. Indeed, it was their very battle cry, 'O Mexica, Courage!' Tenochtitlan means 'City by the Prickly Pear Cactus' and Tlatelolco 'Place of Many Mounds'. Inhabitants of Tenochtitlan were called Tenochca and those of Tlatelolco were Tlatelolca. Both cities were often referred to with the term 'Mexico' such as in Mexico-Tenochtitlan and Mexico-Tlatelolco. The ancient world of the Valley of Mexico, centred around its lakes, was called appropriately Anáhuac (Near the Water). Wherever possible I have retained the spelling that most closely approximates the original personal or place names.

I have relied heavily on quotation of the surviving words of the main characters in order to let them speak for themselves and to give the reader a sense of the rhythm and poetry of Indian oratory. I have also attempted to match the prose style to the colour and drama of these vanished civilisations, whose sense of 'the other', that fundamental difference from our Old World perspectives, is so mesmerising.

The language spoken in Central Mexica from at least Toltec times was Náhuatl which continues in use to this day. Durán refers to it as a language of poetry, infinite metaphors, and great subtlety. All words in Náhuatl are accented on the second to the last syllable. The **x** is pronounced as **sh**; the **h** is spoken with a soft aspiration as in English. The **tl** and **tz** represent single sounds. The **u** used before **a**, **e**, **i**, and **o** is pronounced like the English **w**. **Cu** before vowels is pronounced **kw**. Mexica – may-SHEE-kah and Huitzilopochtli – weets-eel-oh-POHCH-tlee; Tenochtitlan – tay-nohch-TEE-tlahn; Cuitláhuac – Kwee-TLAH-hwac. Many place names were hispanised, simply because Spanish tongues could not pronounce Náhuatl words. Cortés consistently mangled names. Cuauhnahuac (Near the Trees) became Cuernavaca. Tollan became Tula. I have tried to use the spelling that most closely corresponds to the original name, hence Huexotzinco instead of Huexotzingo and Tlaxcallan instead of Tlaxcalla.

I owe a special thanks to the long-dead Spanish friars Diego Durán and Bernardino de Sahagún, and to their anonymous Indian informants, whose labours of love in capturing the passing Mesoamerican world preserved irreplaceable insights into the characters of the ten Mexica rulers and a record of their words. The modern interpreters of Mesoamerican history, Nigel Davies and Ross Hassig, have provided invaluable interpretation of often highly complicated events. The works of Miguel Léon-Portilla and Inga Clendinnen have provided similar explanation of the cultural and religious context of Mexica society. David Freidel and Linda Schele's work on deciphering the history of once hidden events in the Maya glyphs allowed the deeds of Smoking-Frog to emerge from their silence. John B. Carlson's work on the Venus-Tlaloc 'Star Wars' warfare cult has been equally illuminating, and I thank him for providing several of his papers on this subject. I must also thank my colleagues, Terence A. Gardner, for his insights into military techniques, and Vincent Mikolainis for his insights into Native American cultures and for his patient editing. To Christopher P. Tsouras, I am indebted for his superb photographic work.

To Scott Gentling and Stuart Gentling, to whom I have dedicated this book, I owe my heartfelt thanks for making the past come alive with their encyclopaedic and masterful knowledge of the Mexica and for their breathtaking paintings of that lost world. Even more I appreciate the enthusiasm and selflessness of their help. I have tried to do with prose what they have done with their paintings, so that , in Scott's words. . . 'it just might be possible in a very real sense to accompany Bernal Díaz del Castillo when he enters this strange land and be there too when at last he sets foot on the Ixtlapalapan causeway and turns his vision northward to where, dazzling white and green in the distance, out in the vastness of the lake, frightening and grand, the capital comes into view.

Peter G. Tsouras
Lieutenant Colonel, USAR (Ret)
Alexandria, Virginia

THE FIRST CONQUERORS
1
SMOKING-FROG AND THE MAYA WARS (FOURTH CENTURY)

AN IMPORT FROM TEOTIHUACÁN

The world changed for the Maya on the day that the Mexicans came to Tikal in Guatemala. Tikal's subsequent conquest of its neighbour Uaxactún in 378 AD was to knock Maya civilisation into another lane of history. The story of the conquest was the stuff of legend that resounded down succeeding generations.

The names of these war-riors and merchants from Teotihuacán in central Mex-ico are lost. No inscription names them, but their arrival was chronicled on a vase painting, a delegation of turbaned strangers armed with handfuls of atlatl (spearthrower) darts. Undoubtedly, they brought gifts to the king of Tikal, jewel of Maya cities in the

Smoking-Frog name glyph.

southern lowlands of the Petén. Perhaps it was the much-prized dark green obsidian, the razor-sharp edge for tool and weapon. The obsidian deposits near Teotihuacán were one of the foundation piers of empire. 350 obsidian workshops chipped the immense numbers of dart and spear points and the sharp blades for war clubs that were in unquenchable demand everywhere. This monopoly on obsidian and the city's position as the most powerful religious shrine in central Mexico drew power and wealth there like a magnet. By this time, the great construction programme had filled the city centre with immense temples, including what is known today as the Temple of the Sun, an immense stone-faced rubble-cored pyramid greater in volume (1,175,000 cubic metres) than the Great Pyramid in Egypt. Teotihuacán boasted a population estimated at 150,000 in vast single-story apartment-building complexes that included many foreign colonies of merchants and crafts-men. Even the Maya were represented.

About 150 AD a final burst of monumental building in Teotihuacán added the Temple of the Feathered Serpent and its vast Ciudadela com-plex, containing two-thirds the amount of mater-ial in the Temple of the Sun. On this temple, four-ton figures of the gog-gle-eyed Storm god, Tlaloc, and the Feathered Serpent alternate in ascending bands up the structure. They repre-sent the largest sculptural effort in the entire 800-year history of the city. The entire complex was built, as René Millon speculates, when 'an ambitious new ruler with a passion for immortality wished to build a colossal new seat of power and authority. . . The core of the newly emphasized ritual was a cult of sacred-war-and-sacrifice ("Star Wars") associated with the Feathered Serpent deity, the Storm God, and the planet Venus and its cyclical motions.'[1]

The Mexican and Maya worlds had been in steadily increasing contact since the first cen-tury, but the fourth century was to see the beginning of a flood of highland Mexican influ-ence. In the southern Mayan highlands shortly after 400 AD, the Teotihuacános conquered the Mayan city of Kaminaljuyú and rebuilt it as their Mexican capital in miniature. It was no accident that deposits of grey obsidian were located in the vicinity of this new outpost. Monopoly is not only a modern economic term. From there, Teotihuacáno influences in cul-ture, art, and warfare diffused rapidly to the Maya heartland to the north through the

Toltec visitors to a Maya city, found on a bowl at Tikal.

agency of a hardy merchant-warrior (*pochteca*) class. Already a quarter century before, their influence at Tikal was immense. Perhaps the Teotihuacános had chosen Tikal as the funnel of their trade into the rich Maya lowlands and had found willing allies in the kings of that city.

The Teotihuacános bore the emblems of new gods to the Maya lands, the goggle-eyed Tlaloc and the Feathered Serpent, patrons of their great imperial city over 1,100 kilometres to the north. Tlaloc and the Feathered Serpent were fitting twin deities for a city that specialised in weapons exports. They were the imperial essence of Teotihuacán, gods of war, with a complex and compelling theology for waging it, under the aegis of the Great Goddess, chief of the city's pantheon. According to John Carlson, a specialist in Mesoamerican Venus lore, 'Teotihuacán's Feathered Serpent was a representation of Venus, a god of warfare and blood sacrifice, as well as of water and fertility. The goggle-eyed Storm God has also been linked with both warfare and water.'[2] Both gods 'embodied . . . paired attributes of creation and destruction, water and fertility, and warfare

and blood sacrifice. These dual aspects of Quetzalcoatl and Tlaloc, together with the unifying Mother Earth embodiment in the Great Goddess, form the heart of the present inter-

Temple of the Sun, Teotihuacán.

pretation of the Teotihuacán cult of Venus-Tlaloc warfare.'[3] Carlson identifies the role of Venus-Tlaloc warfare:

'. . . the fundamental archetype involves the transformation of human blood into water and fertility, shed under the auspices of these deities through Venus-regulated warfare and ritual sacrifice. This is part and parcel, literally, of the essential Teotihuacán ascendancy in warfare, conquest, and long-distance *pochteca*-style trade and tribute.'[4]

Attempts to strictly identify the sixteenth century Mexica (Aztec) Tlaloc, Feathered Serpent, and Great Goddess of a millennium earlier are difficult. Mesoamerican deities often shared attributes and over time they merged with each other or assumed new attributes. However, the Mexica would have recognised Quetzalcoatl, Tlaloc, and Chalchuihtlicue (Great Goddess) in their own religion.

Venus-Tlaloc warfare (Star Wars) as described by David Freidel, 'involved the conquest of territory and the taking of captives for sacrifice. Most of all, decisions about when and where to do battle became tied to the cycles of Venus and Jupiter. It was a kind of holy war timed by the stars',[5] recently dubbed 'Star Wars'. Venus, the star of strife and ill-omen, became the symbol of war throughout Mesoamerica, and the representative emblem of its cult. As a battle standard, the Teotihuacános carried the War Serpent, which the Maya would call Waxak-lahun-Ubah-Kan. A feather-rimmed disc on a wooden shaft, the War Serpent brought forth the war god when carried into battle. Infinitely more than the symbol of a modern flag, it was the soul of the state or a noble lineage when called forth for battle. 'They saw their great standards of war not only as the representation of the state, but as an embodiment of a potent spiritual being whose presence and performance were critical to their success.' The Teotihuacános also carried a related iconographic device on their persons, a medallion emblazoned with an owl-javelin-shield device repeatedly intertwined with war imagery and sacrifice.

Temple of Quetzalcoatl, Teotihuacán. Feathered Serpent and Tlaloc carvings.

SMOKING-FROG AND THE CONQUEST
OF UAXACTÚN

The Maya had been no stranger to war, but customary Maya warfare, though deadly, was child's play compared to the new arrival from Mexico. Each Maya city possessed a ruling lineage whose ancestors watched over and cared for their descendants and city. These other-worldly ancestors and the gods could only be summoned to advise the Maya and receive their petitions through mystical portals into the other-world. The summoning of these spirits was through a bloody process of auto-sacrifice by the Maya lords. Stingray spines or thorns on knotted strings were pulled through tongues or genitals to produce an ecstasy of pain needed to summon the spirits. Their blood dripped upon paper which was then burnt on the por-

tal's altar, the smoke summoning the ancestors. The blood of captives taken in war was also prized in these ceremonies, and for these captives Maya war was waged. Not just any peasant would do, either. It was only the blood of kings and nobles that was fit for opening the portals. Maya war then was essentially a series of duels among the royal lineages and nobilities of the Maya kingdoms. The level of destructiveness for the common man and his family cannot have been great.

The arrival of the Teotihuacános would change that. Star Wars had built an empire for them in Mexico, whose outposts reached even to Guatemala. Star Wars were for conquest, and conquest demanded armies, sustained operations, and war to the hilt. That was the message the Teotihuacános brought. The lords of Tikal embraced it with overwhelming enthusiasm.

Smoking-Frog, Uaxactún Stela 5.

The recent decipherment of the Maya glyphs has reawakened the names and deeds of these lords: Great-Jaguar-Paw, king of Tikal, and his brother the city's war leader, Smoking-Frog. Of the two, Smoking-Frog was the pivotal figure. The king was an old man when Tikal unleashed the fury of Star Wars on the rest of the Maya world. One can then picture Smoking-Frog as the restless and aggressive younger brother, ready to seize new ideas to further ambition or perhaps a zealous religious convert or both. His image leaps out of the traditional Maya stela depictions of war and sacrifice as a jarring change. He is shown as no Maya lord but is replete in the Tlaloc-Venus war costume of Teotihuacán with its balloon-shaped headdress surmounted by a bird, perhaps the War Emblem Owl associated with Venus. He grips a spear-thrower in his right hand and an obsidian-edged club in his left.

The object of Tikal's ambition was close at hand, the rival city of Uaxactún, less than a day's march to the north. How long the men of Tikal prepared for their first war of conquest is only conjecture. This war of conquest could have been no spur-of-the-moment enthusiasm. But if the Teotihuacános had brought a new theology of war, surely they must have also brought hard lessons on the practical aspects of its execution. The first lesson would have been that advanced ideas of war were based on organisation. It is not inconceivable that Smoking-Frog employed Teotihuacáno captains and mercenaries to train his own warriors. And more than the traditional noble and warrior classes would have been needed in a war of conquest. The Teotihuacános would have advised that numbers as well as skill counted for conquest, especially if the enemy was to be utterly overthrown and occupied. Tikal may have undergone its first mass mobilisation as a large peasant militia was introduced to the concepts of drill and discipline and the handling of weapons. The craftsmen of the city also would have been mobilised to produce the war gear and weaponry needed for such a large force. And here the Teotihuacános would have been helpful with bearer loads of the prized obsidian dart and spear points to be attached to local wooden shafts and the sharp-edged teeth of war clubs inset. War which had been the full-time occupation of maybe a few hundred men in a kingdom such as Tikal, now became the temporary but intense purpose of thousands as they were instructed in the use of new weapons and in the discipline of unaccustomed formations.

The Teotihuacános had introduced the Maya to a thoroughly modern process in the art of war. In contemporary terms coined by Soviet military theorists, the Maya were about to undergo a 'revolution in military affairs', where new ideas mixed with the old to bring about entirely new and superior concepts and methods that would overpower the old. It was not just the throwing spear as an agent of firepower with which the traditional Maya fighting man could not deal, but also the discipline that focused the potential of the new weapon under the guidance of a superior strategy. An analogy is the introduction of the assegai, the short stabbing spear, by the Zulu Shaka over 1,400 years later in Natal. Shaka replaced the light Bantu throwing spear with a

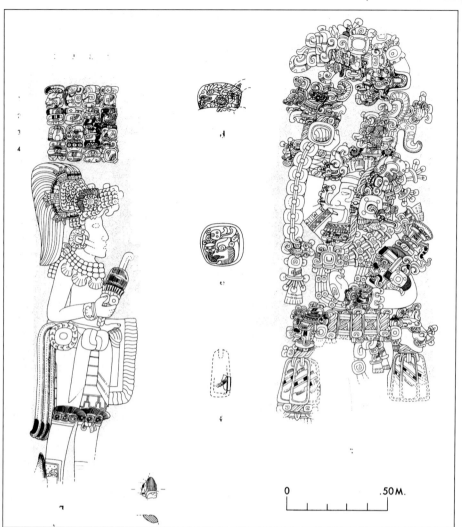

0   .50 M.

stabbing weapon. On the surface it was the opposite of the Teotihuacáno replacement of the Maya stabbing spear with the altlatl dart. However, the essential element that bound the two events was the enhancing force of discipline and strategy over primitive and less bloody forms of warfare.

The two armies that marched from Uaxactún and Tikal could not have been more different. The men of Uaxactún marched out in the traditional way, their king leading the fighting men of his royal lineage and those of the noble lineages that formed the pillars of his kingdom. With them would be the limited number of full-time warriors that formed bands around the king and his nobles. They probably numbered only in the hundreds and were armed with the traditional stabbing spear and hand held weapons. From Tikal came similar bands, but many of them were now armed with the deadly obsidian-tipped atlatl darts and obsidian-edged clubs introduced by the Mexicans. And among these bands were the companies of Teotihuacáno mercenaries in their foreign dress and carriage, comparatively few among the Maya but held in respect by the men they had trained. Behind these were the peasant militia in their several thousands, in plainer dress but clutching bundles of the newly made darts. There was a genuine enthusiasm among the men of Tikal; they could sense they were part of something momentous. Their natural apprehension of change had been swept away by the mysterious powers of the new foreign cult so readily adopted by their king and his feared younger brother, their war leader. A man accustomed to command, he strode at their

14

head of their host in the regalia of the new cult, eager and confident.

Somewhere between the two cities their armies met on 16 January 378 AD. The unsuspecting fighting men of Uaxactún had responded to the traditional challenge to meet their old rivals of Tikal at an appointed place between their two cities. If the men of Uaxactún were suspicious on that day, it did them no good for the new style of war was to strike them like a thunderclap. Perhaps they noticed when the armies arrayed themselves in the stretch of savannah that parted the jungle that there were strange men among their fellow Maya from Tikal. The battle may have begun in the traditional way with challenges issued and met by the various heroes of each city. David Freidel conjures up a vivid picture of when the surprise was sprung.

'It was then that the treacherous enemy lord struck. Smoking-Frog the war chief of Tikal's army, flashed an unseen signal and from the forest came hundreds of hidden warriors. In eerie silence, never once issuing challenge, they hurled a cloud of spears into the thick ranks of the Uaxactún warriors. Shocked and horrified, the king realized the enemy was using spearthrowers, the hunter's weapon, killing people like food animals gathered for slaughter.

'The surprise of the attack was too great and many of his very best warriors fell to the flying lances, unable to get to safety in time. Many died and even more were crippled by a weapon that the king had seen only foreigners use in war, the foreigners who had come into their lands from Teotihuacán, the giant capital to the far west. The hidden hundreds of Tikal's militia advanced, all carrying bunches of light, obsidian-tipped darts and throwing-sticks. He heard one of his kinsmen scream as a spear drove through his cheek, turning his black-painted face red with blood.'[6]

The introduction of discipline and firepower to the Maya battlefield was crushing. The survivors fled to the safety of their unwalled city, thinking the war ended with their defeat. But the men of Tikal and their Teotihuacáno allies were on their heels and followed them among their homes and temples, killing all who resisted. Their king, if he survived the battle, was hunted down by Smoking-Frog as the greatest prize of the war, to be dragged back to Tikal for sacrifice by his brother, the king. How much Uaxactún suffered in its conquest is unknown, but since the city was awarded to Smoking-Frog as his own kingdom, it could not have been much beyond the expected sack and the extirpation of its lineage. The war chief of Tikal would have seen little value in a dead city. More important was a living city whose portal to the other-world he now commanded, for to him the capture of the portal was the culmination of the capture of the city.

'Under the code of this new, foreign battle strategy, Smoking-Frog would be able to bring his own Tikal ancestors to the portal of Uaxactún. He and his descendants would rule not only the people of the city but their venerated ancestors as well. It was an act of audacity beyond imagination: war to take not only the king but also his portal — and if possible to hold that portal captive. For as long as Smoking-Frog and his kin reigned, the people of Uaxactún would be cut off from the loving guidance of their ancestors, a people stripped of their very gods.'[7]

So momentous was the fall of Uaxactún that Great-Jaguar-Paw assumed a new name redolent with his victory — Spearthrower-Owl, which embodied both the new weapon and the Venus War Emblem Owl. He was to enjoy it only briefly, dying the next year in 379 AD. Smoking-Frog then probably assumed the rulership of both cities in this first Maya empire. According to Schele and Freidel, he allowed his brother's son, Curl-Snout, to ascend the throne of Tikal as a vassal on 13 September of that year. An alternative interpretation suggests that Smoking-Frog and Curl-Snout were the same individual with the name Smoking-Frog being only one of this warlord's most important titles. The title, with its fire element, signified that its bearer had introduced to Tikal the Cipactli/Imix fire-drilling cult of Teotihuacán.[8] Curl-Snout is vividly depicted on the stela of his son, Stormy-Sky, in the full war regalia of the Tlaloc-Venus cult, so powerful was the propaganda value and symbolism of Tikal's glory. He was in every respect a Teotihuacáno warrior, bearing Teotihuacáno weapons, the spear-thrower, and wearing 'shell platelet headdresses, a pyrite hip disk, a whole shell collar, and coyote tails. His. . .

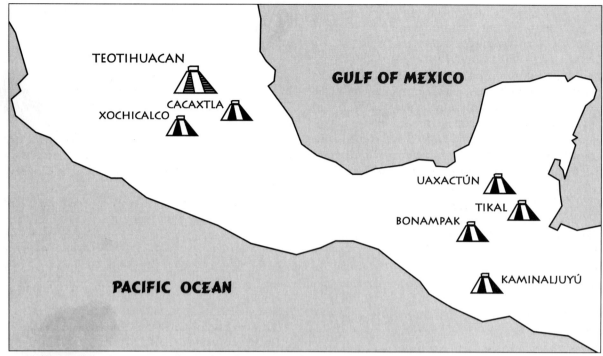

The Realm of Star Wars: from Teotihuacan to Tikal.

shield portrayed a figure with goggles, whole shell earspools, a nosebar, and the "tassel headdress" that identifies the highest ranking Teotihuacános abroad.'9

The goggle-eyed figure was surely Tlaloc, and the disk appears to be the same sort of mirror found on the remains of warriors sacrificed at the dedication of the Temple of Quetzalcoatl at Teotihuacán. Not only the royal lineage exulted in the memory of the conquest. The nonroyal noble lineages as well gloried in the participation of their ancestors in what was to become legend, much as the ancient Greeks proudly claimed descent from the heroes who fought on the plains of Troy.

A striking example was found in the compound of one of the great noble lineages in Tikal. There a ballcourt marker in the shape of an effigy battle standard was erected on 24 January 414 AD by Ch'amak, lineage patriarch, celebrating the participation of the lineage's ancestor in the overthrow of Uaxactún 36 years before. The ballgame had been a feature of Maya culture for centuries by this time, signifying war and sacrifice, but the Maya lord who erected this battle standard marker ordered it built in a thoroughly Teotihuacáno style.

'In the dedication ritual, Ch'amak planted the effigy standard on its platform altar, then called for the Waxaklahun-Ubah-Kan to serve as the path along which the companion spirits of important warriors and lineage heads travelled when they came to participate in rituals. But this same standard could also be used as an instrument for bringing forth the Teotihuacán god of war that these Maya had adopted as their own.'10

The burials of Curl-Snout and his son, Stormy-Sky, are also replete with Teotihuacáno imports. A contemporary burial may even have been that of a high-ranking Teotihuacáno, another indication that a Mexican colony existed at Tikal.

STAR WARS COMES FULL CIRCLE

Smoking-Frog himself ruled at least another eighteen and possibly 26 years before his death. One hundred and twenty-six years later his descendants in Uaxactún were still erecting monuments to celebrate his victory and bask in its reflected glory. For 180 years Tikal would dominate the central Petén, the Maya heartland. Surely its kings must have exploited their new style of war and their lucrative arrangements with Teotihuacán to capitalise on this prestige. So stupendous was the conquest of Uaxactún that Star Wars spread rapidly through all the Maya kingdoms until it had been thoroughly absorbed as an common element of their civilisation, much as the blitzkrieg in 1940 made all armies instant adherents of mobile warfare. One of the last great masterpieces of Maya art, the murals at Bonampak, celebrated an event in another Star War dated at 792 AD.[11] In one of history's ironies, the Mayanised version of Tlaloc travelled back to Mexico and is found in late Classic sites at Cacaxtla and Xochicalco 500 miles away in central Mexico. At Cacaxtla, eighty miles to the east of Teotihuacán, extraordinarily well-preserved murals painted in a magnificent Maya late Classic style adorn the walls of the city's acropolis.

'The jaguar warriors are the obvious winners in the violent encounter with the soldiers dressed as birds. Clothed in tailored pelts arrayed with lavish insignia of rank, grimacing with exertion, they drive flint-sharp lances into the bodies of the bird men, who are unarmed. Many of the vanquished already sprawl in grotesque poses of abject disarray, their blood falling in vivid droplets from hideous wounds. Some, disembowelled in the action, clutch in vain at their exposed entrails.'[12]

Carlson pointed out that, 'The place is crawling with Venus symbols.' Art historian, Breatriz de la Fuente, in awe of the mass of superb artistry, had no doubt, 'The people who made the paintings were Maya.' The people who commissioned them have been identified as the Olmeca-Xicalanca who originated on the Gulf Coast and seized the Teotihuacán corridor linking the trade of the Mexican highlands and rich coast. The Olmeca-Xicalanca were a warrior-merchant people, the very name Cacaxtla means merchant's backpack, and they were most probably seafaring Putún or Chontal Maya, referred to as the 'Phoenicians of the New World'. Their heyday between 650 and about 790 AD when the latest murals were painted, overlapped the decline and fiery fall of Teotihuacán itself around 700 AD. Occupying the rich trade route that had fed Teotihuacán's rise can only have brought Cacaxtla into conflict with the ancient metropolis. The simultaneous rise of the Maya-influenced polity around Xochicalco to the south of Teotihuacán may also have had a hand in the collapse. We know that the religious heart of Teotihuacán, its mile-and-a-half-long avenue of temples, the Street of the Dead, was consumed in fire, and the Cacaxtla culture centred nearby in Cholollan (Cholulla) flourished until destroyed by the Toltecs hundreds of years later. On one of the Cacaxtla murals depicting emaciated captives prepared for sacrifice, there are seven burning temples, the symbols of fallen cities, two in the Teotihuacán style. Can the defeated bird men of the Cacaxtla murals be the lords of Teotihuacán? Was it one of the offshoots of the Maya who burnt the numberless temples of Teotihuacán, and is just such an event painted on the walls of Cacaxtla?[13] If so, the gift of Star Wars to Smoking-Frog 400 years before had come full circle.

1. René Millon, *The Place Where Time Began*, eds. Kathleen Berrin and Esther Pasztory, Thames and Hudson, London, 1994, p. 25
2. John B. Carlson, 'Rise and Fall of the City of the Gods', *Archaeology*, November/December 1993, pp. 61, 64.
3. Carlson, 'Venus-Regulated Warfare and Ritual Sacrifice in Mesoamerica', *Astronomies and Cultures*, ed. Clive L. N. Ruggles and Nicholas J. Saunders, University of Colorado Press, Boulder, 1993, p. 211.
4. Carlson, 'Venus-regulated Warfare and Ritual Sacrifice in Mesoamerica: Teotihuacán and the Cacaxtla "Star Wars" Connection', *Center for Archaeoastronomy Technical Publication No. 7, 1991*, College Park, Maryland, p. 7.
5. David Freidel, Linda Schele, Joy Parker; *The Maya Cosmos*, William Morrow and Company, New York, 1993, p. 296.
6. Linda Schele and David Freidel, *A Forest of Kings*, William Morrow, New York, 1990, p. 152.
7. Ibid., p. 153.
8. Clemency Chase Coggins, 'The Age of Teotihuacan and Its Mission Abroad', *Teotihuacan: Art From the City of the Gods*, eds. Kathleen Berrin and Esther Pasztory, Thames and Hudson, London, 1994, pp. 147-148.
9. Coggins, ibid., p. 147.
10. Freidel et al, *The Maya Cosmos*, ibid., pp. 299-300.
11. Carlson, 'Venus-Regulated Warfare and Ritual Sacrifice in Mesoamerica', ibid., p. 206.
12. George E. Stuart, 'Mural Masterpieces of Ancient Cacaxtla', *National Geographic*, September 1992, pp. 122, 130.
13. Carlson, 'Rise and Fall of the City of the Gods,' ibid., pp. 67-68.

2

TOPILTZIN QUEZALCOATL, OUR LORD THE FEATHERED SERPENT (TENTH CENTURY)

A few hardy conquerors have overthrown kingdoms. Fewer still have overthrown empires — men like Cyrus, Alexander, and Genghis Khan. However, history records only one empire destroyed by a man 500 years in the grave. Such was Topiltzin Quetzalcoatl (Our Lord the Feathered Serpent), the first recognisable personality in ancient Mexican history.

The reality of Topiltzin Quetzalcoatl is dimmed through layers of compounded history and legend. The destruction of the Indian books and the massive die-off of the knowledge keepers from disease only deepened the confusion. One thing is certain. For the Indians of Central Mexico, his achievements were of such a stupendous nature as to make him the progenitor of a golden age of men, a time of greatness. The centre of this Eden was the city of great Tollan and its people the Toltecs. The very name Toltec came to signify perfection in all creative things — the exquisite gem, the supreme artist, and the finest poetry. Driven by the conspiracy of evil men from his throne, he marched east with his followers and set across the fearsome ocean to return to his native land, vowing to return some day to regain his dominion in the year 1 Reed, the year of his birth in the repeating 52-year native calendar cycle.

The collapse of the Toltec empire, with the burning of Tollan about 1168 AD, resounded through Mexican history. The fleeing nobility found refuge in many cities in the Valley of Mexico and nearby, especially in Culhuacán, meaning in Náhuatl 'The Place of Those Who Have Ancestors'. Dead though the Toltec state was, the refugees carried within themselves a

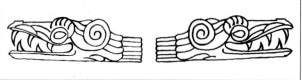

Images of the Feathered Serpent

priceless treasure. In their blood they bore the very legitimacy of this time of perfection. So when a miserable nomadic people, the Mexica, entered the Valley of Mexico in the thirteenth century, craving a place among the civilised peoples they found there, they were careful to acquire, through marriage and adoption, local royalty of the Toltec bloodlines. From this shrewd policy a philosophy of empire was born. The Mexica boldly appropriated the entire Toltec legacy, proclaiming themselves the heirs and regenitors of the Toltec patrimony in a magnificent exercise of imperial propaganda. They had even appropriated the name of the greatest of the Toltec lineages and called themselves the Culhua-Mexica.

Arcane but powerful symbols of the Toltec patrimony were the turquoise diadem and imperial blue mantle of the Mexica emperors. The diadem worn by the Mexica emperors was the exact replica of those carved on royal figures in the ruins of Tollan. The mantle, a simple, tie-dyed pattern of diamonds and dots, stood out in its stark simplicity amid the splendours of the Mexica court. Only eleven of the 38 Mexica provinces provided these imperial cloaks as tribute. At least eight of them were known to have been provinces of the preceding two empires, which both claimed descent from the Toltec lineages of Culhuacán — the thirteenth century Acolhua and fourteenth century Tepanec empires.[1]

Having appropriated the Toltec patrimony with great success, the Mexica did not realise that it contained the seed of their own destruction. Prominent within the Quetzalcoatl legend

The god Ehécatl. (Drawing by Keith Henderson)

was the prophecy of his return to reclaim the patrimony. For almost a hundred years, that remained merely one of the finer and more esoteric points of theology for the Mexica, like the Second Coming of Christ, something unquestioned but so safely distant as to be irrelevant. Then in 1519 the prophecy was seemingly fulfilled with the arrival of Cortés, in the very year in legend that Topiltzin Quetzalcoatl had announced for his return, 1 Reed by the Mesoamerican calendar. The preceding years had been filled with premonitions of doom — strange apparitions, natural disasters, a crushing famine, and sobering lost wars. The moment messengers from the coast brought word of the arrival of Cortés' expedition, the Mexica emperor, Motecuhzoma II, was beaten psychologically. A superstitious and rigid man, he was utterly convinced that the prophecy had been fulfilled. At that moment he was no longer the sovereign of a great empire but merely a caretaker of the dominion of the returned Quetzalcoatl. Cortés was allowed to enter the imperial city, Tenochtitlan, where Motecuhzoma formally abdicated and made submission to the Spanish crown. Despite the incredible blunders by Cortés' subordinates and the subsequent replacement of Motecuhzoma by a less credulous monarch, the Mexica never recovered from this first surrender which helped Cortés break their imperial grip on their subjects. Even after driving Cortés from their city, the Mexica were doomed. Smallpox, Cortés' military genius, and his skill at rallying allies from former Mexica subjects were crushing. When he returned to lay siege to Tenochtitlan, he came not with just a handful of surviving Spaniards but with scores of thousands of Indian allies. In the ensuing siege, Tenochtitlan did indeed become a second Tollan, not the Tollan of the golden age but Tollan of the great fall.

THE MAN WITHIN THE MYTH

Who then was this flesh and blood man who could bring down empires from the grave? That question is one of the greatest mysteries of Mesoamerican history, made more confusing by the fact that the name Quetzalcoatl was both that of a major deity and apparently a title. Ehécatl Quetzalcoatl, with whom our historical figure is associated, was the Wind God as well as a creator god and God of the Morning Star, Venus. The later attribute was closely associated with war in Mesoamerica, and, in fact, was the basis of a war cult that had spread from Teotihuacán to the Maya lands in the preceding Classic era. His emblems were a duckbill mask and conical hat. He was also closely associated with water and fertility and was a god of many faces as most Mesoamerican deities were. There is some evidence that the name Quetzalcoatl was a title of the priest kings of Tollan. The surviving accounts of the history of Tollan and Topiltzin Quetzalcoatl do not always clarify these distinctions and isolate the real and historical man, but:

'One thing is clear. For the Conquest period central Mexican groups within whose corpus of traditional lore this tale occupied a stellar position, it was considered "historical" in a very different way from the frankly cosmological incidents which usually preceded it. Topiltzin Quetzalcoatl, in spite of his concomitant divinity, is essentially a very human figure, who lived at a stated time and who moved through a world very specifically located in space. More striking than his godhead, is his very mundane role as the great ruler of the Toltecs, the fountainhead of all later legitimate political power. Motecuhzoma was clearly claiming descent from a man, not a god.' [2]

The peoples of Central Mexico believed the Quetzalcoatl legend was history as firmly as the Classical Greeks believed in the historicity of Homer's *Iliad*. As with the *Iliad*, trying to sift out the real nuggets of historical information from the embellishments of time is an eternal puzzle. Yet, some shape of the man and his times can be worried out of the tangle.

The rise of Tollan in the middle of the tenth century marked the recovery of civilisation in Central Mexico after the collapse of the Classic world and the great centre of empire at Teotihuacán in the middle of the eighth century. Prominent in Teotihuacán was the image of the god Ehécatl Quetzalcoatl whose image of a feathered serpent even today adorns the ruins of that immense capital. From here the Venus war cult, had spread throughout Mesoamerica. The first genuine historical individual to emerge in the following Post-Classic period is Mixcoatl-Camaxtli. He appears as a catalyst, who set the stage for the remarkable achievements of his son, much as Philip II prepared the way for Alexander.

A conqueror in his own right, Mixcoatl appears to have subdued much of Central Mexico. He is favoured by the goddess Itzpapalotl who periodically explodes creating each time stone sacrificial knives of blue, white, yellow, red, and black. Mixcoatl carries the white knife before him wrapped in a costly mantle, as an adored emblem of divine favour. He first subdues the city of Comallan which offers him food as a peace offering. Next he marches through Cocyama, Huehuetocan, and Pochtlan, bearing before him the white stone knife. Everywhere, his enemies submit. In his last conquest, at Huitznahuac, he meets the princess, Chimalman (Shield-Hand), for whom he develops a tempestuous desire. He finds her alone and naked and proceeds to use her for target practice. The first javelin he aims at her head. It misses as she gently inclines her head. The second strikes her side but bends. The third she catches with her hand. The fourth she catches between her legs. He leaves in bewilderment, and she flees to a cave. But he cannot rid himself of his fascination and returns to search for her in vain. Finally he forces the women of the city to lead him to her. Again she appears before him defenceless and naked, and again he throws the four darts with the same result. Thoroughly impressed, he takes her to bed. Another version, probably closer to the actual event, describes Chimalman as a woman of the Valley of Cuernavaca which Mixcoatl has invaded. He shoots at her with an arrow only to watch her effortlessly deflect it with her hand. 'Amazed by this feat, Mixcoatl left his weapons and took Chimalman as his wife.'[3]

From their union Quetzalcoatl is born. He is also called Ce Acatl (1 Reed) after the year of his birth. His mother died in childbirth, and he is given to her parents to raise. Ce Acatl's ascent to the throne then wound through the travail of a great religious experience. Leaving his grandparents as an adolescent, he spent the next seven years in the mountains alone, doing penance, drawing his own blood as an offering to the gods in supplication for their aid in becoming a great warrior. Now in his young manhood and fortified with the certainty of divine approval, he rejoins his father and accompanies him on further conquests beginning at Xiuhucan where he accomplishes his first deeds of valour by taking captives. Shortly after this victory, the young prince's ascent to the throne was blocked by his uncles, Apanecatl, Zolton, and Cuilton, who conspired to murder him. In one version of the legend, it is his own jealous brothers who repeatedly try to murder him. Enraged by their failure and by Mixcoatl's continuing favour for the young prince, they murder the old man to prevent the succession. With Mixcoatl's protection removed, the royal uncles circle for the kill. Ce Acatl, however, has found his father's remains and desires to inter them in the temple of Mixcoatepetl (Cloud Serpent Mountain). The uncles, looking for the right pretext to eliminate him, insist on dedication rites that the prince cannot possibly meet. They demand he sacrifice ferocious animals such as cougars and eagles. Instead, he enlists these animals in his cause. At the altar Ce Acatl confounds his uncles, and they attack him in the sacred precinct.

'And the uncles were very angry then, and they started at once. Apanecatl led the way, hurriedly scaling the temple. But immediately Ce Acatl rose up, and striking him full in the face sent him tumbling down, and he fell to the base of the mountain. Next he seized Zolton and Cuilton and as the animals blew on the

Topiltzin Quetzalcoatl. (Drawing by Keith Henderson)

fire, then he put them to death; he spread them with chili and slashed their flesh; and when he had tortured them, then he cut open their breasts. And then Ce Acatl set out to make conquests.'[4]

Ce Acatl had struck dead the first of them, Apanecatl, with a sacred vessel. He tore the hearts from the other two in sacrifice to the murdered Mixcoatl.

The legends are silent on the details of Ce Acatl's ascent to kingship except that he was of such martial repute that the people of Tollan chose him for his valour to be their ruler. His decisive elimination of his rivals would also have been an impressive recommendation. It is not certain whether Tollan was the capital of his father's hegemony. In one account, he inherits the rulership of Culhuacán after the victory over his uncles. Some of the legends place him in other cities such as Tollantzinco where he built his house of penance, his turquoise house of beams. In either case, his martial abilities must have been twinned with a powerful religious message for the people of Tollan chose him as their high priest as well as king.

Once established in Tollan, Ce Acatl becomes associated with the name Topiltzin Quetzalcoatl (Our Lord the Feathered Serpent), surely a title. He then ushered in a reign of unprecedented moral and political order and of such prosperity that it forever became synonymous with the perfect state among the peoples of Central Mexico. The state of political order may have been based upon a strong empire, a triple alliance of cities, similar to the Mexica empire that Cortés encountered. Allied but junior to Tollan were the cities of Culhuacán and Otompan. Significantly, Culhuacán was to be the inheritor of Toltec legitimacy after the fall of Tollan. This Toltec triple alliance appears to have lasted 191 years from its possible founding by Quetzalcoatl.[5]

The reign of Topiltzin Quetzalcoatl was the great event in the pre-Conquest history of Mexico that set the pattern for all else to follow. H. B. Nicholson described it:

'His role during this period seems to have been a familiar double one, sacerdotal-secular. It is very likely that he was an important religious innovator, who introduced significant new auto-sacrificial rites and attempted to advance the cult of an older creator-fertility god symbolized by the feathered serpent, whose name he seems to have adopted as a title. In addition, he apparently operated as a patron of the arts and crafts and certain intellectual activities, particularly calendric. Although the central Mexican core group [of histories] does not usually stress this and no formal lists of conquest after his ascension are given . . . he undoubtedly made efforts to build up the political power of his capital, for his role as political legitimizer is so strongly stressed in so many sources. In short, he seems, like Harun-al-Rashid, to have ruled at a time of great prosperity and cultural and political growth, a "golden age", and to have been given a great deal of credit for it.[6]

And golden it was in the memories of the peoples that followed. Quetzalcoatl's vassals, according to the best of the surviving sources, were supreme artisans in all manner of skills such as the working of precious stones, goldsmithing, and featherwork. Together with 'wisdom', all these wondrous crafts began with Quetzalcoatl. He built palaces of jade, gold, red shell, white shell, wooden beams, turquoise, and lustrous green quetzal feathers. His people were also rich beyond measure. The yield of the earth grew to enormous sizes and in rich variation. Squashes were enormous, maize ears as big as the manos that ground the kernels, and amaranth bushes so big they could be climbed like trees. Cotton yielded itself not just in simple white but rivalled the rainbow in its natural colours of red, yellow, rose, violet, blue-green, blue, green, orange, brown, grey, dark yellow, and tawny. The land abounded in priceless birds of brilliant plumage as well as sweet-singing songbirds. Cacao grew copiously and in an array of colours. The people were loaded down with their gold and jade. Scarcity and famine had been banished from the land and the memory of man.

Archaeology supports the memory of great prosperity and cultural achievement that spread its influence and commerce further than that of fabled Teotihuacán, as far as Costa Rica and Nicaragua and the pueblos of the Anasazi in the American south-west. 'A sizeable number of artisans supported a variety of handicraft workshops as witnessed in the vari-ety of wares found throughout the site, including pulque cups, braziers, censers, bowls, cylinder jars, jewelry.'[7] There were comparable skills lavished in the treatment and fine embellishment of its monumental architecture. 'Toltec architecture acquired new contrasts and patterns, becoming one of the finest expressions of artistic integration among America's Indian cultures.'[8]

So great were the artistic and creative powers of the Toltecs in the memories of their successors, that their very name became synonymous with excellence. The name Toltec or *Toltecatl* referred to a 'refined person who had great knowledge and artistic abilities'. The term, 'Toltecayotl' came to mean 'wonderful artist'. The name of the city itself, Tollan, became synonymous with 'great city', 'a place of abundant culture' or 'an authoritative centre of cultural order'. This memory lived on in an Mexica poem:

> 'The artist: a Toltec, disciple, resourceful,
> diverse, restless.
> The true artist, capable, well trained,
> expert;
> he converses with his heart, finds things
> with his mind.
> The true artist draws from his heart;
> he works with delight;
> does things calmly, with feeling;
> works like a Toltec;
> invents things, works skillfully, creates;
> he arranges things;
> adorns them; reconciles them.'[9]

In later times the title of 'Tollan' was transferred only to the greatest of the cultural centres such as Tollan Cholollan (Cholulla) with its great temple of Quetzalcoatl.[10]

The most intriguing element of the Quetzalcoatl legend was Topiltzin's aversion to human sacrifice emphasised by so many of the Indian sources. They relate how he would sacrifice only butterflies and flowers to his namesake deity and attempted to abolish human sacrifice.[11] Some modern scholars tend to dismiss these assertions as desperate attempts by post-Conquest Indians to prove they had at least one semi-respectable deity. Surviving codices show Ehécatl Quetzalcoatl inflicting mutilations on prisoners. His cult in immediate pre-Conquest

Toltec warriors scout the coast of the Maya Yucatán.

times did not seem to show an aversion to human sacrifice. Certainly there was nothing pacific about the Toltecs. The ruins of Tollan abound in evidence of a warrior cult, and other stories of Topiltzin cite him as the creator of military orders of knights such as the Eagles and Jaguars of the later Mexica. Evidence of skull racks have also been found. The most prominent of such features were the 34 atlantes columns of the temple of Tlahuizcal-pantecuhtli on top of the chief pyramid of Tollan, each carved in the shape of an individual warrior.

'The atlantes are typical of the grim men-at-arms who proliferate in the art of Tula: Toltec warriors wore a heavy pad of quilted cotton on the left arm as a protection against arrows and a round shield strapped on the back; their sandals are often decorated with feathered serpents, and their headgear, as worn by the atlantes, is a kind of pillbox-shaped hat, topped by quetzal plumes and carrying in front a bird flying downwards, a favourite Mexican adornment or symbol, both in early times and late.

On their breasts these Toltec warriors wear a butterfly emblem, so stylized as to be barely recognizable as such.'[12]

While the question of the exact nature of Topiltzin's faith must be left hanging, it seems that his downfall was due to a religious conflict within Tollan itself. The sources unite in describing the machinations of a rival god to Ehécatl, the warlike Tezcatlipoca (Smoking Mirror) who conspired to destroy Topiltzin's kingship by undermining his moral authority as a chaste and abstinent ruler. Tezcatlipoca was most likely the high priest of this god, bearing the same name, much as Topiltzin shared Ehécatl's name. He is seen as the cause of disharmony in the evil he causes the Toltecs and conspires with others to depose Topiltzin.

'He must abandon his city; we will live there.
    Let us make some wine, some *pulque*,
And let us give it to him to drink.
    Let us corrupt him,
So that he may no longer live in divine
    favour.'[13]

The likeness of the bearded Topiltzin Quetzalcoatl is perhaps seen in this figure of a Toltec warrior attacking Maya warriors on a gold repoussé diskcfound in the sacred well at Chichén Itzá.

In the guise of an old man, he tricks Topiltzin into getting drunk on exquisite pulque and then encourages him to call his sister, Quetzalpetlatl, from her devotions to join him in his revelry. She imbibes as well, and they both fall into carnal sin. Horrified at his fall from grace, he abandons the kingship of Tollan probably in 987 AD, calling upon the common people to follow him into exile. Perhaps this appeal to the lower classes is an indication of the power of Tezcatlipoca's cult among the aristocracy and warrior classes. The sources show that at this time a great split occurred among the Toltecs as many elected to follow their lord into exile.[14]

After a long journey, Topiltzin Quetzalcoatl and his followers reached Tlallapan (Red Land), thought to be in Yucatán. There he vanishes from history according to the Mexican sources. Some say he throws himself on a funeral pyre, others that he disappears into the sea, or that he boards a raft of serpents and departs to the east vowing that his descendants will return to claim his patrimony in the year 1 Reed. At this distance he has simply fallen off the edge of the world from the viewpoint of Central Mexico. It is this departure and its prophecy that would come back to haunt the Mexica emperor.

THE CONQUEST OF THE MAYA YUCATÁN

Though Topiltzin Quetzalcoatl had disappeared from the chronicles of Central Mexico, there is no doubt that a great Toltec conqueror burst into the Yucatán at exactly the same time, in the Mayan reckoning to a calendar cycle, Katun 4 Ahau, ending in 987 AD. The Mayans whom he furiously assaults and subdues call him Kukulcan, in Mayan *Kukul*, 'feathered', and *can*, 'serpent' — the Feathered Serpent. Is this the same Quetzalcoatl who fled to Tlallapan? If so, the association of Tlallapan with the Yucatán and the coincidence of dates is a neat fit.

This time there is no ambiguity in the native sources. This Toltec Feathered Serpent exults in human sacrifice and the altars of the new kingdom he carves out of the Maya lands drip red with blood. The archaeological evidence also points to a cruel and violent conquest. The Mexicans may have thought Topiltzin Quetzalcoatl disappeared on a raft of serpents to the east, but archaeological finds in Yucatán clearly show that a conquering bearded Feathered Serpent arrived along their coast from the west. The Toltecs may have come in alliance with a sea-coasting merchant people, the Mayan Itzá, who had already been heavily exposed to Mexican influences.[15] The seaborne conquest must have fired the imagination of later generations; its depiction is found on the murals of the Temples of the Warriors and Jaguars in Chichén Itzá and on some of the golden discs found in the city's Sacred Cenote. Michael Coe describes the awesome assault.

'The drama opens with the arrival of the Toltec forces by sea, most likely along the Campeche shore, where they reconnoiter a coastal Maya town with whitewashed houses. In a marine engagement in which the Maya come out in rafts to meet the Toltec war canoes, the former suffer the first of their defeats. Then the scene moves to the land, where in a great pitched battle (commemorated in the frescoes of the Temple of the Jaguars) fought within a major Mayan settlement the natives are again beaten. The final act ends with the heart sacrifice of the Maya leaders, while Feathered Serpent himself hovers above to receive the bloody offering.'[16]

The conquest of the Yucatán was a long and bloody affair. The Mayan kingdoms summoned tremendous powers of resistance. The first Toltec onslaught came straight south from the coastal trading centre at Isla Cerritos against the kingdom of Izamal which boasted one of the largest pyramid temples in the region. Izamal was overthrown in the first rush. Then the Toltecs struck at Yaxuná, an ancient centre, on the border between the two strongest Mayan powers, the kingdom of Cobá and the Puuc states. In the featureless, riverless plain of the Yucatán, Yaxuná had two important geographic markers, its great deep natural well or cenote and its massive pyramids. It was a natural objective, the weak join between two natural allies. At Yaxuná the Mayan alliance stopped the Toltec advance and immediately began construction of the greatest of all Mayan building projects, a stone causeway road over

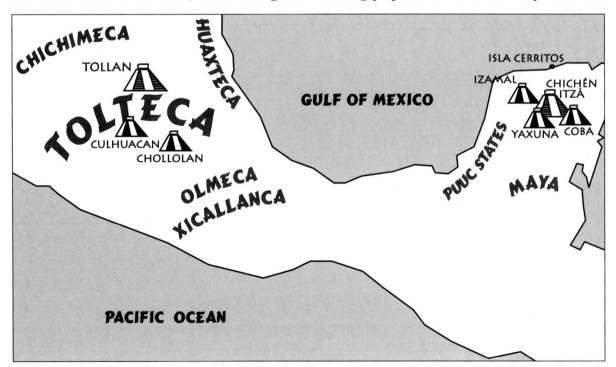

The Toltec World

Toltec warrior on a bas relief at Chichén Itzá.

100 kilometres long, linking Cobá with Yaxuná. The Mayans quarried 750,000 tons of stone for the project. This causeway was not only a political statement of the ownership of Yaxuná but a military highway to speed Mayan armies to the strategic centre of the Yucatán. As the forward defence against the Toltecs, Yaxuná expanded and pushed a screen of outpost settlements halfway to Chichén Itzá.[17]

Temporarily rebuffed the Toltecs established their capital at a nearby site, one that already possessed a great cenote, an old Mayan city probably called Uucil-abnal (Seven Bushes). Later ages would call it Chichén Itzá. From there they continued to wage bitter and relentless war against the Mayan confederacy.

'Ultimately, however, the efforts of the Puuc cities and Cobá to remain in power in the center of the northern lowlands failed. After many years of bitter fighting, Chichén Itzá's armies won the battle on the fields of Yaxuná. The rebuilding of the city ended almost as soon as it had begun. Quarried blocks of stone lay strewn at the base of the ancient platforms,

abandoned in hasty retreat before the masons could use them. The occupants of the perimeter communities likewise fled, leaving their little decorated palaces unattended and their homes to fall into ruin.'[18]

The Puuc states collapsed, and their cities were eventually abandoned. Cobá went into a long and steady decline at the same time. Within short order, the Toltec conquerors extended their sway across the whole of the northern Yucatán, creating the largest state the Mayan lands had ever seen, an empire in the style of Central Mexico and great Tollan. Chichén Itzá grew into a magnificent capital that successfully blended Toltec and Mayan architectural and cultural themes. The conscious blending of cultures was probably the secret of the success of the new empire, for it co-opted and included the conquered Mayans in the scheme of empire. In many ways, though, Chichén Itzá appears to have been created as a conscious copy of great Tollan, over 1,500 kilometres away. Carved Feathered Serpents and warriors are everywhere. Most

Temple of the Warriors at Chichén Itzá. Left, as seen from the Castillo. Right, Feathered Serpent columns of the temple entrance.

telling was the forest of columns supporting a great hall at the base of the Temple of the Warriors, an unmistakable and grander reproduction of one of the most important temples at great Tollan, Pyramid B. Each column was carved with the likeness of an individual warrior, bringing to mind the atlantes in great Tollan. Was this evidence of the yearning of the disposed Topiltzin Quetzalcoatl to replace his lost kingdom with a splendid replica? Was this conquering Toltec warlord indeed the same Topiltzin Quetzalcoatl who founded the glory of great Tollan, left an indelible imprint on an entire civilisation, shepherded a nation on a great migration, and then led them to carve out a new empire? If so, then nothing was beyond this man.

Like Alexander, with whom an earlier analogy was made, the memory of Quetzalcoatl-Kukulcan remained positive in the memory those he conquered. The Spanish chronicler, Bishop Landa, wrote of the Mayan historical sense of the man: 'They say he was favorably disposed, and had not wife or children, and that after his return he was regarded in Mexico as one of their gods and called Quetzalcoatl; and they also considered him a god in Yucatan on account of his being a just statesman.'[19]

HOW MANY QUETZALCOATLS?

The preceding pages have reflected a traditional understanding of the Quetzalcoatl legends. However, the historian, Nigel Davies has presented another conclusion — that Topiltzin was not the first ruler of great Tollan but rather almost the last, some two centuries later. The confusion revolves around the name — Quetzalcoatl, for the god, as a title, and for a particular individual. Adding to the confusion were the different year count systems used by various pre-Conquest sources. By the time of the Conquest, some 400 years after the fall of Tollan, the three had become entangled in a Gordian Knot of legend, myth, and history.

Examples of the similar structures at Tollan and Chichén Itzá. Upper, Temple of Tlahuizcalpantecuhtli, Tollan. (Drawing courtesy © Scott Gentling, photographed by David Wharton). Lower, Temple of the Warriors, Chichén Itzá.

Davies makes the point that the symptoms surrounding Topiltzin's fall are those of a *fin de siècle*, an exhausted and degenerate ending rather than vigorous beginning of empire. The story survives precisely because it marks that very heroic ending of a civilisation, a last brilliant flash of glory, much as the saga of the Trojan War and its heroes survived the collapse of Bronze Age Greece while most earlier sagas disappeared.

The Toltec empire was born of the union of two distinct peoples in the city of Tollan in the early tenth century — the semi-barbarian Chichimeca who arrived from the north-west and the civilised Nonoalca from the Gulf Coast. The latter had been part of the diaspora of peoples from the collapse of Teotihuacán in the eighth century and were the bearers of its remnant high culture. They brought with them the cult of the god Quetzalcoatl, which they had carried with them from Teotihuacán. At the

same time, a Mayan people, the Itzá, from the same region and with whom the Nonoalca had close relations, migrated to Yucatán. The vigour of the Chichemec-Nonoalca hybrid bred an imperial state in which the Quetzalcoatl cult thrived. Tollan alone never had the population base to support widespread conquest, but in league with other cities such as Otompan and Culhuacán respectively at the northern and southern ends of the great lagoon, was able to conquer a considerable tributary empire in Central Mexico. It was in this early period of expansion that Toltec adventurers travelled along well-known Nonoalca-Itzá cultural roads to seize Chichén Itzá and ultimately conquer most of northern Yucatán. The new Toltec centre became something of a twin to Tollan rather than just a colony. Davies ascribes the great similarities of the two imperial cities to a continuous cross-fertilisation of ideas and styles. He contends that the excellence of the monuments of both cities was the result of superior Mayan artisans working under Toltec direction, first in Chichén Itzá. In effect, Tollan is a copy of Chichén Itzá rather than the other way around.

'. . . if the Toltecs brought a new spirit to Chichen, it does not follow that they invented the art forms which it inspired. Not only are certain Chichen buildings older than those of Tula; its art is also richer and more versatile and in this respect Tula's inferiority cannot be denied. One has only to study the two great ball-courts to see that the one flanking the Tula plaza is a pale if not pitiful reflection of its Chichen counterpart. . .'[20]

The historical Topiltzin appears some 200 years later when Toltec power is on the wane. In the north-west the outposts of civilisation have receded close to Tollan itself as more Chichimeca drift into the empire, much as the Goths and other Germans infiltrated the late Roman Empire. The earlier Toltec conquest of the great centre of Cholollan to the south two generations before was now threatened. In another parallel with Rome, about 1125 AD the Toltecs recruit Chichimec war bands to come to their assistance and relieve Cholollan. One such warband, under a leader named Mixcoatl, detours on the road to Cholollan, lured by the more easy pickings in the heart of the Toltec empire. So weak have the Toltecs become that he makes an arc of conquest through the northern Valley of Mexico and finally captures the second city of the empire, Culhuacán. Mixcoatl repeats a sequence already honoured in the Old World, that of a barbarian war leader recruited as a mercenary by a decrepit civilisation that soon finds itself the victim. In another universal move, Mixcoatl married a high-borne lady, Chimalman, whose hand helped facilitate or cement his control of Culhuacán. The annals suggest that he saved the woman from being used by his men for target practice, a more gallant interpretation than the one cited earlier. From this union, Ce Acatl, the later Topiltzin, was born.

Clearly the Toltec empire was tottering if it could not prevent a rogue barbarian from capturing its second city in its own heartland. Tollan must have felt relieved when Mixcoatl was murdered by his brothers. It was a false sense of security for the Toltecs. The young prince Ce Acatl is not faint-hearted and slaughters his uncles to secure his throne. From there he boldly marched on great Tollan itself about 1150 AD, brushing aside any resistance by existent dynasties. The young conqueror now gives Tollan its last flush of glory as he embarks on a career of conquest and assumes the title of Topiltzin Quezalcoatl. It is not clear whether they are reconquests of tribute states broken away or new conquests by a dynamic young warrior king. The list of conquests stretches from the southern Valley of Mexico to Yucatán, and surely has been mingled with legendary and other historical events. Yet a core of mighty events is remembered in this last burst of sunset splendour, *à la* the Trojan War, that became so firmly fixed in the cultural memory of Mesoamerica. Topiltzin's reign, however, almost immediately became ensnared in an array of intractable problems that had led to Tollan's decline. The north-western marches of the empire had receded to a dangerous proximity to Tollan itself. Topiltzin himself was living proof of the power of the Chichimeca pressure within and without. To the north-east, the Huaxtec peoples were exerting a strong pressure on the empire. Internally, the condominium between the earlier Chichimeca and Nonoalca peoples, who had never fused into a

single race, had strained to the breaking point. An element of this strain was reflected in the rulership of Tollan. Most of the accounts of Topiltzin's rule speak of a contemporary figure named Huemac who conspired against him. There appears to have been a joint Toltec rulership in Chichén Itzá which provided a stability that allowed them to rule in Yucatán for 200 years. Perhaps Topiltzin had forced his way into such a joint rulership as a senior member, but it was a rulership deep in decay and without the virility that had built and sustained the empire.

The subsequent struggle between Topiltzin and Huemac was to become one of the great antagonisms of history. Huemac, the villain of the story, appears to have been a Nonoalca and a member of one its ruling dynasties. The Chichimec faction rallied around the new ruler, Topiltzin. The cults of the gods Tezcatlipoca and Quetzalcoatl also seem to have come in conflict. Tradition has Huemac and the Nonoalca favouring the cult of Tezcatlipoca and Topiltzin and the Chichimeca favouring Quetzalcoatl. The annals also speak of this contest in the context of a general moral decadence. Into this nest of faction and conspiracy, enters a woman who plays a critical part in sowing dissention. In this morass, Topiltzin is eventually trapped and his moral authority weakened.

Against this background of conspiracy, Topiltzin was suddenly faced with a major external military threat from a Huaxtec confederation of three kings. Threatened from within and without at the same time, Topiltzin attempted to buy off the Huaxteca with rich gifts but only whetted their appetites. They seized outlying provinces and then marched on Tollan itself. Topiltzin was able to secure a long truce which, considering his weakened position, must have required a substantial danegeld payment. Predictably the Huaxtec kings returned. This time determined to fight it out, Topiltzin had assembled two large armies. The struggle lasted three years. In a great battle in which Topiltzin himself waded into the fray like a Homeric hero, the Huaxteca prevailed. He fled to Tollan with the victors hard on his heels, but the city was now empty of its ancient martial hardness. He must have fled again just ahead of the enemy who thoroughly sacked the city, leaving its imperial

The panorama of Precolumbian Mexican civilisation with Quetzalcoatl departing to the coast in his serpent boat. (Painting by Diego Rivera)

centre of temples and palaces in flame. The year has been given variously as 1168 or 1175 AD. Did he look over his shoulder at the flames licking the horizon as he escaped toward Cul-huacán? As the Huaxtec kings loaded up their loot on the backs of its newly enslaved inhabitants, Topiltzin had found a refuge in the caves of Xico, near Chalco at the southern end of the

Valley of Mexico. One last battle was fought between the invaders and the remnants of the Toltecs led by Topiltzin's sons, Xilotzin and Pochotl. Nothing was spared the fugitive king. The Toltecs were defeated and Xilotzin captured, presumably to end his life on a sacrificial stone.[21]

The fall of Tollan was fixed in the Mesoamerican mind as a cultural cataclysm as firmly as the fall of Rome was in the European mind. The imperial centre of Tollan was put to the torch in a conflagration that turned adobe into burnt bricks. Tollan's vast columned halls that were such a feature of imperial Toltec architecture, roared — their immense wooden roofs burned from end to end in a continuous sheet of flames. Above them, gushing their own flames in single pyres, were the temples atop the pyramids. The 34 giant atlantes – the warrior columns that upheld the temple of the Lord of the Dawn, were wreathed in their own fire as the roof timbers crashed among them.

Huemac emerged as the ruler of a scorched shadow of a once splendid city. The empire had collapsed and with it the tribute wealth that sustained an imperial centre. Much of the population had also disappeared, either in the Huaxtec war or in a number of earlier migrations of disaffected groups of Chichemeca and Nonoalca. Huemac ruled only briefly and none too easily. Within a short time, he too was forced from power and fled for his life. Unlike Topiltzin, though, he was to find no safety. He eventually hanged himself on Chapultepec. Topiltzin may have had the last laugh after all. He appears to have retained control of Culhuacán where he ended his days and where his dynasty is traced to at least 1321 AD.

1. Patricia Rieff Anawalt, 'Riddle of the Emperor's Cloak', *Archaeology*, May/June 1993, pp 30-36.
2. H. B. Nicholson, *Topiltzin Quezalcoatl: A Problem in Mesoamerican Ethnohistory*, doctoral thesis, Cambridge, MA, Harvard University, 1957, pp. 313-314.
3. Fray Diego Durán, *The Aztecs: The History of the Indies of New Spain*, Orion Press, New York, 1964, p. 327.
4. 'Leyenda de los Soles', trans. John Bierhorst, *Four Masterworks of American Indian Literature*, Farrar, New York, Straus & Giroux, 1974, p. 21.
5. Nigel Davies, *Ancient Kingdoms of Mexico*, Penguin Books, Harmondsworth, Middlesex, 1983, p. 143.
6. Nicholson, *Topiltzin Quezalcoatl of Tollan*, pp. 318-319.
7. David Carrasco, *Quetzalcoatl and the Irony of Empire*, The University of Chicago Press, Chicago, 1982, p. 75.
8. Jorge E. Hardoy, *Pre-Columbian Cities*, Walker and Company, New York, 1973, p. 83.
9. 'Códice Matritense de la Real Academia' VIII, fol. 115 v.; Miguel León-Portilla, *Pre-Columbian Literatures of Mexico* University of Oklahoma Press, Norman and London, 1986.
10. Carrasco, *Quetzalcoatl and the Irony of Empire*, p. 76.
11. Topiltzin Quezalcoatl's aversion to human sacrifice and his depictions as being heavily-bearded, highly unusual for an Indian, have led to speculation as to whether he was in reality a Viking or Christian European sailor or adventurer washed up in Mexico over 500 years before Columbus. A Muslim from North Africa, for that matter, under similar circumstances would have shown no less horror at human sacrifice. Until more definitive proof is found, the speculation remains little more than intriguing entertainment.
12. Davies, *The Ancient Kingdoms of Mexico*, p. 134.
13. 'Historia de la Literatura Náhuatl', quoted in Fray Diego Durán, *The Aztecs: The History of the Indies of New Spain*, Orion Press, New York, 1964, p. 327.
14. Perhaps the warrior cult and human sacrifice imprint in the ruins of Tollan were latter manifestations of the triumph of Tezcatlipoca's cult built after Topiltzin Quezalcoatl's exile?
15. Coe, *The Maya*, p. 142. Coe argues that 'According to the late Maya scholar Ralph Roys, the accounts of this great event are seriously confused with the history of a later people called the Itzá, who moved into the peninsula during the next Katun 4 Ahua, in the thirteenth century, and gave their name to the formerly Toltec site of Chichén'.
16. Michael D. Coe, *The Maya*, 5th edition, Thames and Hudson, New York, 1993, pp. 145-146.
17. David Freidel and Linda Schele, *A Forest of Kings: The Untold Story of the Ancient Maya*, William Morrow, New York, 1990, pp. 351-353.
18. Schele and Freidel, *A Forest of Kings*, p. 354.
19. Coe, *The Maya*, pp. 142, 145.
20. Davies, *The Ancient Kingdoms of Mexico*, p. 154.
21. Davies, ibid., pp. 405-407.

Above: Maya Star Wars shown on the murals at Bonampak. Below: Prisoners abase themselves before the King of Bonampak, having already been tortured and bled as shown by their mutilated, dripping fingers. Both illustrations Room 2; watercolour copies by Antonio Tejeda, 1948. Photos courtesy Peabody Museum.

Opposite page: Part of the mural on the west wall of the Upper Temple of the Jaguars, Chichén Itzá; watercolour copy by Adela C. Breton, 1904–6. Photo courtesy Peabody Museum.

Below: A mural of the Toltec conquest of the Yucatán from the Temple of the Jaguars at Chichén Itzá. Toltecs attack a Mayan city employing ladders and a siege tower below. The city is sacked in the upper part of the fresco. Photo courtesy Peabody Museum.

Opposite page:: The Shrine of the Eagles (Cuauhcalli) at Manlinalco. The city, conquered by Axayácatl in 1476, became a fortress, called the Eagles Nest, on the border of the Tarascan Empire. The temple, built by Ahuitzotl, served Aztec military religious life and was headquarters for the orders of the Eagle and Jaguar Knights. (Painting courtesy © Stuart Gentling photographed by David Wharton)

The Sacred Square of Tlatelolco,the sister city of Tenochtitlan, conquered by Axayácatl in 1473. On top of the temple at the right, Axayácatl slew in single combat the King of Tlatelolco and hurled his body down the steps. (Painting courtesy © Scott Gentling, photographed by David Wharton)

'A Military Marketplace'. Tlacaélel, the Snake Woman of the Mexica, was the formaliser of the Xochiyaoyotl or 'Flowery Wars' with special enemy states where the champions of both sides would fight to show their valour and secure the finest captives for sacrifice. These special conquests were designed to meet Huitzilopochtli's perpetual hunger for blood from the finest of the civilised peoples sharing the civilisation of Anáhuac who would come 'like warm tortillas, soft, tasty, straight out the oven' to please the gods. (Felipe Davalos/National Geographic Society Image Collection)

Streets and canals of the Tenochtitlan rebuilt by Ahuitzotl. Below are illustrated houses on the Cuepopan Road, an example of the magnificent rebuilding of Tenochtitlan after the flood of Ahuitzotl. By the arrival of Cortés the capital had achieved a cosmopolitian sophistication unparalleled in the history of Mesoamerica. (Paintings courtesy © Scott Gentling, photographed by David Wharton)

The magnificent palace or 'New Houses' of Motecuhzoma II as seen from the rear. The Sacred Square is to the right. Across the square in front of the palace are the house of song and the palace of Cihuacoatl. The imperial palace may have occupied over 25,000 square metres, sufficient, said one Conquistador for 'thirty knights to run their course in a regular tourney' over its terraced roofs. Even Cortés' famous hyperbole failed him: 'His residence within the city was so marvellous for its beauty and vastness that it seems to me almost impossible to describe. I shall therefore say no more of it than that there is nothing like it in Spain.' (Painting courtesy © Scott Gentling, photographed by David Wharton)

The great southern road looking north towards the Templo Mayor. It is along this road that Cortés entered the Tenochtitlan. (Painting courtesy © Scott Gentling, photographed by David Wharton)

The **Capitana**, *the flagship of Cortés' small fleet of brigantines, tied up at the fortress of Acachinanco after its capture in a sudden descent by the Conquistador. Note the Tlaxcallan shields hung over its sides. (Painting courtesy © Scott Gentling, photographed by David Wharton)*

Above: Distant view of Lake Texcoco and Tenochtitlan as seen from below the Paseo de Cortés. From here the Mexica sorcerers saw the vision of Tenochtitlan in flames before Cortés descended into the Valley of Mexico. (Painting courtesy © Stuart Gentling, photographed by David Wharton)

Below: A Mexica Palace near Chalco. Cortés described such palaces 'as good as the best in Spain in respect of size and workmanship both in their masonry and woodwork and their floors, and furnishings for every sort of household task!' (Painting courtesy © Stuart Gentling, photographed by David Wharton)

3
TEZOZOMOC,
THE MEXICAN MACHIAVELLI
(1320–1426)

In 1371 the birth of Niccolo Machiavelli was 102 years in the future. In that year, a Prince mounted the throne of the Tepanec city of Azcapotzalco on the shores of the sapphire-blue Lake Texcoco in Central Mexico. Tezozomoc (Angry Stone Face) would rule for 56 years and create in that lifetime an empire not seen in Mexico for 300 years, since the glory of great Tollan. He would demonstrate every skill and guile of war and statecraft, for the mere writing of which Machiavelli would later be branded infamous — and taken seriously. If the famous Florentine had already known, his model for the ultimate warrior-statesman, whom he had unwitting described in The Prince, had already grown old and died. He was remembered as:

'. . . a shrewd military strategist who also made effective use of flattery, bribery, assassination and treachery in a career worthy of a Machiavelli. Here, no less than in Renaissance Italy, the pragmatic aims of politics were never confused with idealism, much less with morality. But also like the tyrants of the Italian states, this ruler's accomplishments and fortunes were interwoven with the changing life a civilization.'[1]

For the empire Tezozomoc built would be inherited not by his own seed but by his favoured vassals, the Mexica, who learned the lessons of empire at the knee of this great Tepanec lord. It would be the Mexica in their magnificent capital of Tenochtitlan in the centre of Lake Texcoco, close by Tezozomoc's capital of Azcapotzalco, who would inspire the final flourish of native Mexican civilisation before the coming of Cortés.

Tezozomoc's name hieroglyph.

In a process that predated the Toltecs, the barbaric Náhuatl-speaking Chichimec tribes kept drifting into the civilised lands of Central Mexico from the north. Like the Germans drawn to the rich lands to the south, the Chichimeca were drawn to the attractions of older, more cultured peoples, whom they conquered and by whom they were in turn civilised. The Tepaneca and Acolhua were two such Chichimec groups. The Tepaneca occupied much of the western shores of the lakes in the Valley of Mexico and the Acolhua the eastern. The Mexica were a later group. After the fall of great Tollan in 1168, the history of Central Mexico was the history of the absorption of the Chichimeca and their coalescence into civilised states. The first great Chichimec leader was Xolotl who entered the Valley as a conqueror and whose exploits were aided by the bow and arrow, introduced for the first time into the warfare of Central Mexico. He overwhelmed the men of Culhuacán in 1246. Culhuacán was a great prize - the prestigious centre of surviving Toltec culture that the Chichimeca were eager to adopt. Xolotl forced the Chichimec Huetzin upon the Toltec-Culhua as their king and married his son to a Culhua princess.[2] The fusion of Toltec-Culhua and Chichimec blood was the foundation of all the coming great dynasties of Central Mexico, each equally proud of the Toltec lustre and the Chichimec vigour they had inherited.

The first of the Chichimeca to pick up the imperial idea and compel the unity of the region were the Acolhua under the leadership of Huetzin, who ruled from approximately 1253 to 1274, in alliance with the Tepanec lord of Tenanyocan (Tenayuca), Tochintecuhtli (Rabbit Lord). The Acolhua empire dominated the Valley of Mexico and reached north-eastward as far as Tulancinco but collapsed with the deaths of its founders, just as the Mexica, the last of the Chichimec peoples, were entering the Valley of Mexico. By 1300 the Tepaneca, who had arrived in the Valley about the same time as the Acolhua, began their march to empire when the city of Azcapotzalco slowly began to replace Tenanyocan as the chief city of that nation. Shortly thereafter, in 1320, Tezozomoc was born in Azcapotzalco, son of Acolhnahuacatzin, leader of the Tepaneca, and Cuitlaxaochitzin (Leathery Flower) daughter of the great Chichimec founder, Xolotl. By the middle of the century, power in the Valley was shared by three peoples in a reoccurring pattern dating back to great Tollan. The new triumvirate included the Tepaneca of Azcapotzalco, the Acolhua of Coatlichán, and the Toltec-Culhua of ancient Culhuacán, surviving member of the Toltec triple alliance.[3]

This delicate balance of power had already collapsed when Tezozomoc came to the throne of Azcapotzalco in 1370, a situation perfectly suited to a man of his talents. Culhuacán had simply disintegrated, probably pushed along by a Mexica attack in the last decade. There were also other powerful independent states in the region such as Chalco and Xochimilco in the southern region of the Valley, each with their own vassal cities and towns. The system of vassalage was loose enough for a cunning man like Tezozomoc to use it as an endless series of levers and wedges to create shifting alliances that relentlessly increased his power.

'His very longevity gave him ample opportunity to expand his realm and to display his talents both in war and diplomacy. A firm believer in the principle of divide and rule, he showed a

Tezozomoc, King of the Tepaneca.

rare skill in isolating his rivals and in crushing them one by one. For this Machiavellian monarch, tomorrow's victim was his ally against today's adversary.'[4]

FIRST CONQUESTS AND SPECIAL VASSALS

Tezozomoc's eye did not allow even the smallest pawn to go unnoticed. The Mexica had been driven from their attempted settlements in the southern parts of the Valley onto the small, barren islands in Lake Texcoco near his capital of Azcapotzalco. Their twin settlements of Tenochtitlan and Tlatelolco elected new kings the year after Tezozomoc came to the throne and were his nominees. Up to this time the Mexica had tried to avoid vassalage to any power, but their precarious position now drove them to swear fealty to Azcapotzalco and pay tribute in exchange for protection. The Mexica of Tenochtitlan were determined to do more to advance themselves. For the next two generations, the Mexica used the protection of the Tezozomoc to gather power by serving as loyal vassals who supplied increasingly important military service in his wars. Tezozomoc was glad to use such a particularly warlike and ferocious people.

Tezozomoc's first victim was the broken down polity of Culhuacán. Its value lay in its very weakness and in its genteel heritage, priceless in establishing legitimacy from the Toltec golden touch. The later Mexica histories were to describe the takeover as an act of mercy, so badly had the city deteriorated. Tezozomoc's reward to his Mexica vassals was to put a Mexica prince on Culhuacán's tarnished throne.

The absorption of Culhuacán had been the first in a series of rapid conquests of other cities in the southern part of the Valley of Mexico. Xochimilco, Cuitláhuac, and Mizquic, all valuable agricultural cities in the chinampa (floating lake gardens) region, followed quickly. Those conquests brought Tezozomoc's power into contact with the powerful Chalca confederacy of thirteen states directly south of the three newly conquered cities with whom they had had close and friendly relations. Chalco had enormous prestige as a civilising force and lay astride the southern part of the Valley of Mexico in the modern state of Morelos which put it in close contact with surrounding peoples and all the riches they had to offer. In 1376 Tezozomoc attempted to detach the Chalca dependency of Techichco and ignited a bloody war that would flare and sputter until 1410. Initially, the war was a Tepanec affair, but Tezozomoc eventually turned most of the fighting over to the Mexica which sparked one of the great enmities of Mesoamerican history. For almost a hundred years thereafter, Chalco was a bitter enemy of the Mexica. By the first decade of the new century, Tezozomoc's proxy war between the Mexica and Chalca was reaching a crescendo of violence. Then about 1407 the Chalca suffered a crushing defeat at the hands of the Mexica due to internal dissention among their leaders. The Mexica victory was so thorough that they installed their own rulers on

many Chalca cities. But the Mexica victory so upset the regional balance of power and alarmed the courts of central Mexico that a coalition was formed to free the Chalca. Even armies from outside the Valley poured in to force the Mexica to disgorge their enormous conquest. Even Tezozomoc took a hand. His vassals had become too powerful and, it has been suggested, had the effrontery to act more as partners than as vassals. Faced with such a coalition, the Mexica king, Huitzilíhuitl, dropped his prey in 1410. The Chalca rulers resumed their thrones. Tezozomoc apparently was satisfied with this chastisement of the Mexica. However, he was caught on the horns of a dilemma. The Mexica had proven how powerful they could be and how easily they could slip the leash. On the other hand they were just too valuable, as the obsidian teeth in his sword, to suppress. Since they were a major means to the empire he coveted above all things, the latter argument seems to have prevailed.

In 1404, the Mexica sought to strengthen their position by the tie of blood with Tezozomoc and requested one of his daughters for Huitzilíhuitl. It was not an impertinent request. Tezozomoc had skilfully married his children and grandchildren among the kingdoms of the Valley to cement alliances and create a strong web of common interest. The Mexica had become valuable vassals, and he was not adverse to binding them closer to himself. So when the Mexica emissaries came to him begging a wife for Huitzilíhuitl, they spoke in terms of strengthening Tezozomoc's power:

'Great lord, accede to our plea. Have pity upon your servant, the king of Mexico; upon the city which is among the reeds and rushes, where Huitzilíhuitl rules and protects your vassals. He is single, still to be wed. What we ask of you is that you surrender one of your jewels and precious plumes — that is, one of your noblewomen. She will not go to an alien place but will stay within her own land and country, where she will be in command. Therefore, O lord, we beg you not to refuse that which we ask of you.'[5]

Tezozomoc saw another web spinning out to bind his power, and responded:

'O Aztecs, your words, your humility have overcome me and I find it difficult to answer. I have daughters and the Lord of All Created Things has destined them for this end. Behold my beloved daughter called Ayauhcihuatl. You are welcome to take her.'[6]

A son was born in 1407 to the Tepanec princess to the delight of Tezozomoc who selected the child's name, Chimalpopoca (Smokes Like A Shield), from the signs under which he had been born. The tie of blood was now working well to the advantage of the Mexica as Ayauhcihuatl quickly became a partisan of her husband's people. Child in arms, she approached her father and begged him to reduce the heavy tribute of the Mexica. He easily relented and essentially excused them of all but a symbolic tribute of a few ducks, frogs, and fish. From this indulgence, envy and distrust grew among the princes of Azcapotzalco.

In 1395 a dynastic succession in the city of Xaltocan in the northern part of the basin of the Valley provided Tezozomoc with the opportunity to expand in that direction. Tzompantli, The new ruler of Xaltocan, a city of the non-Náhuatl speaking Otomis, allowed his subjects to go on a rampage and plunder nearby towns. Tezozomoc was encouraged by the ruler of Texcoco, Techolatlallatzin, to destroy the Otomi city. In the name of order, Tezozomoc organised an expedition to suppress the Otomis. To his own Tepanec forces he summoned those of his Mexica vassal. Joined by the forces of Texcoco, they crushed the Otomis from east and west, forcing Tzompantli to flee. Hailed as a liberator from Otomi depredations, Tezozomoc annexed not only Xaltocan but most of the cities in the north, going as far as Tollan itself. But the tribute he levied on the conquered Otomis was so harsh that many fled to the protection of Texcoco, the centre of Acolhua power on the eastern shore of the lake. The kaleidoscope of alliances was taking another turn. Techolatlallatzin foolishly allowed his central authority over his own Acolhua cities to devolve upon a number of jealous vassals.

THE WARS AGAINST TEXCOCO

By the turn of the century, Tezozomoc had firmly established his rule in the western, northern, and much of the southern regions of the Valley basin. The Mexica had begun campaigning heavily in the west as far as Morelos for him, although they would later claim these were their own conquests. His armies also fought their way through the old Toltec zone of Tollan itself and the Tolluca Valley and southward to Izucar. Now only the eastern shore of the lake stood against him. Patiently, Tezozomoc worked over the next years to weaken the Acolhua. His spies and emissaries quietly encouraged pro-Tepanec factions among Texcoco's vassals and in Texcoco itself. Like Cromwell, he believed that it is not enough to strike when the iron was hot — it was necessary to strike to make the iron hot. Techolatlallatzin's fracturing of Acolhua power among his vassals gave the wily Tepanec opportunities in plenty. Eventually Tezozomoc was ready to challenge the power of the Acolhua more openly. His opportunity came when their new king, Ixtlilxochitl (Black-Faced Flower), rashly claimed the title of Lord of the Chichimeca (Chichimecatl or high king of all the Chichimec-descended peoples of the Valley) as his legacy from his ancestor Xolotl. This was the very title Tezozomoc coveted for, as he growled, was he not also Xolotl's grandson? Tezozomoc then sent Ixtlilxochitl a load of cotton requesting him to weave it into mantles for the Tepaneca. In the diplomatic language of the day, his request was blatant demand that Texcoco swear fealty to Azcapotzalco; the mantles would be tribute. Ixtlilxochitl defiantly gave the cotton to his own vassals and proceeded with his coronation.

Tezozomoc had raised the art of destroying an enemy's power base to a high order. So much treason was afoot in Ixtlilxochitl's kingdom that he dared not leave his capital while Tezozomoc's forces ate away at its borders bit by bit. Eventually Ixtlilxochitl suppressed the disloyal towns and consolidated his power in his loyal ones, but the damage had been done. Tezozomoc had preoccupied Ixtlilxochitl's attention thoroughly on internal security. So much so that Tezozomoc was able to raise an army from his western and southern vassals and march secretly into Texcocan territory before Ixtlilxochitl could raise and concentrate an army. The Tepanec army attacked the loyal Texcocan vassal city of Itztallopan in the southern part of the kingdom. The attack began in the morning, and after a

Anáhuac: The world of the Valley of Mexico

day-long battle, overwhelmed it. Tezozomoc's campaign continued as he subdued more of Texcoco's vassals to the north: Otompan, Acolman, Tepechpan, and Tollantzinco. Although the war ended without the conquest of Texcoco, Ixtlilxochitl had been clearly defeated. The altars of the gods in Azcapotzalco and Tenochtitlan ran red with the blood of Acolhua captives.

It was not Tezozomoc's policy to finish off Ixtlilxochitl in one campaign. He had humbled his only rival and would peel off his remaining loyal towns one by one. Texcoco remained far too strong to attack directly. Ten years after the victory at Itztallopan, Tezozomoc struck again

at one of Texcoco's most loyal allies, the nearby city of Huexotla to the south along the lake. For the first time, the Tepanec armies and their vassals came by water, in a great fleet of canoes. The scene is vividly described by Frances Gillmor:

'Then the sun rose one morning on the lake covered with canoes of the enemy. They had come by Huexotla. And the water of the lake was red that day as the eagle and tiger warriors fought. The water was foul with the bodies of the dead. Still the canoes came over the water, and the armies clashed day after day. The warriors died, and went to suck the honey of the

skies with the hummingbirds of Huitzilopochtli.'[7]

The attack across the lake may have been a
Mexica idea for they had been specialising in
the military use of the canoe. The advantage of
this technique was logistical. An army travelling around the lakeshore would have to sub-
sist on what its own men or bearers could
carry, and in enemy territory, supply quickly
became a problem. By coming across the lake,
that problem was solved; supplies could easily
move across the lake to support an army. The
battle was fought both on land and on the lake
as the Acolhua met the Tepanec fleet with their
own. The fighting lasted many days with the
Tepaneca attacking in the day and returning to
their bases at night. Tezozomoc was again
working on two fronts. While his armies pinned
down those of Ixtlilxochitl, his agents were sowing more discord among the Acolhua and their
vassals, fanning the strength of the peace
party. And again, Ixtlilxochitl was caught
between two fires.

As before, the war was not decisive, but Tezozomoc was drawing the noose tighter and
tighter around Texcoco. Three years passed,
and the lord of the Tepaneca resumed the war.
His army marched north around the lake
against Texcoco. At Chiucnauhtlan, north of
Texcoco, Ixtlilxochitl defeated him in a great
battle. Tezozomoc fell back to find allies to the
north and south of Texcoco, in Chalca and
Otompan. But Ixtlilxochitl was emboldened by
his victory and gathered many allies to him.
With this new host he went onto the offensive
and took the war to Tezozomoc, retracing Tezozomoc's route around the lake, conquering city
after city. He drove the Tepanec armies before
him until he had shut up Tezozomoc in
Azcapotzalco, but the city continued to be supplied by canoe from the lake, probably by his
Mexica vassals. Other Tepanec armies ravaged
the undefended towns of Texcoco. Nevertheless, Tezozomoc saw that the odds were against
him in the present war and he sued for peace,
promising to swear fealty to the Texcocan king.
Accepting the promise, Ixtlilxochitl marched
home and disbanded his allies.

Over the next year, Tezozomoc's royal kin
began travelling throughout the Acolhua lands,
visiting their many relatives, themselves the
descendants of the ancient Tezozomoc. He was
gathering the strands of his vast web. His wisdom in spreading his seed among the greatest
houses in all the Valley of Mexico would now
bring him back from the edge of defeat. In 1418
he raised a new alliance and struck now in
deadly earnest at Texcoco, but first he baited
his trap. The royalty of the Valley were converging on Chicunauhtla for a great hunting
festival, and Tezozomoc pleaded a special
favour from Ixtlilxochitl. Would the Texcocan
allow him to swear fealty there rather than
make another long and wearying trip to Texcoco itself? The regularly gullible Ixtlilxochitl
agreed. As he was about to set out, he was
warned that Tezozomoc planned to assassinate
him. His brother who resembled him went in
his stead and was duly murdered and flayed,
his skin stretched over a rock. The warning had
done Ixtlilxochitl little good for though Tezozomoc's plot to murder him had failed, his work
of the last year had not. Ixtlilxochitl's kingdom
collapsed immediately attacked from without
and betrayed from within; Tezozomoc had even
suborned factions within Texcoco itself to
attack the king's supporters. Ixtlilxochitl
attempted to flee to Tlaxcallan over the mountains but was hunted down and killed while his
young son, Nezahualcoyotl watched in hiding.
Had Ixtlilxochitl been a less resilient and defiant enemy, Tezozomoc would likely have
returned his throne to him as a vassal. The old
Tepanec had anticipated Machiavelli's advice
on what to do with defeated enemies: kill them
or befriend them. The latter had been a good
policy in most cases, but the Texcocan king
would not bend and had to die. Texcoco needed
another lesson to cure it of its resistance as
well. All through the land, Tezozomoc's warriors travelled and asked each child under the
age of seven, 'Who is your king?' If they
answered as they had heard their parents talk,
Ixtlilxochitl or Nezahualcoyotl, they were
butchered on the spot by swift blows from the
obsidian-edged sword.

NEW RIVALS

Now, at the moment of his complete victory,
remorseless age was closing at last about the

The divine sign that showed the Mexica where their mighty city would take root and flourish, the eagle clutching serpent on a cactus. (Painting courtesy © Scott Gentling, photographed by David Wharton)

conqueror. Wrapped in his blankets as braziers glowed around him to supply the warmth his body could no longer provide, he waited in contentment for the end.

'In Azcapotzalco the old king shivered with age and death coming. . . . His wars were ended. His sons and his grandsons were placed strategically in all the great towns of the kingdom. In Acolman, in Coatlichan, in Tenochtitlan itself . . . Maxtla in Coyohuacan — a city rich and powerful . . . he need not take offense that he was not to rule in Azcapotzalco . . . Tayauh would be better there. . . . Everything was settled now . . . and the tribute was pouring in . . . the men of the conquered towns were planting corn for Azcapotzalco . . . the land was settled.'[8]

The old man was mistaken. The land was not settled. With the final lesson ground into the Acolhua, Tezozomoc distributed the cities and towns to his allies and even to his two prized Mexica vassals, Tenochtitlan and Tlatelolco. Yet the heir to the Acolhua kingdom had not fallen into his net. Nezahualcoyotl seemed to be everywhere, seen first in one Acolhua city, then in a village, or in the courts of the powerful neighbours, Tlaxcallan and Huexotzinco. But as year followed year, the ephemeral prince

receded from his concerns as no danger materialised. Then great ladies from the royal house of Tenochtitlan, his own relations and Nezahualcoyotl's as well, came with gifts of rich jewels to beg and wheedle his forbearance of the young prince. Tezozomoc relented and allowed Nezahualcoyotl to live in Tenochtitlan where the Mexica vouched for his behaviour. He accompanied the Mexica to war and took captives, presenting them to Tezozomoc as an act of vassalage. The old man's fears were successfully allayed, and he allowed Nezahualcoyotl to live in his own city of Texcoco. Then a hideous nightmare reawoke his fears, and he resolved to kill the prince. He would do it by indirection and bribe a close friend of the Texcocan prince to turn assassin.

'Listen, Coyohua, it is for this that they came to fetch you. I dreamed another thing that was truly evil: that an eagle came upon me; that a tiger came upon me; that a wolf came upon me; that a snake came upon me, huge, brightly coloured and very venomous. Coyohua, may it not be that Nezahualcoyotl destroys me; may it not be that he seeks out his father Ixtlilxochitl. . . may it not be that he himself resumes the war against my sons, lords and princes?'[9]

But Coyohua only pretended to fall in with the plot. Instead, he warned the prince who fled over the mountains to safety. Tezozomoc's last trap had been sprung. He suddenly had more important worries at his very threshold.

With the conquest of Texcoco, the Mexica found themselves with tributaries of their own. Now the relationship of master and vassal began to sour. Ross Hassig pointed out the change, 'A militarily powerful Tenochtitlan was a desirable ally, but with Texcoco subdued, Tenochtitlan looked less like a necessary ally and more like a potential challenger.'[10] The flash point apparently was the request of the Mexica that the Tepaneca supply them with building materials to construct an aqueduct from the springs of Chapultepec to their island cities. The request was seen correctly in Azcapotzalco as tantamount to a demand for tribute, a reversal of roles between master and vassal. Tezozomoc did not betray his anger but merely replied to the Mexica that he would consult his council, whose spokesman replied:

'Lord, monarch, what is in the mind of your grandson and of his advisors? Do they think that we are to be their slaves? Is it not enough that we sheltered them and admitted them within our territory, that we permitted them to build their city? Have we not given them the water that they asked for? Now they demand, in a shameless manner, without respect for your dignity, that you and all of us build them a pipe for their water? We do not wish it; it is not our will. We would rather lose our lives! Even though King Chimalpopoca of Mexico is your descendent and friend of the Tepanec nation, we refuse to be commanded in this manner. He is only a child and what he has done has been provoked by his advisors. We would like to know where they found such daring and insolence.'[11]

The tone of the council's reaction was a clear indication that power was at last slipping from the old man's fingers. He was swept along by his council which roused the population of Azcapotzalco against the Mexica and imposed an embargo on all trade with the twin island cities, blocking every road and causeway. The council, and especially the king's son, Maxtla, was determined to destroy the Mexica. Maxtla had more on his mind than just the Mexica. He coveted the throne of Azcapotzalco that his father had assigned to another brother. Tezozomoc wanted them to spirit away his much beloved grandson from Tenochtitlan, but they refused. Chimalpopoca, they said, may have been a Tepanec on his mother's side, but he was a Mexica on his father's, the side that counted and the side to which he would cleave. They demanded his death. Durán records then the last pathetic days of the great Tezozomoc before his death in 1426 at the incredible age of 106:

'The king was so distressed when he heard this response, so saddened to see that he could not pacify his vassals, that he became sick with sorrow, and soon after died of his grief. He died a very old man.'[12]

Thus passed into history, Tezozomoc, lord of the Tepaneca, one of the most remarkable monarchs of all time. His empire was a monument to his own genius and the work of a single lifetime — and that only, as his successor would prove.

1. Richard F. Townsend, *The Aztecs,* Thames & Hudson, London, 1992, p. 66.
2. Frederick Peterson, *Ancient Mexico,* Capricorn Books, New York, 1962, pp. 75-76.
3. Nigel Davies, *The Ancient Kingdoms of Mexico,* Penguin Books, Harmondsworth, Middlesex, 1982, pp. 166-167.
4. Davies, *Ancient Kingdoms of Mexico,* p. 175.
5. Fray Diego Durán, *The Aztecs: The History of the Indies of New Spain,* Orion Press, New York, 1964, p.42.
6. Durán, p. 42.
7. Frances Gillmor, *Flute of the Smoking Mirror: A Portrait of Nezahualcoyotl Poet King of the Aztecs,* The University of Arizona Press, n.p., 1968, p. 25.
8. Gillmor, p. 50.
9. *Anales de Cuauhtitlan,* published in *Codex Chimalpopoca,* Imprenta Universitaria, Mexico City, 1945, p. 41; in Davies, Nigel, *The Aztecs,* University of Oklahoma Press, Norman and London, 1989, p.69.
10. Ross Hassig, *Aztec Warfare: Imperial Expansion and Control,* University of Oklahoma Press, Norman, OK, 1988, p. 139.
    11. Durán, p. 48.
12. Durán, p. 49. In the notes to this edition of Durán, the editor cites a reign of 83 years for Tezozomoc, from 1343 to 1426.

4

NEZAHUALCOYOTL, THE POET WARLORD (1402–1472)

HIDE AND SEEK WITH DEATH

The sixteen-year-old prince hid in the tree as the pursuers swarmed up the canyon on Mount Tlaloc. Nezahualcoyotl watched as the men wearing the insignia of Otompan, Chalco, and even his own city of Texcoco came plainly into view. His father, the king, Ixtlilxochitl (Black-Faced Flower), waited for them with his two remaining captains. The king's last words filled his ears, 'Hide,' in this 'tree, remembering that if you die, with you ends the ancient line of the Chichimecan kings. Go later to your relatives at Tlaxcallan and Huexotzinco and ask for help from them. Remember that you are a Chichimecatl recovering your kingdom.'[1]

Nezahualcoyotl peered from between the leafy branches as the vassals of Tezozomoc spread out to surround the three men of Texcoco. Their words dripped with the forms of deference, carefully adding the respectful 'tzin' to the end of his name. They were asking him to honour the Tepanec gods at their festival. Nezahualcoyotl shuddered at the thought of the honour they were asking of him, that which would throw him on the stone of sacrifice. It would be just the sort of final exquisite victory the ancient Tezozomoc would savour and the gods too, for the blood of kings was especially sweet to them.

Tezozomoc recently had reduced the Acolhua kingdom of Texcoco on the eastern shores of the lakes in the centre of the Valley of Mexico to ruin by the death of a thousand intrigues. He

Nezahualcoyotl's name hieroglyph.

already ruled the other great Náhuatl-speaking peoples of the Valley, the Tepaneca who controlled the western shores of the Valley. Great wars had been waged around the lakes of the Valley of Mexico for the mastery of Anáhuac, as this ancient lake-centred world was called. Ixtlilxochitl had initially beaten Tezozomoc in that arena, bringing his capital under siege and finally extracting peace from the Tepanec king and a pledge to acknowledge him as the high king, or Chichimecatl, the legitimate successor of the Toltec patrimony. But it had been a poisonous peace, in which Tezozomoc had suborned the Texcocan vassals and allies, many of them co-opted by his skilful web of marriages to his own children and grandchildren. The trap had been so carefully sprung in 1418 that the power of Texcoco fell away from Ixtlilxochitl in an instant.

The wily old Tepanec had come across the lake to a great hunt and begged the younger Texcocan king to spare his old body the rigour of a second trip to pay him homage. Ixtlilxochitl had been prepared to do so and take Nezahualcoyotl with him when he was warned of treachery by his brother, Acatlotzin. Returning to Texcoco from Tezozomoc's capital of Azcapotzalco, he warned of a plot to kill him. In the cloaking greyness of dawn he had heard the Tepanec lords discussing the plan to bring down the Texcocan king. At the suggestion of the royal tutor that a double be sent instead of the king, he asked to take the king's place; his resemblance was close enough to fool the

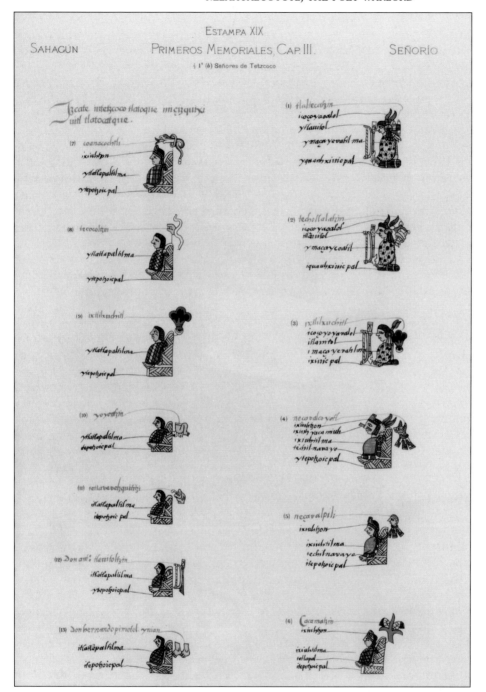

The lineage of the kings of Texcoco. Ixtlilxochitl is No. 3; Nezahualcoyotl is No. 4.

Tepaneca. He only asked that the king see that his wife and children and vassals never wanted. In tears, Ixtlilxochitl agreed. He had no choice. The armies of Texcoco were scattered by the peace, and his vassals and allies had turned in his hand. Acatlotzin then went bravely to the death meant for the king, but he had bought time. His retainers had escaped to bring the news that the trap had been sprung and that Tezozomoc had been deceived, but the deception would last only a short time. The royal family barely had time to flee to their summer home in the mountains ahead of Tezozomoc's warriors.

From there the king sent another son, Chihuaquequenotzin (He Who Laughs at Women)

58

to beg help from Otompan, a city Ixtlilxochitl had once punished for its allegiance to Tezozomoc. This prince was Nezahualcoyotl's half-brother, son of the Tepanec Flower, Tezozomoc's own daughter. Tezozomoc had sought to use her to bind the Texcocan king to him but found only insult in the connection. Ixtlilxochitl had kept her only as his concubine; Nezahualcoyotl's mother was his wife and queen, and he would not set her aside for the Tepanec woman. This woman who had won Ixtlilxochitl's heart was sister to the ruler of the Mexica, Chimalpopoca, in Tenochtitlan, the island city across the lake, vassal to Tezozomoc. This flower of the Tepaneca bore four sons for Ixtlilxochitl, three of whom inherited none of their grandfather's treacherous nature. Chihuaquequenotzin was one of these. He too asked that his family be cared for upon his death. The prince arrived in Otompan at the time of religious festival when the population of the town had gathered in the plaza. The military governor turned away the prince's request, telling him to ask the people of Otompan from the temple steps. The crowd howled its reply and the governor proclaimed his loyalty to Tezozomoc. He Who Laughs at Women died in a hail of stones, and the warriors of the town vied to take a piece of his flesh home for a sacred festival meal. Ixtlilxochitl knew all was lost as the messenger brought this tale and its final dregs — that his son's fingernails were worn by the governor of Otompan as a necklace. Flight over the mountains to his wife's other relatives in Tlaxcallan was now the only hope. Taking only Nezahualcoyotl and two captains, he slipped away.

Now he was surrounded in the canyon. He threw back Tezozomoc's invitation. Then the Tepaneca attzcked. His captains fell around him, and then he was alone laying about him until he too disappeared in the slashing obsidian. They stripped him of the royal insignia, the blue crown and mantle of the Toltec kings, and left. For the rest of the day, Nezahualcoyotl huddled in the tree, too afraid to show himself. The next morning more men came, but these reverently retrieved the body, dressed it in royal blue insignia, and paused to praise the dead king and his missing heir. At last the prince emerged from his tree to show himself to these last loyal retainers. They burned the body upon a funeral pyre in the style of the Toltec kings.

With this small band Nezahualcoyotl headed over the mountains to Tlaxcallan. Huddled in the canyons he found many of the still loyal lords and priests of Texcoco who had fled Tezozomoc's onslaught. What he had seen from the tree had transformed him. He was no longer the heir, but the king charged by his father with recovering his kingdom. He told the frightened group to go home and submit outwardly but to wait for him when he should return from exile to reclaim his throne. Then he turned his back on Anáhuac and walked into exile and adventure that would become legend.

With him to Tlaxcallan went his nephews, the sons of his brother, Chihuaquequenotzin, who were now his charge. Also with him were the other sons of the Tepanec Flower - Cuauhtlehuanitzin and Xiconocatzin. Like their martyred brother, they were loyal to the core. Redoubtable in battle and counsel, they would be two right arms to their young king and brother. The fourth brother, Tilmatzin, was the true seed of Tezozomoc's line. He lingered behind and gladly allowed his grandfather to place him on the throne of Acolman on the lake shore to the north of the capital.

In Tlaxcallan, the mountain-rimmed republic to the northeast of the Valley of Mexico, Nezahualcoyotl and his small band of followers found refuge among his mother's relatives. There he began the four years of exile and preparation for the moment when Tezozomoc's grip on Texcoco would slip. They would be years of wandering and danger. The young king was not inclined to hide in the safety of Tlaxcallan. In this time, the meaning of his name, Hungry Coyote, would be fulfilled. Hungry he would be and hunted but never still and always playing the game for the highest prize. It was not long after Tezozomoc fastened his grip on Texcoco that the rumours of the boy king began seeping through the land. He was seen in one place then another always disappearing like the mist when Tezozomoc's men closed in upon the rumour. Tezozomoc's rule sat uneasily on Texcoco despite the web of alliances by blood and interest that anchored it. He veered between terror and paternal favours to win over the Texcocans. His soldiers visited every village to ask the children the name of the king. If they answered Ixtlilxochitl or Nezahualcoyotl, as they had heard their parents speak, the soldiers killed them on the spot. The word spread ahead of them forcing the people to teach their children to mouth the name Tezozomoc with the word king. With the terror, there also came honey to sweeten the taste of Tezozomoc's rule. The king's herald gathered the people from Texcoco and the surrounding towns to hear the Tepanec's words to his new subjects. From a pyramid he spoke of Tezozomoc's love for them as a father and of his forbearance of their tribute for a full year so that they might repair the ruin of war. They would be ruled by their own local lords and suffer no Tepanec governors. The vast crowds roared in approval. Close by on the hill of Cuauhyacac, a boy listened to the clear voice of the herald even at a distance, and heard one more of Tezozomoc's bribes to the people of Texcoco. Great would be the rewards to him who brought before Tezozomoc the prince Nezahualcoyotl, dead or alive.

Tezozomoc had used marriage alliances to his great advantage, but most weapons have more than one edge. The Mexica ruler in Tenochtitlan was his grandson but was also Nezahualcoyotl's cousin. His aunts in the Mexica royal family pleaded his case with their Tepanec liege and relative and brought rich gifts. They argued well that in all these years that had passed, Nezahualcoyotl had raised no conspiracies or armies against him. He had simply whiled away his time in ball games and other concerns of youth. Let him come to live with them in Tenochtitlan. Were they not loyal vassals and kin of Tezozomoc? What safer place to keep the young man where he could be watched? In time the old man's guard dropped, and Nezahualcoyotl came to live in Tenochtitlan in 1422. For two years he lived quietly and in friendship with his young cousin Chimalpopoca and especially his uncle, Itzcoatl (Obsidian Serpent), whom he greatly admired. In these impressionable years, he found his first if tenuous security under the protection of his Mexica relatives, and must have become very Mexica in outlook. He accompanied his relatives to war and took prisoners, the vital first step to create the military reputation vital for a ruler. He even offered them up to Tezozomoc, saying with a

disarming coolness remarkable in one so young, 'My lord, O Tezozomoc, a fatherless orphan enters your presence to make his offering.'

Several years later his aunts again pleaded for their nephew. Let him return to live in the palace of his father in Texcoco. He is harmless as he has proven himself over the last two years. Does not Texcoco pay its tribute directly to Tenochtitlan as you so ordered, and does that not still bind the land to your loyal vassal? What harm is there in his going? And so they pleaded, and their words fell pleasantly into the ears of Tezozomoc who knew he was approaching the end of his days. The cold-blooded enmity had melted out of him in his last years, and he agreed, provided the young man not go beyond Texcoco, Tenochtitlan, and Tlacopan, the Tepanec city on the mainland from which the causeway to the island city of the Mexica began. And so Nezahualcoyotl returned to the city of his father, and for two more years occupied himself with the pleasures of the good life — the ball game played for high stakes and the joy of young women. And with subtlety he made his way back into the hearts of his people who had never entirely forgotten him.

But again Tezozomoc's heart hardened. The image of Nezahualcoyotl came to him in a dream as his devourer in the shape of a jaguar, a wolf, and then a serpent. Utterly shaken by the dream, he again plotted the young man's death. First he sought out Nezahualcoyotl's friend and fellow countryman, Coyohua, to murder him. Coyohua instead warned the prince and excused himself to the old king that too many friends surrounded Nezahualcoyotl. So Tezozomoc sought to murder him when he came with the other lords of Texcoco to offer their yearly tribute. And again, the warning of this friend saved his life. With that the last chance slipped away. Death came to Tezozomoc in 1426, huddled in his blankets set in the sun to warm himself.

The rule of his empire Tezozomoc he left to his son Tayauh. To another son, Maxtla, he left the rich city of Coyohuacan. They had inherited their father's fear and hatred of Nezahualcoyotl, and to this they added a hatred of the growing power of their own Mexica vassals. Still, they stayed their hands when Nezahualcoyotl attended the funeral of Tezozomoc at Azcapotzalco. Murdering a guest at their father's funeral was bad form. Maxtla had other plans. As his father's pyre sent its smoke skyward, he stunned the assembled lords by declaring that he, as the eldest of Tezozomoc's sons was the rightful heir. As the arguments surged back and forth, Nezahualcoyotl slipped into his canoe and made his way across the lake to Texcoco.

Maxtla faced down his brother. Later he would murder him. He next turned his attention to the hated Mexica and their king, Chimalpopoca. The young man lost his courage, and Maxtla held his life in his hand. He marvelled to see Nezahualcoyotl reappear before him in his palace at Azcapotzalco to beg for his kinsman's life. 'Oh Lord, great and powerful, I come to plead for the life of Chimalpopoca. He has been a precious plume over your head, and you are throwing it away. He has been a necklace of gold and jewels about your neck and you are unloosing it.'[2]

Maxtla must have enjoyed toying with his enemies for he bade Nezahualcoyotl to visit Chimalpopoca and reassure him. Turning to his steward he said, 'Does it matter whom I kill first — Nezahualcoyotl or Chimalpopoca or Tlacoteotzin (king of Tlatelolco) — kings of three cities and enemies all three!'[3]

Nezahualcoyotl found his young kinsman imprisoned in a cage in his own city. It was apparent that, dear as he was to the Texcocan, Chimalpopoca had quailed at the prospect of war with Maxtla. That was the last time they would meet. He returned to Texcoco, and the news followed him across the lake that Chimalpopoca was dead; it was said at first to be at the hand Maxtla's vassals from Tlacopan. But then new rumour whispered that his death had not been at Maxtla's hand but at the hand of his own people disgusted at the thought of so weak a king. Again Nezahualcoyotl returned to Azcapotzalco to weave a disarming shield of harmlessness with talk of peace. This time he also brought his brother by the Tepanec Flower, Xiconocatzin, Maxtla's own nephew. He had come one time too many into the lion's den. So palpable was the danger that even Maxtla's steward warned him of the danger. He laid flowers before Maxtla as a sign of peace,

but the Tepanec king turned away from him. He withdrew in silence. Outside, one of Maxtla's concubines approached and said her lord would meet him in the cool summer house of straw in the courtyard. He pulled his brother aside to warn him to melt into the crowds and return home. Then he disappeared inside, by all appearance entering his death chamber. Immediately he dug his way out of the back and raced through the city and across the causeway towards Tlatelolco, Tenochtitlan's sister city on the lake. Behind him raced the Tepanec warriors who had expected to find him in the straw summer house. But the prince was young and fit and unburdened by the weapons and armour of soldiers and easily outdistanced them to reach safety in Tlatelolco. From there he swiftly sped by canoe across the lake to Texcoco. The transparent peace had been torn away.

Barely had Nezahualcoyotl returned to Texcoco when the king of Tlatelolco sent to him begging for refuge. He was fleeing across the lake with his warriors and treasure ahead of Maxtla's vengeance. Quickly upon this message came the news that Tlacateotzin had not been swift enough. Maxtla's warriors had fallen upon him and crushed his skull. Danger was leering over Nezahualcoyotl as it had not since he fled the canyon of the flashing obsidian. Yet Maxtla attempted to strike with intrigue. Through Nezahualcoyotl's brother, the traitor Tilmatzin, he sent an invitation to a feast. Tilmatzin had been playing both ends against the middle while Tezozomoc's power had been slipping from his ageing fingers, warning his half-brother of the old man's plots. But now he would take no chances with a violent man like Maxtla. But again, the trap was too obvious, and again the aged royal tutor suggested that a double be sent, the same trick that had saved the life of Nezahualcoyotl's father. A young man was found who was willing to offer his life for his king. Maxtla was happily deceived by the head of the double. He found it a deliciously gruesome warning to send to Chimalpopoca's successor as king of Tenochtitlan. To Maxtla's rage, Itzcoatl, uncle to both Chimalpopoca and Nezahualcoyotl, had been chosen as the new king. The rage was justified for Itzcoatl was a man of great ability and courage. As the

Tepanec messenger displayed the head of the supposed Nezahualcoyotl to Itzcoatl, the living Texcocan came out of the shadows to stand behind his uncle. 'I am immortal. Behold, you bring my head as an offering to Itzcoatzin. And I am here before you offering my congratulations on his election.'[4]

Maxtla now decided that a more direct approach was needed. He dispatched a delegation of generals to Texcoco to murder Nezahualcoyotl outright in his own feasthall. He was exercising in the ball court with Tilmatzin, who was all honeyed words. He had denied knowing of the murder planned by Maxtla, but when he saw the Tepanec lords arriving, he hurriedly excused himself. Nezahualcoyotl played the perfect unsuspecting host at a feast for the generals, but in a haze of incense smoke he slipped out of a hole in the wall behind his throne and fled to the mountains. Again the Tepaneca spread a wide net for him throughout the Acolhua lands, offering a huge reward for his capture. None of the Acolhua would betray him even upon the threat of death. Nevertheless, the danger was real as the Tepanec patrols swept through the countryside. He tried to persuade his loyal retainers and kinsmen to leave him and find safety in their homes.

'Go back to your houses and do not seek to die for me. Do not for my sake fall into disfavor with the tyrant, and thus lose your homes and lands." Quauhtlehuantzin and Tzontecochatzin and all the others replied that they only desired to follow him and die where he died. On hearing this, Nezahualcoyotl was deeply moved, and began to weep, together with all those who accompanied him.'[5]

It was obvious that he would need a more secure base from which to finally make his move. He then made his way across the mountains surrounding the Valley of Mexico to the court of Huexotzinco.

ARM OF THE LION

It was from Huexotzinco that the final journey back began. He was there when a delegation from Itzcoatl arrived to seek allies against Maxtla's growing hostility. The timing was perfect. Nezahualcoyotl used the opportunity to present his case both to the Mexica ambassadors and to his hosts. Now was the time to gather his strength and free his kingdom. The years with his relatives across the mountains in Tlaxcallan and Huexotzinco, the years of wandering among his own people, the years of winning back their hearts as the golden prince while spinning a web of diffidence before the Tepaneca — were all over. His words were decisive, and the alliance that would bring down the Tepaneca, was forged. The messengers sped across the mountains, throughout Texcoco, and even to old rivals of Texcoco such as Chalco, at the southern edge of the lake. And they came — the hosts of Huexotzinco and Tlaxcallan, the fighting men of Chalco, and his own Acolhua from their villages in the mountains and plain.

Nezahualcoyotl, was now resplendent in the brilliant feathered armour of a king, an image immortalised by a post-Conquest codex painted in Texcoco. He strides into battle with a blue and orange feather-covered shield (*yaochimalli*) advanced and an obsidian-edged sword (*macuahuitl*) beginning its striking arc. His wrists are encircled with turquoise bracelets, and his biceps and calves with golden bands. He sports a magnificent golden-serpent lip plug in his lower lip. On his head is a helmet in the shape of a coyote, his name sign. The helmet and his quilted cotton armour (*ichcahuipilli*) shimmer with a carpet of Toltec royal blue feathers. Below the armour, he wears a feathered kilt (*ehuatl*) of green, red, yellow, and blue. On his back is a small blue drum to give commands in battle.[6]

Now with the power and insignia of a king, he directed the pincers that would rip his kingdom from Maxtla's grasp. The Tlaxcallans he sent to drive his brother from his city of Acolman north of Texcoco. The men of Chalco he sent to take the city of Coatlichan south of Texcoco. He himself would lead the men of his own kingdom to take back his capital. The campaign was swift, taking Maxtla completely by surprise. Nezahualcoyotl's allies overran the cities to the north and south of Texcoco, isolating Texcoco as Nezahualcoyotl closed in. Maxtla's troops were driven through the city to the shoreline and fled across the lake in their canoes as the population accorded their king a joyous hero's

Nezahualcoyotl in his war costume. The drum on his back was to sound commands.

welcome. Flowers rained across his path and clouds of incense sweetened the air of his triumph, and he remembered his father's words before the flashing obsidian, 'Remember that you are a Chichimecatl recovering your empire.'

Texcoco now served as the base for operations by the anti-Tepanec alliance. However, a pause appears to have occurred in which many of the allies returned home. Chalco dropped out of the alliance The Chalca had been happy to loosen the Tepanec grip on the eastern shore of the lake, but an alliance with the hated Mexica to carry the war to the Tepanec western shore was asking too much.

When the allies moved again, Tenochtitlan was under siege by Maxtla, who had assembled the might of the Tepaneca to break the Mexica. They gathered at the ends of the causeways

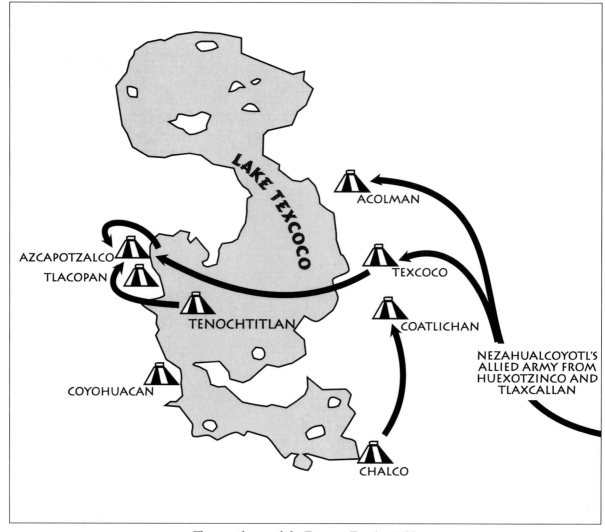

The overthrow of the Tepanec Empire, 1428

that led to the island city and particularly at Tlacopan where the main causeway was anchored to the mainland. Nezahualcoyotl and the Huexotzinco king served as joint commanders of the army assembling at Texcoco and decided to steal a march on Maxtla and land an army by canoe in his rear. But first Nezahualcoyotl had to deal with a morale problem among his own troops. The allies that assembled in Texcoco came dressed in a glitter of war finery unequalled in the world. The eagle and jaguar warriors, from their warrior societies, wearing their tight-fitting costumes of feathers or jaguar pelts and their faces framed by helmets in the shape of the great raptors and the spotted hunting cats. Brilliant blue-green quet-zal feathers shimmered from the helmets of kings and lords, as did the turquoise, jade, and gold and the rainbow of colours of their clothing and armour. From their backs on wicker frames, floated their standards worked in exquisite feather work and multi-coloured cloth, tricked out with gold and precious stones. And strewn throughout this rainbow river of fighting men were the sharp, glittering black obsidian spear points and sword edges. But in all this stream of colourful splendour, only the men of Texcoco were humbly dressed in plain white cotton. And they were not happy about it.

'Does he mean to belittle us in the eyes of all men that we should go so ill equipped to war?

64

That we should go in white, unadorned, while our allies march in their companies in colour?' With that fine touch of leadership that breathes a natural and contagious confidence, he walked among them. His pride in them was manifest.

'I feel happy and amused to see you among such an array, brilliant with every colour; it seems as if I was in a garden filled with a variety of flowers, and in which you, the fragrant blossoms of the jasmine, with no more adornment than a simple whiteness, are supreme among the blooms. External decorations do not increase the valour of those who sport them, but that of the enemy, whose greed drives him to victory, to obtain the spoil.'[7]

'In this battle you will win the adornments you seek. Look at the splendor of your enemies that now only weighs them down in battle. When the war is over, their splendor shall be yours.'[8]

And when he had finished they were suddenly proud of their efficient simplicity.

With that settled, the army pushed off into the lake in thousands of canoes to approach the shorefront of Azcapotzalco. They had achieved a complete surprise. In turn, they were surprised by the new shorefront fortifications that made a landing impossible. Still, their operational surprise overcame the tactical surprise they had met. They simply landed north of the city. Maxtla, however, was thoroughly panicked when he heard of the sudden appearance of an army in his rear and near his capital. He immediately abandoned his siege of Tenochtitlan and rushed his forces back to the area around Azcapotzalco.

With the land end of the causeway abandoned, the Mexica poured across from their city and overran the Tepanec first line of defence, a wide ditch. A Tepanec counterattack threw them back across the ditch and back to the lake shore itself, and there the fighting raged. At the same time, another Mexica force overran Tlacopan which offered a feeble feigned resistance. Their king was secretly in sympathy with the Mexica. Itzcoatl resumed the attack and again breached the ditch forcing the Tepaneca to retire to their last line, a circle of earthworks around Azcapotzalco itself. Now Nezahualcoyotl's army arrived to complete the siege ring

A human sacrifice. (Drawing by Keith Henderson)

around the city. The Mexica occupied the north, south, and eastern portions of the circumvallation. Nezahualcoyotl's army filled into the western part, the place of honour, for it was most exposed to a relief army from the Tepanec heartland behind it. The war now settled down to a siege of months enlivened by numerous Tepanec sorties in which the casualties on both sides were heavy. But the power was draining from the Tepaneca. Unlike the allies, they could replace no losses.

After 114 days of siege, starvation was stalking the city. Maxtla had been pleading with the Tepanec cities in the hinterland to come to his rescue. Now as a relief army finally appeared from the north-west, he threw his army into a great sortie hoping to crush his enemies between them. Those enemies between the converging Tepanec forces were the Texcocans and the men of Huexotzinco. Like the Romans at the siege of Alesia, they must have fought desperately front and back. Tepanec hopes died when their chief general, Mazatl, was struck down by a sword stroke. They fled with the allies on their heels.

As the allies rushed through the streets of Azcapotzalco slaughtering and looting, Nezahualcoyotl headed straight for the royal palace to hunt out Maxtla. He found him cowering in his own bathhouse. Nezahualcoyotl dragged him out and ordered a platform built in the temple square. He later ringed it with the mass of the alliance's fighting men, the Mexica and the others in their colours and his own men of Texcoco in their blood-stained white. Maxtla was pushed onto the platform stripped of his royal raiment and thrown across a sacrifice stone, his arms and legs held by four black-clad priests. Nezahualcoyotl raised the obsidian knife aloft, and then in one swift slash, tore open his chest and pulled out his still-beating heart. Holding it high, he scattered the blood to the four corners of the world.

It was a supreme moment for Nezahualcoyotl, as described by Richard Townsend:

'The ritual action brought to an end the power of the Tepanecs. On one level the performance may be seen as an expression of personal vengeance by Nezahualcoyotl and an assertion of his status as a *tlatoani* (although he would not in fact be crowned ruler of Tetzcoco until 1431). But the act of offering the vanquished king's blood to the four quarters had deeper implications, reaching to the very soil and its life-sources. Sacrificial human blood was regarded as the primary ritual fertilizing agent, ensuring the earth's regeneration in the planting cycle and the arrival of water, especially at the critical annual change from the dry to the rainy season. In a similar manner, war and sacrifice were linked to the renewal of the state in coronation rites, when society was transformed from dissolution to reintegration and production. Thus Maxtla's sacrifice transformed death into life. On another level, Maxtla's demise signalled the fertilization of conquered alien land and joined it with the land of the victors. Finally, the sacrifice marked a major social turning point, because the formerly subservient city-states of Tenochtitlan and Tetzcoco themselves became sovereign.'[9]

Not only sovereign but rich beyond all dreams — Azcapotzalco had been the centre of an empire, and its accumulated treasure houses and the riches of its slaughtered inhabitants had been spilled into the hands of the victors. Even after the allies from outside the Valley had been loaded down with plunder for their return journey, the riches were immense. Now began the sharing out of the real treasure of conquest, the lands and tribute of the con-

quered, between Tenochtitlan and Texcoco. The men of Texcoco had returned home in glory singing the praises of their king, awarding him the epithet, 'Arm of the Lion'.

After a while, murmurs of discontent began to float across the lake from Texcoco because Nezahualcoyotl had not returned to his native land with his troops but stayed in Tenochtitlan with his Mexica relatives and his uncle Itzcoatl. There he built a splendid palace and supervised public works for the Mexica, including the building of an aqueduct across the lake from the mountain springs. He also busied himself with new wars to subdue more of the remaining independent states of the Valley. Yet the murmurs against him in Texcoco and in the other towns of the Acolhua grew to cries of rebellion at the absentee king. Even his traitor brother, Tilmatzin, had found his way back to lead a revolt among the disaffected cities. What was Nezahualcoyotl doing so long from home when the affairs of his kingdom were crying out for a strong hand? None of the annals are clear about this. His subsequent actions, however, give an important clue. This man who achieved a later reputation as a sage statesman surely was not giving in to indolent pleasure in feckless disregard of his own interests. He was simply cementing his ties to the emerging great power of Anáhuac. It was vital that he secure a place within the new reality of power. His father had opposed the similar hegemony of the Tepaneca and been ground to dust by it. Nezahualcoyotl was ensuring that Texcoco would be an integral part of the next hegemony. He had no illusions that Texcoco could dominate it. Clearly he was willing to acknowledge pride of place to the power of the Mexica. But his fine hand was seen in the creation of the internal balance of this hegemony. Its twin pillars were obviously Tenochtitlan and Texcoco, but the tradition of empires beginning with the Toltecs had always included three pillars for such a power structure. Nezahualcoyotl suggested to Itzcoatl a wise alternative to the cowardly Tlatelolco, Tenochtitlan's Mexica twin city. Tlatelolco had joined the alliance only late in the struggle and fought with no distinction. To Itzcoatl's surprise, he recommended that the Tepanec city of Tlacopan be raised up. He advised that,

'. . . it would be wise to give a share in the alliance to Tlacopan. They did not fight long against us, though they were of the Tepaneca blood. Their hearts were with us. And it will secure the peace if the dignity and tradition of the Tepaneca are saved by our giving them the remnant of honor still. After all, the Tepanecan blood runs in the veins of nearly all our cities; Tezozomoc saw to that.'[10]

Like Machiavelli and Tezozomoc, Nezahualcoyotl understood that there were two options with a defeated enemy. Befriend or destroy him. So was born the Triple Alliance, with Tenochtitlan and Texcoco each receiving two-fifths of all tribute and Tlacopan one-fifth. And when the time came, that power would restore the wavering towns of Texcoco to his control. In 1431 the combined armies of Nezahualcoyotl and Itzcoatl marched through his kingdom returning the rebellious towns to their allegiance. Then in Tenochtitlan, each of the three alliance kings took his formal title. Nezahualcoyotl was declared the Acolhua Tecutli – Lord of the Acolhua, the Great Chichimecatl.

LAWGIVER AND POET

His kingdom was now safely in his hands — for the first time since he had been declared heir by his father more than fifteen years ago. However, that fifteen years playing cat and mouse with death had made a shrewd realist of him. Th-- were havens for all the rebellious lords that Itzcoatl and he had driven away in their recent campaign. He was all too aware of the dangers represented by so many dispossessed hereditary princes and their relentless conspiracies. In a bold stroke of enlightened self-interest, he pardoned most of them and returned fifteen to their towns. Itzcoatl advised strongly against it, arguing for a more strongly centralised state. But so effective were the results in securing stability that he quickly followed Nezahualcoyotl's example, restoring nine lords. The king of Tlacopan similarly restored seven such princes. The trick to Nezahualcoyotl's clemency was that the restored lords were required to reside most of the year in his court at Texcoco, anticipating Louis XIV's taming of the French aristocracy by almost 300 years.

Under the royal eye they were not off in distant towns inflating their own importance and sense of independence.

With the threat of rebellion subdued, Nezahualcoyotl turned to the management of the kingdom and midwifed one of history's golden ages. The years of wandering had done more than make a political realist of him. They had given him time to dream. He was already possessed of a princely education, an artistic temperament, and a keen intellect. The years of wandering must also have instilled a hunger for creation and permanence. Now this pent-up desire to create had its canvas. His first effort was to give the kingdom laws and the order that would flow from them. Like Hammurabi, he created a unified law code to replace tribal law. This 'legalist' system was 'designed to ensure government by severe but standardized laws that favoured the rule of the state.' This system defined 'behaviour and responsibilities with punishments meted out with strict impartiality. Rules prescribed exclusive and concrete solutions to specific types of disputes, and these rules were mechanically applied, with no regard to mitigating circumstances.' The eighty laws in the code were supplemented where they were inappropriate with a traditional system of justice based on 'the reasonable man', which was based on 'notions of reasonable behaviour' and thus was able to modify the harshness of the legalist system.[11] Nezahualcoyotl clearly understood the power of example. He executed the law with harsh impartiality in the blood of his own family by putting to death two of his own sons under the law. 'Let my son die. On those of noble blood a heavier responsibility rests than on a villager. It is the law that a man die for adultery. Let my son die. Yes, and the woman too, according to the law.' For another son who was proven guilty of sodomy, he said, 'I myself will kill him.'[12] He was especially vigilant to punish corrupt judges and in doing so increased the efficiency and reliability of justice. A surviving codex shows corrupt judges being strangled in their own courts. By these measures, confidence in justice grew. His code also unified the diverse peoples and cities of his growing kingdom into a single system, curbed the power of his vassals, and disciplined the whole people to the power of the state. His innovation of such a law code was revolutionary in Mesoamerica and the benefits so quickly manifest that again the kings of Tenochtitlan and Tlacopan copied his example.

Though he executed his draconian laws with the utmost evenhandedness, his humanity comes through in the folk memories. Once, under his law, he had to condemn to death a man who had stolen seven ears of corn to feed his family. Touched by the pathos of such a punishment for nothing more than the sin of poverty, he ordered that the waters' edges and road sides be planted with corn, beans, and squash from which anyone in need could take without fear of punishment.

The stories about Nezahualcoyotl survived even the Spanish conquest and reflect Mexican society's image of the just ruler in his primal role as protector, as much as that of the man himself. They depict a man of character driven by a sense of duty and justice and a man firmly in control of his passions for the sake of his people. He is repeatedly shown seeking firsthand information about the condition of his realm by wandering the land in disguise or listening to the words of ordinary people from a balcony of his palace. From these wanderings came the idea for his code of laws.

Once he overheard a woodcutter straining under his load complain, 'The man who lives in this palace has everything he needs, while as for us, we are worn out, and we die of hunger.' Nezahualcoyotl ordered the terrified man brought before him. 'So you are angry because the king has riches. Do you think I carry no burden of responsibility for all the people of this land? I am their final judge and guide. On me is the burden of defense.' Turning to a servant, he ordered, 'Bring cotton mantles and cocoa.' Then to the woodcutter he said, 'These things are now yours. Take them and speak no ill of the king again. Know that although he has riches he has nothing.'[13] At other times he would watch from his balcony the market where the poorest vendors offered little piles of salt or beans, and on the days when they sold little, he would order his servants to go out and buy everything at double price and give it away to the neediest. He made provisions that widows, orphans, and the war-maimed did not go hungry. Once wandering in the country in one

Judges and the administration of justice. The royal diadems signified that they acted in the king's name.

of his disguises, he came across a crying boy gathering small fragments of wood on a cold winter day. He asked why the boy did not go into the woods behind him to gather the plentiful deadwood. The boy cried out in fear that it was death to break the law that forbade taking wood from a royal reserve. Like the woodsman, the trembling boy and his parents were ordered into the royal presence, and to their surprise loaded down with gifts.

'I called you to give you and your family corn and cocoa and fine cotton clothes, and to thank you for teaching me a thing I needed to know. From now on all men may go into the forest and take the dry wood they need. The boundaries of the reserve are blotted out. We will leave one law only, to protect our wood for the future. No one must cut down a living tree on pain of death.'[14]

Nezahualcoyotl was far more than a lawgiver. He was a magnet for the creative vitality of Anáhuac. His encouragement attracted talent and innovation — and they came from everywhere. The colonies of craftsmen, artisans, and artists that had been originally attracted to Azcapotzalco's seat of empire and had survived the war now moved to Texcoco. Also came goldsmiths from Xochimilco; coppersmiths, featherworkers with their rainbow skills; weavers of fine cotton cloth, painters of books on maguey fibre or on the beaten bark of the amatl tree or on softly-tanned deerskin; the painters of frescos and artists in stone to adorn the new palaces and temples arising in Texcoco; jewellers in jade, turquoise, and rock crystal; men skilled in carving wood; and the creative men of music and the spoken word, the poets held in much esteem by the speakers of the elegant Náhuatl, a language rich in symbolism and metaphor and made for poetry. Even Itzcoatl sent skilled men to his nephew's capital. Nezahualcoyotl instituted fairs and festivals at which performances were heard and judged for their beauty, and the artists either rewarded or punished for their work. Nezahualcoyotl's memory survived the Spanish conquest as not only a ruler who encouraged the arts to flourish but, as Gillmor described him in the subtitle to her book, *The Poet King of the Aztecs*, he was a gifted artist in his own right. Who but a poet would exempt the musicians, painters,

and makers of books from taxes and tribute. For it was said that 'Theirs was a tribute of beauty.'[15] Nezahualcoyotl's residence glowed and echoed with the splendour of a renaissance court where a poet could recite:

'I, am the singer, I make the poem
  That shines like an emerald
A brilliant, precious and splendid emerald.
  I suit myself to the inflections
Of the tuneful voice of the *tzinitzcan*. . .
  Like the ring of little bells,
Little golden bells. . .
  I sing my song
A scented song like a shining jewel,
  A shining turquoise and a blazing emerald,
My flowering hymn to the spring.'[16]

Nezahualcoyotl's reputation as a builder rivalled that as a patron of the arts. His palace at Texcoco measured 1,000 by 800 yards, boasting 300 rooms. It became in Mexico a byword for magnificence, again anticipating Louis XIV's Versailles by almost 300 years. Besides the royal apartments reserved for the kings of Tenochtitlan and Tlacopan, there were his own private rooms, his considerable harem, and rooms for a host of retainers and relatives. Gardens filled the rest of the palace complex:

'with many fountains, ponds and canals, many fish and birds, and the whole planted with more than two thousand pines . . . and there were several mazes, according to where the king bathed; and once a man was in he could not find the way out. . . and farther on, beside the temples, there was the bird-house, where the king kept all the kinds and varieties of birds, animals, reptiles and serpents that they brought him from every part of New Spain; and those which were not to be had were represented in gold and precious stones — which was also the case with the fish, both of the sea and those that lived in the rivers and lakes. So no bird, fish or animal of the whole country was wanting there: they were there either alive or figured in gold and gems.'[17]

Nezahualcoyotl's country retreats, particularly at Tetzcotzinco, were marvels of delight. His post-Conquest descendent, Ixtlilxochitl, described a water and flower wonderland. The water was brought by immense aqueducts from another mountain that fed a large reservoir adorned with exquisite bas-reliefs. From there the water ran through the gardens in two directions filling large basins surrounded by carved stelae whose images shimmered in the water. From out of the basins the water

'leapt and dashed itself to pieces on the rocks, falling into a garden planted with all the scented flowers of the Hot Lands, and in this garden it seemed to rain, so very violently was the water shattered upon these rocks. Beyond this garden were the bathing places, cut in the living rock . . . and beyond them the castle that the king had in this park and in which still other rooms and halls were seen, and many of them; one was a very large hall with a court in front of it, and it was there that he received the kings of Mexico and Tlacopan and other great lords when they came to enjoy themselves with him: the dances and the other spectacles and delights took place in this court . . . The whole of the rest of this park was planted . . . with all kinds of trees and scented flowers, and there were all kinds of birds apart from those that the king had brought from various parts in cages: all these birds sang harmoniously and to such degree that one could not hear oneself speak.'[18]

There was more to Nezahualcoyotl's energy for creation than the simple delight in the new and the beautiful. He seemed to be expressing the Mexican concept that true spirituality was found in artistic creation, and of that the most pure was the most ephemeral – that of the spoken and sung word. This search for the spiritual led him to the teachings of the men of letters and philosophy and from there to the devotion of 'unknown god, creator of all things', Tloque Nahuaque, 'he who invents himself', 'he of the immediate vicinity' or Ipalnemohuani, 'he by whom we live', 'the Creator of Life, the god of the 'With and the By', 'the Close and the Near', the god of the 'Immediate Vicinity'. He built a temple to this god with no blood altar and no idol, the same impulse of the human spirit that built an unadorned, bloodless altar to the 'Unknown God' on the Acropolis in Athens. On the great pyramid of Texcoco stood a unique temple of nine stories 'which stood for the nine heavens, and the tenth, which finished these nine stories, was painted black and studded with stars outside, while the inside was

adorned with gold, gems and precious feathers.'[19] Instead of human hearts, Nezahualcoyotl's offerings to Tloque Nahuaque were flowers, symbolic of poetry and art. Although he did not reject the other gods, his absence at the human sacrifices to them became conspicuous and a matter of concern among the people. Out of the shining folk memory of this remarkable man, this aversion to sacrifice, so strange in Mesoamerica, stands out boldly. A poem of his to The Giver of Life survives:

'In truth no one is intimate with You,
  oh Giver of Life!
Only as among the flowers
  we might seek someone,
thus we seek You,
  we who live on the earth,
we who are at Your side.

'Your heart will be troubled
  only for a short time,
we will be near You and at Your side.

'The Giver of Life enrages us,
  He intoxicates us here.
No one is at His side
  to be famous, to rule on earth.

'Only You change things
  as our heart well knows;
no one is at His side
  To be famous, to rule on earth.'[20]

Suffusing the legends and poems of this man is a sense of the vanity of all earthly things, of the omnipresence and inevitability of death to wither every flower and crack every jewel. At the feasts to mark the opening of each new palace he would address his guests:

'Listen with attention to the lamentations which the king, Nezahualcoyotl, make upon my power . . .

'O restless and striving king, when the time of thy death shall come, thy subjects shall be destroyed and driven forth; they shall sink into oblivion. Then in thy hand shall no longer be the power and the rule, but with the creator, the All-powerful.

'He who saw the palaces and court of the old king Tezozomoc, how flourishing and powerful was his sway, may see them now dry and withered . . . all that the world offers is illusion and deception . . . everything must end and die . . .'[21]

Within this aching understanding of death was a search for the eternal, and a realisation of the mystery surrounding the Giver of Life. Miguel León-Portilla wrote that 'Nezahualcoyotl sought in his heart songs and flowers that would endure forever. Aware of death, he hoped that at least these might be carried to the innermost house of the Lord of the Close and the Near, where dwell the birds with golden feathers':

'They shall not wither, my flowers
   They shall not cease, my songs.
I, the singer, lift them up.
   They are scattered, they spread about.
Even though on earth my flowers
   may wither and yellow,
they will be carried there,
   to the innermost house
of the bird with the golden feathers.'[22]

WARS FEIGNED AND REAL

Having settled the internal affairs of Texcoco, Nezahualcoyotl then set himself to measure the kingdom's external security. He remembered how Tezozomoc had broken Texcoco. Without a doubt, the Mexica would be even more fierce and unrelenting enemies if provoked. To liberate his kingdom, Nezahualcoyotl had needed allies, not only from Tenochtitlan but from the major powers of Tlaxcallan, Huexotzinco, and Chalco as well. To suppress rebellion he had needed the Mexica again. He measured the power of Texcoco and Tenochtitlan and concluded that if he attempted to stand alone outside the alliance, the Mexica would grind Texcoco to bits and with far less indirection and restraint than Tezozomoc. To attempt to place himself at the head of the alliance would provoke the same reaction from the Mexica. By formally accepting second place, Nezahualcoyotl would ensure the security of Texcoco. His power was vital to the Mexica, and as long as it did not threaten but instead benefited them, his kingdom would

remain secure. There was more than sheer calculation here. He was related closely to the large Mexica royal family. He had not forgotten that they had saved his life repeatedly from Tezozomoc nor the years he had spent as a protected relative in Tenochtitlan. These connections had been vital to his survival. The bonds of affection and shared hardships in war are powerful motives in even the most objective statesman.

With the death of Itzcoatl in 1440 and the election of his nephew, Motecuhzoma I, Nezahualcoyotl found the time appropriate to cement Texcoco securely to the alliance.[23] Motecuhzoma was his cousin. They knew each other well. Motecuhzoma once had even saved his life with a timely warning while they paid court to Tezozomoc in Azcapotzalco. In the siege of Azcapotzalco, they had fought as the commanders of the two allied armies. Had not he himself, as the senior of the kings of the Triple Alliance, put the Toltec royal turquoise diadem upon Motecuhzoma's head when he had been chosen as king of the Mexica upon Itzcoatl's death? Nezahualcoyotl made his decision. He gathered his vassals and addressed them:

'I beg you, lords, brothers, to treat the Aztecs well! Flee from their enmity and from any conflict with them. Let us keep an eternal peace and inviolable friendship. You know them; I do not have to say more regarding their ways. . . Should we oppose them we would only gain wars, trouble, deaths, robbery, the shedding of our blood, and desolation to our kingdom. Therefore be in peace and quiet and urge the people of the cities in my kingdom . . . to do likewise.'[24]

He chose the most exquisite treasures of Texcoco as coronation gifts for Motecuhzoma – gifts meant to soften the ground for his words – golden jewelry cunningly worked, the finest polished stones of jade, turquoise, and carnelian in soft dyed doeskin bags, ear and lip plugs of gold and gems, the most exquisite featherwork, shimmering like captured rainbows, elegant and deadly weapons, shields, quilted cotton armour meant to excite the admiration of an old soldier, and mantles and loincloths of the finest dyed and embroidered cotton. They wove their spell, and Motecuhzoma was much pleased. Then Nezahualcoyotl spoke to him privately with great eloquence.

'I have come here, O lord, to tell you of the misery, the affliction that reigns in your province of Texcoco. In your greatness deign to lift it and ennoble it and shelter it from other nations. You well know, great prince, that all your vassals, nobles as well as common people are under your shade and you have been planted here like a great cedar under which men wish to rest in order to take pleasure in the freshness of your friendship and love. Those who need you most are the old men and women, orphans and widows, the poor and the destitute. All of them are like feathers on your wings and feathers on your head. Also think of the little ones who are beginning to crawl or are still in their cradles, who do not feel, not hear, nor know, nor understand. They have no hands to defend themselves or feet to flee from the wrath of the Aztecs. All these, and I in their name, beseech your clemency. Preserve us in peace and concord and do not allow Mexico to attack us. If I, without purpose or aim, waged a war, I would do so knowing that the fury of the Aztecs is measureless, limitless. Therefore I beg of you to receive my people as children and servants. They love you like a father and mother who consoles them and they hold all Aztecs as friends.'[25]

Motecuhzoma was even more pleased with Nezahualcoyotl's speech — and no wonder. The first part of his reign was to be spent in consolidation of the growing empire and administrative reform. His cousin had lightened his burden immensely. Still, he could not accept the offer out of hand. At this time, the Mexica kingship was not absolute. He ruled, as did most Mesoamerican monarchs, with the advice of a council of the great men of the kingdom. And he listened carefully, for the determined opposition of the council was an effective veto. Speaking for the council, Tlacaélel, Motecuhzoma's half-brother and first counsellor, concurred with the arrangement but argued that there was an important propaganda element to Texcoco's submission that must be engaged. Texcoco must be seen to bend to force as an example to all others of the might of Tenochtitlan. A voluntary submission might leave the impression that it might be as easily cast off. He recommended that both Tenochtitlan and Texcoco engage in a massive charade and stage a mock battle in which the Acolhua would flee. No one would be hurt, and the Mexica would have their object lesson. Nezahualcoyotl could only agree. Both sides sealed their borders with each other and spread rumours of war.

The war was carefully choreographed. The two armies met on the appointed day at Chiquiuhtepec outside of Texcoco. Most of the soldiers on both sides had been kept in the dark but under strict control. The 'battle' began with the usual chants and insults hurled across the small space between them. As soon as the Mexica surged forward, though, the Texcocans, on command, turned and fled the field. Their army poured back into Texcoco with the Mexica in pursuit. In one of the small towns leading into the capital, Nezahualcoyotl was waiting. Watching his men pass by, he gave orders for the town's small pyramid temple to be fired, the act of surrender in Mesoamerican warfare. With that, the Mexica pursuit came to a swift halt. The Mexica army was promptly turned around and marched home, to the disgust of the soldiery who went home empty-handed. No one had been harmed and nothing stolen on pain of death. The leaders fared better. They were welcomed into Texcoco as honoured guests and presented with lavish gifts and estates. Thus by surrendering did Nezahualcoyotl disarm his potential enemies and make them friends.[26]

Nezahualcoyotl's recognition of the supremacy of his Mexica cousins did not end the wars of Texcoco. After his return to his kingdom in 1433, he had led his Acolhua in numerous campaigns either as a single venture of Texcoco or as a contingent of the Triple Alliance. The list of tribute towns that poured treasure into Texcoco continued to grow fast enough to support his ambitious building programme with more to spare. But as the years passed, he campaigned less and less himself in order to devote himself to the affairs of Texcoco. The interests of the kingdom, however, on the battlefield were well-represented by his numerous warrior sons — he was to sire 60 sons and 57 daughters.

After the great drought of the early 1450s that put a hiatus on warfare, a final settlement with the recalcitrant kingdom of Chalco was won. By then the Chalca were the last independent people in the Valley of Mexico. Late in Motecuhzoma's reign about 1459, the Chalca war resumed. As part of the Triple Alliance response, Nezahualcoyotl's son and first minister, Ichautlatoatzin, led an army to bring back the elderly king of Chalco dead or alive. The younger man taunted the old Chalca, who had to be carried to war in a litter, that he was too feeble to be killed and would be dragged to Nezahualcoyotl for judgement. The old man was more cynical.

'Have the lords of Texcoco sent this boy against me? Though I am old and blind, seated in my house and my tent I will give him such a greeting that they will know it is not safe to send a boy against me. I will whip him as a boy has never been whipped before. I will give the king a punishment that will lash his heart.'[27]

The Chalca king sprung an ambush on the overconfident Texcocans in the mountains and drove them away with heavy losses. Nezahualcoyotl bided his time to prepare for a new war. The priests complained that the altars had not drunk enough blood for the gods to favour Texcoco with victory. So the sacrifices resumed as they did in Tenochtitlan, but still the king waited to resume the war. In those years, two of Motecuhzoma's sons and two of his own went hunting and never returned. Then a woman demanded audience with the king and said:

'Are you the king who holds the cities of all the land subject to you? How then do you let the death of your two sons and the two Mexican princes go unavenged? I was a captive and a slave in the house of the king of Chalco. But when I saw their dried bodies standing in the four corners of the great hall to hold the torches, I risked my life to bring them to Texcoco.'[28]

The armies of Texcoco marched, again under the same sons who had been defeated before. Nezahualcoyotl travelled to his country retreat at Tetzcotzinco and prayed this time to Tloque Nahuaque for victory. With the host was a sixteen-year-old son, Axoquentzin, new to war. Around their campfire, his older brothers mocked him as a stripling who should have stayed at home to hold his mother's skirt. Axoquentzin walked away from the fire in silent

fury. That night he crept into the Chalca camp, slew the king's guards, and carried the old man off on his back. He approached his brothers' fire and presented his captive to the stunned group. Nezahualcoyotl greeted Axoquentzin on his return, 'If I had not know that you were my son, yet would I know it by the valor you have shown this day.'

'I THOUGHT THEY WOULD BE MERCIFUL.'

In the years of building, Nezahualcoyotl's mind turned to thoughts of an heir. His palace was filled with concubines and children. His favourite, whom he had spirited away from Maxtla's pursuers, had given him many strong and intelligent sons, who were skilled in war, law, and even the arts. Many of these would have made a worthy heir, but he wished for a perfect bride for his queen, a dream of perfection. He ordered his brother, Quauhtlehuanitzin, to choose quietly from the daughters of the lords of Texcoco this perfect bride, and he picked the young daughter of the lord of Coatlichan. As she was still too young for marriage, Nezahualcoyotl told him to take her into his own household and raise her as a queen. The years passed, and his brother died. And more years had passed until it was ten years (1443) since he had returned to the rule of Texcoco. He thought again of the child who would now be a woman ready for marriage and called for her. In fury he listened to the royal messengers say that his brother's son had married her. The young man pleaded that he had known nothing of the king's intention to marry her, for his father had kept the king's wish secret. Nezahualcoyotl was overcome with such anger that even in his heart he threw away the royal justice, the jewel of his reign. He ordered his nephew brought before the judges, but they absolved him of any guilt in the very face of the king's anger, so well had he built justice into the land.

In his rage he walked into the countryside through town after town until he came to the home of Quaquauhtzin, one of his councillors. Overcoming his shock at the king's appearance alone at his door, Quaquauhtzin welcomed him and ordered a meal set before the king. The young woman that served the king was striking in her grace and beauty. She was Quaquauhtzin's new wife, the king's own cousin, Azcalxochitzin (Ant Flower), daughter of Temictzin of Tenochtitlan, and he had paid a rich bride price for her. Upon the king's return, his household was pleased to see that his anger had fallen away. Then he sent a messenger to Tlaxcallan with whom Texcoco would be fighting a ritual 'flowery war' for the purpose of testing the courage of their warriors.

'This month in the war of flowers Quaquauhtzin will go to battle in the ranks of the Texcocans. You know him of old, a brave captain. But now he has committed a great crime, of which I do not wish to speak. I send him into battle that he may have the chance to die the death of flowers with honor. See that he dies.'[29]

And to his own captains he gave the same order, 'See that he dies.' And they obeyed.

With great circumspection and after a decent interval, Nezahualcoyotl courted the widow through his sister as match-maker. She humbly accepted. To the wedding of his heart's desire he invited the kings of Tenochtitlan and Tlacopan and their great vassals to mingle with the lords of his own kingdom to wish him joy and many sons. The cycle of feasts and ceremonies was said to have lasted four months.

Their son was the joy beyond measure — Tetzauhpiltzintli. He became known as the Prodigy so quick at everything was he, the arts of gem-cutting and the making of glimmering pictures in feathers, and like his father, his words were turning into golden poems. But as the child flourished to his parents' delight, the land shuddered in a succession of natural disasters. In 1446 a plague of locusts stripped the harvests and created a food shortage. In 1449 the rains swelled the lake until it inundated Tenochtitlan and other lakeside cities. Motecuhzoma asked for the master builder, Nezahualcoyotl's help. He designed a seven-mile long embankment to hold back the waters. The two kings carried the first loads of stone themselves as an example to high and low alike. The next year began with unheard of snowfalls that collapsed houses and killed off plants and trees. The following sharp frosts of the spring blighted the young green plants in the fields so that there was no harvest. The land then withered in a scorching drought that staggered from one year to another. Nezahualcoyotl had opened his storehouses to the hungry people, but even his wealth was exhausted as one hungry year followed another. Then the Acolhua, like the Mexica, sold themselves and their children to the peoples of the Hot Lands for food. It was not until the rains returned in abundance in 1455 that the crisis was over.

With the return of the rains, the land blossomed in the riches of the earth. Finally Nezahualcoyotl was satisfied in his heart. The land abounded in order and plenty. Beauty was everywhere to be seen and heard. His sons and daughters had given him joy and were a strength to him, especially his Prodigy. One day his favourite concubine presented him a wondrously carved turquoise jewel fashioned by one of her many gifted sons, Huetzin. He delighted in its beauty and exclaimed that he would make a gift of it to Tetzauhpiltzintli. The concubine suggested that Eyahue, another of her sons take it. This prince found his favoured brother in his own palace at vigorous practice with arms. The Prodigious One had also inherited his father's skill in war and had already won fame in battle. He admired the jewel but remarked that Huetzin would do better to practice with sharp-edged obsidian weapons than the delicate tools of the jeweller. Then he showed him his large array of weapons hanging from the walls of his palace, delighting in their well-shaped deadliness.

Eyahue repeated Tetzauhpiltzintli's words to his mother. This was her chance to push one of her own sons towards the throne. A few careful twists in the prince's words, and she had transformed an innocent statement into one reeking of treason and planned rebellion. Nezahualcoyotl ordered men to look into the arms collected by his son. The concubine whispered to them that should one of her sons inherit the throne, they would not be forgotten. The inspectors reported that the prince was indeed collecting arms, more than any one man could use, enough for an army. Nezahualcoyotl was staggered; the law's answer to treason was stark — death. Though he had committed murder to acquire as wife the only woman he had ever loved, he could not now break the law to save the son of his heart. He asked the kings of Tenochtitlan and Tlacopan to come and judge the case, hoping they would spare the son he could not. They came to Texcoco to sit in judgement and there the concubine sent them the same witnesses she had already bought, and they suggested that the proceedings be held in secret. The prince rushed forward to greet his uncles, the two kings, as they entered his palace. They threw a garland of flowers around his neck as if a token of friendship — and strangled him with the hidden cord.

In horror Nezahualcoyotl heard the messenger of his brother kings. 'We have followed your request. We have done justly.' His heart breaking, the king cried out, 'Better that I had been judge myself. Why did I not sit on the throne of judgement? I thought they would be merciful.'[30]

He shut himself up in his gardens at Tetzcotzinco away from the world, broken by the horror of his deed. Only time pulled him back to Texcoco and the burdens of kingship. Motecuhzoma requested his help in building the great aqueduct from the hill of Chapultepec to Tenochtitlan. Then war with Chalco broke out again, and he found himself back at Tetzcotzinco praying to the Giver of Life for victory while his army marched to war. There an apparition of a man in shining clothes appeared to him, promising that another son would be born to him. The next day came the news of his son, Axoquentzin's capture of the king of Chalco. That night when he went to his bed, happy in the thought that he had worthy sons to succeed him, his wife whispered to him, 'We are to have a child.'

Nezahualcoyotl lived to place the turquoise diadem on the head of another king of the Mexica, Axayácatl, in 1469. The final years drifted by in peace as he watched his young heir, Nezahualpilli (Hungry Prince), grow in healthy, precocious childhood. He felt the end coming, sharpening his yearning to have something of himself survive his death. He ordered the greatest artisans in Texcoco to fashion his likeness in their different materials — gold, gems, feathers, wood, pottery, paint and stone. Shaking his head as he examined them all, he said, 'Men will steal the gold and the precious stones for greed; the pictures in plumes and in paint will be worn and erased with time; the pottery

Nezahualpilli, the son and successor of Nezahualcoyotl.

will break at last. But the stone on the hill of Tetzcotzinco may endure, and my children and grandchildren may remember me.'[31]

The end came in his seventieth year. The anterooms of his private chambers were filled with royal quetzal feathers — the kings of Tenochtitlan and Tlacopan were there to honour the last founder of the Triple Alliance and his four most able older sons, each a pillar of state and leader of a council, those of crime and government, the arts, trade and tribute, and war. To the last of the four, Acapipioltzin, for his mature good judgement, he passed the regency and protection of his heir, charging him to be father to little brother.[32] The two kings he pledged as guarantors of his will. The words of an Otomi poem came to him then:

'The fleeting pomp of the world is like the green willow . . . but at the end a sharp axe destroys it, a north wind fells it . . .'[33]

These were the thoughts of a man drifting into the shadows. Perhaps he had said it better in the sunlight of his life:

'They shall not wither, my flowers
   They shall not cease, my songs.
I, the singer, lift them up.
   They are scattered, they spread about . . .'[34]

1. Gillmor, ibid., p. 34. Gillmor has Ixtlilxochitl telling his son to hide 'under' a fallen tree. However, most of the other accounts, which I have followed here, have Nezahualcoyotl hiding 'in' the leafy branches of a tree.

2. Gillmor, ibid., p.57.

3. Gillmor, ibid.

4. Gillmor, ibid., p. 63.

5. Ixtlilxochitl, vol. II, p. 125; in Davies, ibid., p. 70.

6. Serge Gruzinksi, *Painting the Conquest,* Flammarion, Paris, 1992, p. 120-121.

7. Nigel Davies, *The Aztecs,* The University of Oklahoma Press, Norman, OK, 1989, p. 74; citing Veytia, Mariano, *Historia Antigua de Mexico,* Vol II Editorial Leyenda, Mexico City, 1944, p. 135.

8. Gillmor, ibid., p. 78; citing Fernando de Alva Ixtlilxochitl, *Obrás Históricas,* Vol I, *Relaciones*; Vol II, *Historia Chichimeca*, Publicadas y anotadas por Alfredo Chavero, Mexico City, 1891.

9. Richard F. Townsend, *The Aztecs,* Thames & Hudson, London, 1992, p. 70.

10. Gillmor, ibid., p. 86.

11. Townsend, ibid., pp. 84-85.

12. Torquemada, Juan de, *Monarqúia Indiana,* Madrid, 1723, and Polmar, Juan Bautista, *Relación de Texcoco* (written 1582); in Gillmor, ibid., p. 107.

13. Ixtlilxochitl, *Historia Chichimec*, ibid., pp. 229-234; in Gillmor, ibid., p. 107.

14. Gillmor, ibid., pp. 109-110.

15. Gillmor, ibid., p. 88.

16. John H. Cronyn, *Aztec Literature,* in *XXVII Congrès international des Américanistes,* Mexico, 1949, Vol. II, p. 328-331; in Jacques Soustelle, *Daily Life of the Aztecs,* Stanford University Press, Stanford, CA, 1970, p. 237.

17. Soustelle, ibid., p.124.

18. Ixtlilxochitl, ibid., pp. 208-212; in Soustelle, ibid., p. 125.

19. Ixtlilxochitl, ibid., p. 227; in Soustelle, ibid., p. 118.

20. 'MSS Romances de los Señores de la Nueva España' (Collection of Náhuatl songs and poems preserved at the Library of the University of Texas) fol. 4 v.-5v; in Miguel León-Portilla, *Pre-Columbian Literatures of Mexico* University of Oklahoma Press, Norman and London, 1986, pp. 67-68.

21. Ixtlilxochitl, ibid., pp. 234-235; in Gillmor, ibid., p. 119.

22. León-Portilla, ibid., p. 89. 'Cantares Mexicanos', fac simile reproduction of the manuscript in the National Library of Mexico. Edited by Antonio Peñafiel, Mexico City, 1904.

23. While Durán puts this episode of Texcoco's submis sion to Tenochtitlan at the beginning of the reign of Motecuhzoma, others such as Ixtlilxochitl put it in Itzcoatl's preceding reign.

24. Durán, ibid., pp. 87-88.

25. Durán, ibid., p. 88. Although this account is written from the Aztec viewpoint, Náhuatl was a language of great elegance and metaphor, and great men were accustomed to speak in these terms.

26. Durán, ibid., note, p. 342. Durán's account is drawn from Aztec sources and is probably much overstated. On the other hand, Nezahualcoyotl's descendent in post-Conquest Mexico, Ixtlilxochitl, wrote a history of Texcoco, *Historia Chichimeca*, in which he portrays a genuine war between Texcoco and Tenochtitlan. In this account Nezahualcoyotl led 50,000 into a direct attack on the Mexica city which he subdued after seven days of fighting. Although the Aztec accounts are surely overblown, it is hard to credit Ixtlilxochitl's account as more than Texcocan boosterism. For in the end, Nezahualcoyotl did accept a subordinate if honoured position in the alliance after Tenochtitlan, hardly something that would have occurred had he so decisively humbled the Mexica.

27. Gillmor, ibid., p. 139.

28. Gillmor, ibid., p. 140.

29. Gillmor, ibid., p. 113.

30. Gillmor, ibid., p. 137.

31. Ixtlilxochitl, ibid., p. 237; in Gillmor, ibid., p. 147.

32. Gillmor, ibid., p. 171, n.21. The three other brothers later unsuccessfully attempted a conspiracy against Nezahualpilli and their brother the regent. Nezahualpilli's reign over Texcoco was almost as long and brilliant as his father's.

33. Granados y Galvez, *Tardes Americanas,* Mexico, 1778; in Gillmor, ibid., p. 147.

34. 'Cantares Mexicanos', fol. 16 v.; in León-Portilla, ibid., p. 175.

5
THREE HARD MEN OF TENOCHTITLAN
(1428–1469)

THE TRIUMVIRATE OF ITZCOATL, MOTECUHZOMA, TLACAÉLEL

Seated on reed mats, the three lords of the Eagle Clan, the Mexica royal kin, reached a momentous decision in 1427 — their king must die. The weakling Chimalpopoca was threatening to undo the patient, bloody work of his more able predecessors to build the power of his race. The elder of the three lords was Itzcoatl, brother of the previous tlatoani (Revered Speaker), Huitzilíhuitl, and therefore Chimalpopoca's uncle. Both Huitzilíhuitl and Itzcoatl were sons of the first of the warrior kings, Acamapichtli, Tezozomoc's nominee for the throne of his new Mexica vassal state. Itzcoatl was the *Tlacochcalcatl* or Captain General of the Mexica, having served his brother and now his nephew.[1] To his military leadership could be attributed much of the rise of Mexica fortunes.

The two other lords were Chimalpopoca's younger brothers, Motecuhzoma (Angry Lord) and Tlacaélel (Liverish Lord), and were therefore, Itzcoatl's nephews. The destinies of all three were bound together, but the two brothers were to make Mexica arms resound across Mexico and dominate the century.

'Year 10 – Rabbit (1398)
At this time, as the ancient Mexicans knew, was born Motecuhzoma the elder, *Ilhuicamina,*

he who shines like resplendent jade,
who came into the world when the sun had risen.
His mother was a princess from Cuauhnáhuac (Cuernavaca).
Her name was Miyahuaxiuhtzin.
And Tlacaélel was
born on the same day, in the morning,
when the sun, as we say, was about to rise.
So it is said that Tlacaélel was older.
His mother was named Cacamacihuatzin;
she was princess from Teocalhuiyacan.
Each one had a different mother,
but they had the same father, Huitzilíhuitl II, king of Tenochtitlan.'[2]

Even in their twenties, both brothers were warriors of extraordinary courage and judgement. Tlacaélel was more, a warrior priest, special servant of the Mexica patron god, Huitzilopochtli. Led by Itzcoatl, the three were a rare team of determined and intelligent men of action, hard and ruthless, true sons of the Mexica royal house. They despised the aberration Chimalpopoca.

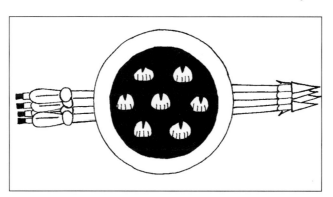

Mexica symbol of war.

There he sat like a slave, in a wooden cage in his own city, terrified of his own uncle, the new Tepanec emperor, Maxtla. No longer the pampered vassal of his dead grandfather Tezozomoc, he cowered under his uncle's animosity for the now too powerful Mexica. Tezozomoc had used the warlike Mexica to build his empire and had married a daughter to their

Tenochtitlan in the midst of Lake Texcoco. (Painting courtesy © Scott Gentling, photographed by David Wharton)

king Huitzilíhuitl as a sign of his favour. He had doted on the child of that marriage and future king, Chimalpopoca, to the rage of his son Maxtla who saw every favour and concession to the Mexica as contributing to the creation of a rival to Tepanec hegemony.

Now Tezozomoc was dead, and his rash successor was determined to humble the Mexica. Before Tezozomoc's death, he had demanded Chimalpopoca's death in fear of growing Mexica power, but now he had a better reason. Chimalpopoca had plotted clumsily with Maxtla's brother, Tayauh, to kill Maxtla. The plot had been betrayed by a dwarf page of Maxtla, and the lordship of a city had been his reward. Tayauh died, strangled by the same garland of flowers intended for Maxtla. He then raped two of Chimalpopoca's women and returned them with threats. Terrified, the young Mexica had panicked and threatened to commit suicide, in a desperate ploy to rally the Mexica to him. Toying with him, Maxtla then put him in a

wooden cage for his own safety. To Itzcoatl, the pathetic king made a poor contrast to his cousin, Nezahualcoyotl, dispossessed prince of the Acolhua kingdom on the eastern shore of the great lagoon. Itzcoatl himself had led the Mexica contingent in the Tepanec conquest of the Acolhua which had led to the death of Nezahualcoyotl's father and the prince's exile. Itzcoatl's sisters had intervened to beg Tezozomoc to allow the prince to reside in Tenochtitlan under the Mexica royal family's protection. There he had grown to young manhood, a brilliant warrior and wise beyond his years. He had accompanied Itzcoatl to the wars against Chalco and had impressed the Captain General greatly.

Leaderless, the Mexica now wavered in fear at Maxtla's all-too-obvious intentions and were all too ready to humble themselves. The three men of the royal kin had other ideas and were not about to let craven public opinion reverse the Mexica's long, hard climb to power. A conspiracy was spun quickly with the Tepanec lord of Tlacopan, an enemy of Maxtla. On a dark and unguarded night Tepanec captains entered the city and killed not only Chimalpopoca but his child heir as well.

The assassinations immediately accomplished two important goals: the succession was opened to a more vigorous man, and the city was shocked out of its paralysis. The game of empire was in play again. The murder of Chimalpopoca's only child was critical to the success of the future Mexica empire. It made the principle of primogeniture irrelevant in this election. Without an heir, the choice was among a numerous and able royal clan. The first speaker among the council of elders was clear on that course.

'The noble lineage of Mexico does not end
  here
Nor has the royal blood perished.
  Turn your eyes, look about you.
You will see the noblemen of Mexico around
  you —
Not one or two, but many excellent princes,
  Sons of Acamapichtli your true king and lord.
Choose freely ' . . .[3]

Apparently that was not necessary. Itzcoatl clearly outshone all his surviving brothers. A man in his prime at the age of 46 or 47, he was associated as Captain General with Mexica military successes of the last two reigns and possessed a sterling reputation for character and ability. That he was the son of Acamapichtli by a concubine from Azcapotzalco was overlooked in the enthusiastic rush to unanimously elect the best man. The council did not realise that they had chosen a man who would make history pivot on his will. They had elected the king of a minor vassal state. Like Napoleon, he would crown himself emperor but with a diadem of imperial Toltec turquoise.

TLACAÉLEL'S EMBASSY

That imperial diadem now rested uneasily on the head of Tezozomoc's successor in Azcapotzalco. Maxtla's murder of his father's chosen heir, had unsettled the legitimacy of

succession in the eyes of his many brothers, each of whom now felt he had an equally good claim to the crown. He had unsettled the Tepanec heartland and now threatened the harmony of Tezozomoc's empire. He had also discredited his claim, so hungrily pursued by his father, to the ancient Toltec legitimacy. The Tepanec empire was becoming dangerously unstable. It was a moment ripe with opportunity for Itzcoatl who was ready to cast off the vassalage of his people.

Maxtla was enraged to find that the pliant Chimalpopoca had been replaced by someone as obdurate as his name — Obsidian Serpent. He immediately blockaded the causeways to Tenochtitlan, cutting off its food supply. Mexica public opinion trembled at the display of Tepanec wrath. Itzcoatl may have been a king, but it was a greatly circumscribed kingship that he held. He depended mostly on the numerous royal kin, the nobility, and the warrior class all of whom had a vested interest in freeing themselves of Tepanec control. Unfortunately, they held relatively little economic power. Tenochtitlan was a poor island city whose wealth, other than its warriors, was in the intensively cultivated floating gardens controlled by the city clan-based wards. The king controlled relatively little wealth, especially compared to richer cities, and had few means to reward those who excelled in war and government. He was therefore not blind to the implications of the city's loss of nerve. Most of the common people and many of the nobility wanted nothing more than to placate Maxtla by carrying the image of their patron god, Huitzilopochtli, to Azcapotzalco. In a frightened panic they rushed to the temple and loaded the idol upon their shoulders. Tlacaélel stormed up to them and shouted, 'What is this, O Aztecs? What are you doing? You have lost your wits. Wait, sit still! Let us consider this matter more fully. Are you such cowards that you feel you must take shelter in Azcapotzalco?'[4]

He turned to Itzcoatl and said, 'Great lord, what is this, how can you permit such a thing? Speak to your people. Seek a way to defend our honor.' The young warrior-priest had temporarily halted them with the force of his personality, but it was only temporary. The silent tension balanced on the thinness of an obsidian flake;

one breath could tip it either way. Then Itzcoatlspoke. The tone of certainty swept across thousands of upturned faces.

'Are you desirous of going to Azcapotzalco? This seems to me a slavish act. We must move with pride. Which of you will appear before the king of Azcapotzalco to hear his decision? The messenger will surely be killed. But, if you insist — whoever wishes to do this — let him rise and go.'[5]

No one came forward. He had fixed the crowd to the pavement. They had seen their abasement as a form of safety. Itzcoatl had painted it over as certain death. Suddenly no one wanted to be the first to die. Except for one — Tlacaélel, whose clear, strong voice rolled across the square.

'I offer myself to carry the message, since I do not fear death. I well know that I must die some day and it matters little whether it be today or tomorrow. How could I have a better death than by defending the honor of my homeland? Therefore, O lord, I will go.'

Itzcoatl gravely assented,

'I am gratified, dear nephew, by the bravery and courage of your decision. If you undertake this task, I will reward you with great liberality, and if you die in this mission your children will receive my favor. You will be remembered eternally for this brave act.'[6]

Then he commanded him to go. The crowds parted in silence for this bold young man, marching to a death sentence. There was no code of immunity for ambassadors. He was a sight as hard as death — dressed in tight-fitting black, his face painted black, and his hair smeared to a hard, snaky crust with dried human blood of sacrifice. What the crowd did not realise was that Itzcoatl had thrown for great stakes. Tlacaélel did not carry a message of self-abnegating peace but of war.

Rarely has history seen a bolder and more daring young warrior. He wore audacity like a shield. Striding up to the Tepanec guards at the gates of Azcapotzalco who had had strict orders to kill all Mexica on sight, he bullied his way past them.

'I well know what you have been commanded, but it is also well known that messengers are not to be blamed. And I am an envoy to your king from the sovereign of Mexico and his chief-

tains. And so I beg you to allow me to pass. I assure you that I will return by the same way. If you then wish to slay me I will put myself in your hands.'

The guards waved him in. He strode straight into Maxtla's palace and presented himself. Maxtla took a moment to overcome his surprise that the young man had eluded death at the city gates. Then Tlacaélel presented his message — the Mexica asked for peace. Obviously caught off guard, Maxtla temporised by saying he must consult his council. Return the next day for my answer, he commanded. The young Mexica asked for a safe-conduct, but Maxtla, all too used to toying with the Mexica, replied that his own cunning must serve.[7]

So Tlacaélel left by the way he had come and again talked his way through the guards.

'My brothers, I have just spoken to your sovereign and I carry an answer to mine. If you will allow me to pass I will be grateful. I have come to talk of peace and I deceive no one. I must return to Mexico to settle this matter. Whether you kill today or the next day matters little, since I give you my word that I will place myself in your hands tomorrow.'[8]

Itzcoatl heard him out. Maxtla must be pushed over the edge.

'Ask him if his people are determined to leave us in peace and admit us again to their friendship. If he answers that there is no remedy, that he must annihilate us, then take this pitch with which we anoint our dead and smear it upon his body. Feather his head as we do to our dead and give him the shield, sword and gilded arrows, which are the insignia of a sovereign, adding that he must be on his guard since we will do everything to destroy him.'

The next day when Tlacaélel strode through the gates of Azcapotzalco, the guards stood aside in respect. Tlacaélel demanded an answer of war or peace from Maxtla. Even now, though he had an abiding hatred of the Mexica, Maxtla attempted to push the blame for war onto his council and lords. Tlacaélel brushed aside the excuses.

'Very well, O lord, your vassal, the king of Mexico, sends you this message: Take care, be strong, prepare yourself — at this moment he challenges you and your people. He is now your mortal enemy, and either you or we will be slain upon the field or become a slave forever. You will deeply regret having begun a thing which you cannot conclude in victory.'

Then in silence he approached Maxtla and smeared his face with pitch and presented him with the shield, sword, and gilded arrows.[9]

The declarations of war had been exchanged. Tlacaélel fully expected to die. Maxtla was a violent man who had murdered kings with little thought. But he stood and asked Tlacaélel to thank Itzcoatl for his message. Then, in open admiration for the Mexica's courage, he said,

'Son Tlacaélel, do not go out by the main gate because there they await to kill you. I have ordered a hole made in the back of the house, through which you may escape. However, I do not wish you to leave without a gift since you are a friend and a brave man. Take these weapons, this shield and sword, and defend yourself with them if you are attacked.'

With this salute from his enemy, Tlacaélel slipped out through the hole in the wall and found a path out of the city. Then turning on the guards he shouted,

'O Tepanecs of Azcapotzalco! How poorly you carry out your task of defending the city! Prepare yourselves! Soon there will not be a Tepanec left in the world. Not one stone will be left upon another; no one will be spared. Prepare yourselves to perish in fire and blood. Itzcoatl, king of Mexico, has challenged you.'

The bewildered guards came after him, but he attacked them boldly. The dark green obsidian-edged sword flashed in his hand as he killed one Tepanec after another and only withdrew when reinforcements arrived.[10]

MOTECUHZOMA'S EMBASSY

Tlacaélel's mission had succeeded in frustrating the peace party in Tenochtitlan by provoking an outright state of war. But that was only a first step. Allies were needed if Azcapotzalco were to be pulled down. Chief among them was his nephew Nezahualcoyotl. The young Acolhua prince had been the first to seize the opportunity caused by Maxtla's unsettling grip on his father's empire. He had raised allies from relatives in the princely houses of Tlaxcallan and Huexotzinco outside the Valley of Mexico and

from the Chalca confederation. In a rapid campaign, the allies had driven the Tepaneca from the Acolhua kingdom and installed Nezahualcoyotl in his capital of Texcoco. Now Nezahualcoyotl was pulling his allies to the aid of Tenochtitlan — except for the Chalca.

Between the Mexica and the Chalca existed a bitter hatred engendered by the ferocity of Itzcoatl's campaigns as a vassal of Tezozomoc against Chalco in the previous decade. The Chalca had had no love for the Tepaneca and had been happy to help crop their arrogance by aiding Nezahualcoyotl. Itzcoatl had relied too heavily on this evidence of anti-Tepanec feeling in agreeing to Nezahualcoyotl's suggestion that the Mexica seek help from the Chalca as he had. After Tlacaélel had delivered the Mexica defiance, both sides had immediately sent out embassies seeking allies. The ambassadors from both Azcapotzalco and Tenochtitlan had first gone to Chalco. Itzcoatl's chief ambassador was Motecuhzoma accompanied by a brother of Nezahualcoyotl. Such was their hostility for the Mexica that the Chalca seized the ambassadors at the border. Motecuhzoma was howled down by the Chalca. There would be no alliance — only death on the stone of sacrifice. But the Chalca king sent the ambassadors to Huexotzinco offering them as sacrificial victims in a devious attempt to transfer the guilt of murdering ambassadors. The Huexotzinco nobility turned aside the ploy and returned the ambassadors, in effect telling the Chalca to do their own dirty work. This the Chalca resolved to do, first notifying Maxtla of their intent and even receiving the assurance from a traitorous Mexica peace party delegation that no protest would be made.[11]

Such a sacrifice was not only a religious event, but a political statement. The Chalca declared a festival and invited guests from all the lakeside cities, again to share the blame if need be. They were shocked when no throngs of guests arrived by canoe, a subtle diplomatic signal from the other cities that the Chalca would have no support in this matter. So Motecuhzoma and his companions languished in their wooden cage while the Chalca king postponed the sacrifice in the hope that guests would come eventually. That night, in what surely was one of history's better examples of *deus ex machina*, their guard said to them, 'I dreamed tonight of the greatness of Tenochtitlan. Go free, although I die for it.' The three crept out of the sleeping city and made their way to the lake in search of a canoe. They found one in which an old man and woman were fishing and called out to them, but the old couple were fearful and pushed away. Motecuhzoma said, 'They must die; we must have the canoe.' The Mexica plunged into the water and dragged the old couple to their deaths.[12] The Chalca had only just begun to regret the time Motecuhzoma had spent in a cage in their city.

Motecuhzoma and his companions eventually arrived in Huexotzinco to enter a dangerous diplomatic struggle. Maxtla's delegation had preceded them, offering rich gifts of jewels, weapons, and brilliantly feathered golden insignia. Another delegation had arrived from Cuauhtitlan, an island city cruelly conquered by Maxtla. Their gifts were so poor that the lords of Huexotzinco imprisoned them to await sacrifice for their insult. The arguments of the diplomats were so finally balanced that the ambassadors from Cuauhtitlan were released to present their story. Their tale of Maxtla's cruelty was so convincing that Motecuhzoma's plea for alliance was granted and the Tepanec ambassadors themselves were sacrificed, cut to pieces with obsidian knives.[13]

ITZCOATL'S BARGAIN

With the anti-Tepanec alliance firmly in place, Itzcoatl prepared to move on Azcapotzalco when again the Mexica peace party upset his plans. The enormity of the gamble unnerved the commons. There was very much a class element to the decision to go to war. The nobility and warrior classes were very much in favour of war; they had grown in power and prestige in the many wars they had waged on behalf of Tezozomoc. Warfare had elevated Tenochtitlan from a miserable vassal to a veritable partner of Azcapotzalco in the last years of Tezozomoc's reign. From being tribute payers they had become the receivers of tribute. War provided new sources of wealth and status outside that traditionally allocated by the wards of the city.

These rising men had no stomach for the amount of humiliation Maxtla would force on them. They were ready to gamble everything on the chance for glory and wealth. The commons, on the other hand, were acutely aware of which class would be squeezed relentlessly by Maxtla's tribute imposed on a defeated Tenochtitlan. Many wanted to leave the city or again attempt to carry the idol of the patron deity in submission to Maxtla.

As all this wrangling might indicate, Mexica monarchs were hardly absolute. They were bound not only by their councillors but by public opinion as well. A loss of nerve was about to abort a powerful alliance and frustrate the imperial ambitions of a number of very capable and ruthless men.

The council house of Tenochtitlan had echoed with speeches for hours. The peace party was making its final play. The square outside was filled with people straining to hear the wisps of speeches, the shouted arguments, and the buzz of voices, that echoed out of its wide doorway. Inside the lords and commons of the Mexica were arguing the fate of the race. At this point in their history, the Mexica were not a rich people. Most of both classes inside still wore rough maguey fibre clothing instead of finespun and embroidered cotton. The gap between them was not vast. Itzcoatl with his lords attempted to reassure the commons massed before them. Durán recounted the words of the historic confrontation: 'Do not fear, my children, we will free you and no one will harm you.' They were not reassured. A spokesman replied, 'And if you do not succeed, our sovereign, what will become of us?' Itzcoatl stood up and stepped forward. A man of renown and presence in the full vigour of his manhood, his hard, black eyes commanded attention. He was a jaguar among deer, and he knew it. He let the silence clear the air of every other thought. When he spoke, he offered what was surely one the most daring social contracts in history,

'If we do not achieve what we intend, we will place ourselves in your hands, so that our flesh becomes your nourishment. In this way you will have your vengeance. You can eat us in the dirtiest of cracked dishes so that we and our flesh are totally degraded.'

Something of his boldness must have jumped like a spark. The representatives of the commons conferred, then spoke.

'Let it be as you have said. You yourselves have delivered your sentence. We answer: if you are victorious, we will serve you and work your lands for you. We will pay tribute to you, we will build your houses and be your servants. We will give our daughters and sisters and nieces. And when you go to war we will carry your baggage and food and your weapons upon our shoulders and we will serve you along the way to battle. In short, we will sell and subject our persons and goods to your service forever...'[14]

While later more autocratic ages may have blown this contract out of proportion, Itzcoatl had done what was necessary to bring a unified people to war. He had also set the stage for a fundamental realignment of Mexica society. His immediate problem was to put the city on a war footing. He ordered Tlacaélel, as the king's most trusted adviser, Cihuacoatl (Snake Woman), to appoint officers and commanders from among the royal kin to lead the fighting men of Tenochtitlan and to see to the manufacture of weapons and armour for the mass of the soldiery that would be provided by the reluctant wards of the city.[15]

THE SIEGE OF AZCAPOTZALCO

However united the Mexica were, they were still left with the unenviable position of being besieged in their own island city, with all the causeways to the mainland held by strong Tepanec forces. Now the alliance began to pay dividends. Nezahualcoyotl led his Acolhua and allied armies straight across the lake in a fleet of canoes and directly threatened the Tepaneca lakeside capital. Thwarted by its shoreline defences, he landed his forces to the north of the city and marched inland. With such a powerful enemy in their rear, the Tepanec armies abandoned their blockade of Tenochtitlan and fell back to the outer defences of Azcapotzalco itself.

As his allies were landing, Itzcoatl stepped boldly upon the stage of empire and addressed the host of Tenochtitlan.

'The king spoke before the soldiers, urging them to conquer or die, reminding them of the glorious history of the Aztec nation. He reminded them that this would be their first great battle and that from it they would bring such honor that other nations would tremble before them. He told them not to be timorous, that the large number of Tepaneca was unimportant, what really mattered were their own courageous hearts. He commanded the men to follow their officers, and thus began the march toward Azcapotzalco.'[16]

The Mexica streamed across the Tlacopan causeway, apparently under the direct command of Tlacaélel, and fell upon the eastern defences of Azcapotzalco and the main body of the Tepaneca host.

'When they reached a spot known as *Xoconochnopallitlan*, "the Place of the Cactus That Bears Green Prickly Fruit", the warriors of Azcapotzalco came out in good order to meet them, carrying shields with insignia richly done in gold, silver, jewels and feathers and with splendid ornaments upon their backs. When the Aztecs saw them coming, Tlacaélel was filled with boldness, and he commanded all the officers and common soldiers to assemble upon an elevation and to wait for the sound of the drums which would be the signal for the attack. He also told certain common soldiers who were lacking in spirit to remain in the rear.'[17]

'Here occurred the hardest fight, the Mexica rolled back the enemy in their initial advance, and made them withdraw a fair distance, capturing a wide and deep ditch constructed near a place called Petlacalco . . . However, the enemy turned against the Mexica with such fury, that they drove them back over the captured trench, and forced them to retire to the shore of the lagoon.'[18]

Apparently even at this point, the peace party was to blame for this reverse, having held back. Another Mexica force under Motecuhzoma conducted a feigned attack on the Tepanec stronghold of Tlacopan. The city, which had connived with Itzcoatl to remove his predecessor, surrendered with only a token resistance and went over to the Mexica side. Meanwhile, Tlacaélel rallied the main Mexica force and led them into another attack on the enemy's works and carried them in hard fighting, forcing the Tepaneca to retreat into the earthworks that surrounded the city itself. By then nightfall had ended the day's fighting. The sun had indeed set on a remarkable day's achievement in which the Tepaneca and Mexica had exchanged roles. In the morning Tepaneca were besieging Tenochtitlan; in the evening the Mexica were besieging Azcapotzalco. The leaders of the anti-Tepaneca alliance agreed that the city was too strong to be taken by storm and settled down to a siege. They divided the circumvallation into four parts. Nezahualcoyotl's forces stood guard to the west while the Mexica filled in the other cardinal directions. Itzcoatl commanded the eastern section, Tlacaélel the north, and Motecuhzoma the south.

Both sides settled down for a siege that bled on from month to month in a deadly series of Tepaneca sorties and allied assaults on the various forts in the city's defences. Finally, the increasingly desperate pleadings of Maxtla to the other Tepanec cities brought the hoped for army of relief. On the 114th day of the siege, the defenders of Azcapotzalco issued out to attack the besiegers at the same time.

A great battle was fought to the northwest of the city as the forces of the entire Tepaneca nation struggled with the Mexica and their allies. The issue was finally decided when the Tepaneca commander was cut down. Even the peace party now saw which way victory pointed and threw themselves vigorously into the fray. The Tepaneca lost heart and fled, leaving the way open to Azcapotzalco. Its defences were unmanned, and the allies rushed into the stricken jewel of Tezozomoc's empire. Itzcoatl strode through the gates and cried havoc — the general massacre of the population. The treasure house of the Tepaneca empire, so carefully amassed over 50 years, was given over to a blood-drunk army. The butchery lasted all day with the survivors fleeing to the foothills of the valley.

'The Mexica following up their bloody victory, like meat-hungry dogs, filled with fury and rage, followed those who had fled into the hills. There they found them prostrated upon the earth. The vanquished surrendered their weapons, promising the Aztecs lands and service in their homes and fields. They promised stone, lime and wood as tribute, as well as

The fall of Azcapotzalco in the year One Knife (1428).

foodstuffs such as maize, beans, *chian* seeds, chili, and many other things.'[19]

Tlacaélel spared them and called off the pursuit. In the city itself, Maxtla was dragged out of his hiding place in a steam bath. With great ceremony, Itzcoatl's nephew, Nezahualcoyotl, sacrificed Maxtla in revenge for the murder of Nezahualcoyotl's father by Maxtla's father. So ended the great empire built over a lifetime by the brilliant Tezozomoc, now all flames and blood-soaked rubble, stripped of its treasures, and inhabited only by its multitude of corpses. Itzcoatl left only one thing in Azcapotzalco, the slave market of the Valley of Mexico.

ITZCOATL, THE OBSIDIAN SERPENT (1428-1440)
THE SPOILS OF A NEW ORDER

Itzcoatl now moved to call in the marker left by the Mexica commons and began the process of centralisation that would lead to the autocracy that the Spanish would encounter in 1519. The Mexica had inherited the bulk of the landed wealth of the Tepaneca. Itzcoatl did not begrudge the men from Tlaxcallan and Huexotzinco who marched homeward over the mountains loaded down with loot of fine cloth, jewels of turquoise and jade, brilliant featherwork, gold and silver, and slaves. He had the greatest treasures — the land and its labour to till it and make it fruitful; and the steady tribute from the conquered. And it was all within his gift. His bargain with the commons had made it clear on that point.

The greatest rewards and offices went to Itzcoatl's brothers and nephews. Chief among the latter were Tlacaélel and Motecuhzoma who received the most splendid fiefs of all. Each was given ten estates spread among the lands of Azcapotzalco. Other military commanders received two estates. The common soldiery, save those who had distinguished themselves by conspicuous bravery, received nothing. The clan-based wards each received one estate for the support of their temples. In humbling the wards, Itzcoatl was not so foolish as to insult the gods or worse, their priests. Even with this generosity, the majority of lands remained in the possession of the state, all in the king's potential gift. At one stroke, Itzcoatl had created a new and dynamic social order among the Mexica. The able and ambitious man was no longer constrained by the control of Tenochtitlan's finite resources by the city wards. Napoleon was not the first to establish the principle that careers were open to talent. Now among the Mexica talent had its reward, earned along a sword's obsidian edge. Power gravitated to the king now that war had made him economically independent. That power and the ruthlessness to use it drove the influence of the wards and the commons into the shadows from which they were never to emerge.

Itzcoatl's name hieroglyph.

Itzcoatl further concentrated power by formalising a four-man council of advisers drawn from his own family. Tlacaélel inherited Itzcoatl's old position of *Tlacochcalcatl* (The Man of the House of Hurled Spears) or Captain General of all the Mexica forces, and Motecuhzoma became *Tlacateccatl* (Cutter of Heads). These titles came to become synonymous with commanding general and general. His brothers Tlacahuepan and Cuauhtlecoatl became *Ezhuahuacatl* (Shedder of Blood) and *Tlillancalqui* (Dweller in the Black House of the War God).[20]

Itzcoatl was shrewd enough, even on the crest of good fortune, to recognise that the Mexica could not have succeeded without allies. It was an ancient tradition — Toltec Tollan and even Tezozomoc's Azcapotzalco had had two formal allied cities to share the burdens of war. Tenochtitlan's obvious ally was Nezahualcoyotl and his Acolhua kingdom with its capital at Texcoco, made even more attractive by the fact that he was as much a nephew of Itzcoatl as Tlacaélel and Motecuhzoma. Still, a dual alliance was not traditional, and the two victors had to consider the resentment of the Tepaneca who were still a numerous and powerful people in the Valley of Mexico. The two monarchs selected, in essence, a dummy third wheel to the alliance by admitting the Tepanec city of Tlacopan into what would be known as the Triple Alliance. The power still lay with the Mexica and Acolhua as indicated by the division of spoil. The two former states each received 40 percent while Tlacopan had to settle for 20 percent.

Itzcoatl's first campaign after the destruction of Azcapotzalco was to shore up the new alliance. Although Nezahualcoyotl had been the key to bringing crucial allies from outside the Valley of Mexico to the war, he had not consolidated control of his own kingdom outside his capital of Texcoco. Tepanec-installed rulers still controlled most of the cities of the Acolhua. Itzcoatl led the Triple Alliance armies across the lake and helped Nezahualcoyotl reduce them one by one. The mighty empire that Cortés would encounter almost 100 years later was the spoil, not just of Mexica prowess, but that of the Acolhua and to a much lesser extent of the Tepaneca as well. Considering that it was the creation of Itzcoatl and three very able nephews, it was very much a family concern.

DOMINATING THE VALLEY OF MEXICO

The Triple Alliance did not automatically inherit Tezozomoc's empire. By Mesoamerican standards, the fall of Azcapotzalco merely freed

Itzcoatl rewards successful warriors with the plunder and tribute of conquest.

its vassals and allies. The Triple Alliance would have to bully back into submission those it could and defeat those it could not. Itzcoatl's first problem was the recalcitrant remnant of the Tepanec confederation. Azcapotzalco's fall and Tlacopan's membership in the Alliance did not cause all of the Tepanec cities to submit. Coyohuacan, in particular, nursed a bitter hatred of the Mexica. The pretext for war was delivered in the usual way by an affront — three Mexica women travelling to market in Coyohuacan were robbed and raped. Unfortunately for the leaders of Coyohuacan, their attempts to gather allies against the Mexica had failed utterly.[21] They then made a curious attempt to add insult to injury. As if no original insult had already been given, they invited the king and leading men of Tenochtitlan to a feast in Coyohuacan. Tlacaélel, sensing a trick, persuaded Itzcoatl not to go and went in his stead.

The Mexica were royally entertained and feasted, and when the banquet was ended, the men of Coyohuacan presented to the Mexica, instead of gifts of flowers, women's skirts and blouses. Tlacaélel allowed himself to be dressed in the women's clothes and returned to Tenochtitlan to the presence of the king, grandly parading his humiliation and a splendid reason for war. Rarely had a city committed so feckless a suicide.

The Mexica army carefully advanced upon Coyohuacan. Alert for ambush, Tlacaélel ordered a scaffold built to survey the approaches to the city. From there, he observed smoke coming from a field of rushes. Believing the Tepaneca to be hiding in wait, he ordered his captains to stay behind while he slipped into the reeds alone to conduct a personal reconnaissance. He found no Tepaneca but three nobles of Culhuacán, come to offer their services to the Mexica for glory. He also observed that the field of rushes offered an equally good ambush site for the Mexica as for the Tepaneca. Charging the men of Culhuacán to kill any Tepanec that entered the field, he returned to the Mexica army. At that moment his watchman on the scaffold shouted the approach of the army of Coyohuacan. Tlacaélel quickly advised Itzcoatl to attack while he led a company of Mexica into the field of rushes. There he presented the insignia of Tenochtitlan to the Culhua nobles as the noise of battle erupted. Tlacaélel's company fell upon the Tepanec rear with complete surprise, shouting 'Mexico, Mexico, Tenochtitlan!' In the ensuing slaughter, Tlacaélel himself surpassed all other Mexica in prowess so that no Tepanec would come near him, a Mexica Achilles whose murderousness made men flinch before him. The Tepaneca fled to the safety of their city and its fortified temple compound, but Tlacaélel was quicker and led a company to seize and burn the temple first. The population fled to the hills with the Mexica harrying and killing as the city burned behind them. They begged for mercy, pledging their submission, and again Tlacaélel relented. Humbled, tribute-paying subjects were valuable as both a resource and an example.

The Mexica 'returned to their city, rich in slaves, gold, gems and precious feathers,

The Mexica sequence of war. Upper, battle. Centre, burning the enemy's temple signified victory. Lower, immediate sacrifice of prisoners.

shields and insignia, clothing and many other spoils.' The great share of the spoils went to the Crown to support Itzcoatl's growing household and administration. Tlacaélel was rewarded with eleven estates while to other distinguished nobles two and three were given. Tlacaélel brought out the two captains and three men of Culhuacán and praised them for their courage and deeds to Itzcoatl who rewarded them well. The three Culhua adventurers were significant in that Mexica power was now attracting aggressive and ambitious men of talent. With the fall of Coyohuacan, many of the remaining Tepanec cities submitted as well. Now the Mexica, through the Triple Alliance, had control of two of the three power centres of the Valley — the Acolhua east and the Tepanec west. The third power centre was to the south and there the Mexica looked next.

The southern rim of the valley was the richest agricultural resource of the valley. The kingdom of Xochimilco (Country of Flowery Fields) grew rich on the fertile floating gardens in the southern reaches of the great lagoon. Its possession would place a major, secure granary at the doorstep of the Mexica. Xochimilco also controlled the two passes leading out of the valley to the south into the present day state of Morelos. Durán recounts the self-serving Mexica story that they had humbly asked Xochimilco for stone and wood for the construction of a new temple to Huitzilopochtli. They were shocked when it was refused. In fact, the request was a symbolic demand for submission. Then Mexica merchants were mistreated in Xochimilco, probably a reaction to the initial Mexica demand, and thus provided Itzcoatl another pretext for war. Apparently, Itzcoatl had such a weak case for provoking war with Xochimilco that he felt he had to goad things along even more by sending a group of men to devastate some of its cornfields and attack whoever came out to stop them. Finally, in an act of great coolness, he sent a high-ranking delegation to Xochimilco on an ostensible mission of peace. They were met at the border by armed men and turned back with the message that all of Xochimilco was ready for war. Itz-coatl was now only too happy to oblige.

Tlacaélel assembled the army and addressed it,

'O valiant warriors, the entire land of Xochim-ilco is against us and they outnumber us, but let this not trouble you. Strength and spirit are what matter! Be informed that the enemy is very near us . . . . Therefore, O Aztecs, make your name ring out as you have always done.'[22]

They met the enemy host gathered on the plain of the lake's south shore.

'The Xochimilca were so numerous that they totally covered the plain, and the gold, jewels, precious stones and plumes that they carried on their weapons, insignia and shields were so splendid that they shone in the sun as they reflected its rays. What a spectacle it was! Weapons of many hues: green, blue, red, yel-low, black, multicolored!'[23]

So strong and numerous was the Xochimilca host that the Mexica were thrown back in their first attack. Itzcoatl summoned reinforcements from Texcoco, Azcapotzalco, and Coyohuacan and led them into a renewed attack.[24]

The Mexica began the battle with an arrow storm and rain of atlatl darts that 'darkened the sun' and staggered the Xochimilca. When the mass of Mexica swordsmen threw them-selves into the enemy ranks, the Xochimilca wavered. Tlacaélel himself entered the fray and again performed prodigies of valour that encouraged the Mexica. The Xochimilca forma-tions began to unravel despite the attempts of their captains to rally them. Then with a rush, they broke and fled to the safety of a large ram-part that shielded their capital. Now was their chance to inflict casualties as they shot through the loopholed wall into the closely packed Mexica. Tlacaélel urged them on over their dead to literally tear the rampart apart. Again the Xochimilca fled. Their leaders quickly emerged from the capital and surrendered, swearing to become the vassals of the Mexica. Tlacaélel coolly held his army from sacking the city, promising to reward them later. It was an act of supreme confidence for Xochimilco was one of the richest cities in the valley, and its plunder would have been immense.[25] Then he ordered the Xochimilca to build a causeway from their city to Tenochtitlan as their first act

of submission. This they did with goodwill and efficiency, tying themselves to Tenochtitlan with a stone and earth structure five yards wide, with numerous intervening bridges. Then Tlacaélel rewarded his soldiers for their missed loot, giving each a good field from the lands of the Xochimilca. Itzcoatl took special care to compensate the Xochimilca and ensure their continued goodwill by the subsequent mildness of his rule. He gave the Xochimilca king unprecedented access to himself, made him a special counsellor (an honour given to no other vassal) and the right of consultation on any matter concerning his kingdom.

From Xochimilco, Itzcoatl turned to the nearby island city of Cuitláhuac and again pro-voked war, claiming that the Cuitlahuaca had insulted the Mexica by refusing to attend a reli-gious festival in Tenochtitlan and were interfer-ing with trade. Cuitláhuac felt secure enough on its island to defy the Mexica despite the inti-mate proximity of the object lesson experienced by Xochimilco. They had even declined to seek allies from among the last powerful confedera-tion, the Chalca which occupied the south-east tip of the valley, a fact Itzcoatl was careful to ascertain. He then ordered Tlacaélel to assem-ble and train an army of boys, sixteen to eigh-teen years old. It was a sign of contempt for the Cuitlahuaca, for the teenagers were not yet of military age. Nevertheless, Tlacaélel took no chances and assigned captains of proven steadiness to command them. Soon the ranks were filled as the young men streamed into the assembly area from the schools of every ward of the city. Having been exposed to a continuous series of glorious wars in which their fathers and older brothers had won renown, they were wild with enthusiasm. Although not of military age they had been training for it as part of every young Mexica's school of life. They were outfit-ted in quilted cotton armour and issued weapons from the city's armouries and then marched to an embarkation point where they were met by a fleet of a thousand canoes. The canoes were already crewed with archers and warriors who could expertly protect the boys by deflecting enemy arrows with their shields. As the Mexica fleet approached the island and began its landings, the Cuitlahuaca issued out 'all in canoes and very well arrayed with their rich and colourful insignia, the canoes themselves being adorned with shields and richly hued feathers with which the oarsmen were covered. And the fighting men were all very well armed and bedecked with feathers, white, red, yellow, blue, green, black, and every colour, all with different plumes on their heads and backs; round their necks they wore many jewels of gold, set with stones, as well as bracelets of brilliant gold; and above their feet, anklets of gold, to complete the arms which they wore from head to foot.'[26]

All this martial finery was no match for the reckless bravery of the Mexica youth dressed in plain cotton armour. The air between the fleets was filled with arrows, darts, and sling stones, causing heavy casualties on both sides. The battle quickly shifted to the land leaving the lakeside drifting with empty canoes, oars, shields, spent missiles, and wounded men struggling to stay afloat. The king of Cuitláhuac quickly came to the same conclusion as his colleague at Xochimilco as the Mexica wildly pressed into his city — he surrendered. Tlacaélel's forbearance at Xochimilco had paid rich dividends, convincing the enemy king that there was an acceptable alternative to the bitter end. When the king offered submission, Tlacaélel immediately ordered an end to the fighting.

About 1434 Itzcoatl campaigned in the north of the valley, forcing the submission of the last of the old Tepanec vassals in the Valley of Mexico. So great was the Mexica reputation at this time that very little if any fighting was needed to bring these cities to heel. Among them was Tollan, former capital of a legendary golden age and home of the hero Topiltzin Quetzalcoatl. Politically, Tollan may have been one of the most important long-term political acquisitions. It was not a city of great wealth or military significance. Rather it held the aura of legitimacy from the Toltec era of wonders — a cross between Camelot and the Rome of 800 AD in which Charlemagne was happy to receive the crown of a dead empire, the prestige of which was still so great that it held more power than armies. From a practical standpoint, this campaign took the Mexica further from the Valley of Mexico than they had ever marched before. More campaigning in northern Guerrero

rounded up more former Tepanec vassals with little fighting as well. One final campaign was conducted to aid the city of Xiuhtepec conquer another city. Itzcoatl mobilised three armies, one from each of the Triple Alliance cities, and sent them on converging paths to their objective. This campaign was a milestone in Mexica warmaking. It was the deepest penetration outside the Valley of Mexico, requiring probably a five-day march for the Mexica, three for the army of Tlacopan, and seven for the Acolhua. The coordination of three separate armies was a difficult command and logistics problem and represented a new level of Mexica skill. Three armies spread the logistic burden and the danger that a single army would be bottled up in a pass in the mountainous region. Not surprisingly, both cities then became vassals.[27]

The capture of the island city of Cuitláhuac was to be followed by the conquest of Cuauhnáhuac (Cuernavaca), a garden-like land on the descent from the harsher highlands of the Valley of Mexico. Itzcoatl had already been ill as these latter victories were added to the Mexica realm. As death clearly approached in 1440, he summoned Nezahualcoyotl and pledged him to remain at peace with his Mexica relatives who had given him shelter from the murderous wrath of Tezozomoc and who had helped him recover his kingdom. He enjoined his nephew to stay on good terms with his Mexica relatives. This Nezahualcoyotl pledged, and in return Itzcoatl settled formally the precedence of the Alliance. After Tenochtitlan was Texcoco and then Tlacopan. The Texcocan king was the real pivot upon which the Triple Alliance rested. Although the second power of the Alliance, it still possessed significant military power. If Nezahualcoyotl chose to oppose the Mexica, he could easily gather allies. That military potential and Texcoco's proximity to Tenochtitlan would fundamentally destabilise the Mexica basis of power.

Itzcoatl then charged his heir, Motecuhzoma, to rebuild the temple of Huitzilopochtli more splendidly than before and to carve the images of the line of Mexica rulers in stone. His death was followed by 80 days of mourning and ceremony to which came not only the rulers of all the lands allied and tribute to the Mexica but throngs of peasants as well. The Mexica were disconsolate. Itzcoatl had been a man larger than life, and in the words of the Spanish chronicler, Durán, he was 'a dauntless king, of invincible spirit, a man who made the Republic great and who had lifted high the glory of his nation.'[28] He had seized the kingship when Mexica fortunes were at a dangerously low ebb and raised them to heights of empire and had crowned himself with the turquoise diadem of Toltec fame.

Tenochtitlan was desolate, for Itzcoatl's greatness had not been left to later ages to recognise. The Mexica knew that an extraordinary man had left the stage.

TLACAÉLEL AND THE IDEA OF EMPIRE

If Itzcoatl had marched the Mexica onto the stage of empire, it was Tlacaélel who would provide the imperial spark. To his fame as a priest, warrior, general, and statesman he would add that of propagandist and philosopher as well.

When Itzcoatl led the Mexica to overthrow their Tepanec overlords, there was little to mark them as the progenitors of empire. They were a people on the make, to be sure, with a reputation for exceptional cruelty and military skill. They were also considered still semi-barbarous newcomers to the world of civilised men. They had felt this stigma early after their arrival in the Valley of Mexica and had gone so far as to beg as a king, the son of the royal house of Culhuacán. The Toltec-descended royal house of Culhuacán carried a blue blood of particular potency, infusing any descendent with the aura of Tollan's majesty as the foundation of civilisation. Culhuacán was believed to have been the original home of the hero Quetzalcoatl before he seized the rule of Tollan and his final refuge after Tollan and its golden age had disappeared. Historically, the blue blood of Tollan was purest in Culhuacán. It is no accident then, that Itzcoatl

The hieroglyph for the flint knife, a day in the calendar. Here it is depicted as a sacrificial knife.

had been quick after the fall of Azcapotzalco to style himself Lord of the Culhua and his people the Culhua-Mexica. He had also been quick to destroy all the books of history in Tenochtitlan that did not support the imperial destiny of the Mexica or that assigned them a secondary or unflattering role in great events.

'They preserved their history
But it was burned at the time that Itzcoatl reigned in Mexico.
The Aztecs' lords decided it, saying:
"It is not wise that all the people should know the paintings.
The common people would be driven to ruin and there would be trouble,
because these paintings contain many lies for many in the pictures have been hailed as gods.'[29]

Significantly, Tlacaélel had been a participant in this decision to burn their books and those of Azcapotzalco even before the embers of the ruined Tepanec capital had cooled. The reference above to the 'common people would be driven to ruin' by the retention of old books is probably an echo of the strong peace party that had had to be bullied into war. By destroying the books, and especially by replacing them with 'approved' versions, the peace party would be morally disarmed while the legitimacy of the transformed kingship and the warrior classes was strengthened. Itzcoatl has been credited with the burning of the books, but the argument probably was Tlacaélel's considering his subsequent efforts to codify the Mexica imperial destiny.

The first step had been obvious. The second step was far more subtle and breathtaking in its boldness. Tlacaélel embarked upon a propaganda campaign to transform Huitzilopochtli from the mere patron deity of the Mexica to the most powerful of all gods in a cult that would encourage and justify Mexica imperialism. Tlacaélel was bold indeed. To the rest of the

Priests of Huitzilo-pochtli. Tlacaélel, the warrior-priest and genius behind the Mexica imperial idea, raised this local patron deity to the top of the pantheon. It was Tla-caélel who established the connection between Mexica military success and the patronage of Huitzilopochtli who required an ever grow-ing number of human sacrifices. (Drawing by Keith Henderson)

Mesoamerican world, Huitzilopochtli (Left-Handed Hummingbird) was 'a late-developing and strictly local divine patron, possibly a union of a Mexica god-hero with a more ancient water deity of the southern lakes.' It was Tla-caélel's bold genius that identified this nobody of a local deity

'with Tezcatlipoca and Tonatiuh, the warrior sun. He was now the Tezcatlipoca of the south (the White Tezcatlipoca), the "young" sun (the growing sun of the spring and summer), and was also identified with the daily warrior sun, Tonatiuh, who battled his way across the sky. In fact Mexica dogma now held that Huitzilopochtli was one of the four sons of the creator gods, the deities at the very top of the Mesoamerican pantheon.'[30]

Tlacaélel actively nursed the new cult along so aggressively that his efforts were well-remembered by the post-Conquest Náhuatl historian, Chimalpain. 'The first in war, the strong and courageous man Tlacaélel, as it may be seen in the books of the years, went

about persuading the people that their supreme god was Huitzilopochtli.'[31] Tlacaélel's office was particularly helpful in the further-ance of this new imperial idea. As *Tlacochcal-catl*, he was more than captain general of the Mexica; he was the keeper of the records of the Mexica people and attendant of the dead, the very custodian of the spirit of the tribe. It was a unique position, recognised as a great but noble burden, from which to spark a fire in the minds of his people.[32]

The imperial theme was already in play fol-lowing the victory over Coyohuacan when Itz-coatl proclaimed:

'Lords and great princes:
  I know of your great deeds!
I am also aware of the dauntless spirit
  With which you have resisted our foes.
You have now concluded your task in enlarg-
  ing our city, our water and our lands.
This is also the task of our god Huitzilopochtli
  And that is why he came to us.

He gathers, he draws to his service
All the nations with the strength of his chest
　　and of his head.'[33]

Tlacaélel tied the Mexica to Huitzilopochtli in the deity's association with the sun, claiming for them the title, 'People of the Sun.' It was then Huitzilopochtli who laboured to keep the sun alive, the sun who nourished the earth. A hymn captures the essence:

'Huitzilopochtli, the young warrior, who acts above! He follows his path! "Not in vain did I dress myself in yellow plumes for I am he who has caused the sun to rise."'[34]

From this argument, Tlacaélel made a tremendous leap. To preserve life on earth, Huitzilopochtli himself required nourishment, the most precious of all — human blood. Human sacrifice was nothing new in Mesoamerica. Recent excavations have discovered over 200 human sacrifices made at the dedication of the Temple of Quetzalcoatl at Teotihuacán about 250 AD. But now, Tlacaélel was to tie the shedding of blood through sacrifice to the imperial idea. It would become the duty of the Mexica to wage war to obtain prisoners for sacrifice. War and the extension of empire were religious duties to Huitzilopochtli who in turn nourished the earth with the life of the sun and rewarded his chosen people with wealth, power, and dominion over the world. It was wonderfully effective in creating an assurance of divine favour among the Mexica. It was also wonderfully rewarding for the Mexica who grew richer and stronger the more diligently they supplied victims to stain the temple of Huitzilopochtli with torrents of blood.

The scale of human sacrifice was entirely new in Mesoamerica. Where the other gods might take victims singly and rarely, Tlacaélel's new cult began consuming them by the hundreds and thousands and even tens of thousands as the fifteenth century progressed until the survivors of whole cities, defeated in war, were 'processed' with all the efficiency of the twentieth century's Final Solution. The great famine of the early 1450s, which will be discussed below, was the impetus for the acceptance of this massive increase in human sacrifice. It was clearly understood that the gods had punished the Mexica for some omission or sin. Tla-

The war costume of the Tlacochcalcatl.

caélel was quick to point out that it was the failure to feed hearts to Huitzilopochtli on a scale to match the deity's appetite.

Normal wars of conquest, however, could not always be depended upon to supply the necessary sacrifices. Try as they might, the Mexica could not always be at war, and Huitzilopochtli was always hungry. Tlacaélel again had a solution.

'Our god need not depend on the occasion of an affront to go to war. Rather, let a convenient market be sought where our god may go with his army to buy victims and people to eat as if he were to go to a nearby place to buy tortillas . . . whenever he wishes or feels like it. And may our people go to this place with their hearts and lives, those precious stones, jade, and brilliant and wide plumes . . . for the service of the admirable Huitzilopochtli.'[35]

He went on to suggest that only the independent neighbours of the Mexica (Tlaxcallan, Huexotzinco, Cholollan and others) be engaged

Huitzilopochtli. (Drawing by Keith Henderson)

Tlaloc. (Drawing by Keith Henderson)

in this form of war: the 'flowery war', *xochiyaoytl* in Náhuatl or *guerra florida* in Spanish. These neighbours were all Náhuatl-speaking, civilised peoples, obviously far more tasty to Huitzilopochtli than distant non-Náhuatl-speaking peoples who were like 'old and stale tortillas.' He explained,

Costume of a warrior who has taken four or more prisoners.

'Our god will feed himself with them as though he were eating warm tortillas, soft and tasty, straight out of the oven. . . And this war should be of such a nature that we do not endeavor to destroy the others totally. War must always continue so that each time and whenever we wish and our god wishes to eat and feast, we may go there as one who goes to market to buy something to eat. . . organized to obtain victims to offer our god *Huitzilopochtli.*'[36]

In this way, the ambitious fighting men of Tenochtitlan could have an almost constant opportunity to show their prowess in single combat and in the taking of prisoners for sacrifice. From such demonstrations of prowess came rank, wealth, and prestige. And from such opportunities came a flood of young men willing to seek the deadly path to glory and divine favour.

MOTECUHZOMA I, THE EMPIRE BUILDER (1440–1469)

Succession has frequently been the weak joint of new empires. A jealous brother had murdered Tezozomoc's chosen heir and weakened the Tepanec empire enough for the Mexica to destroy it. The Mexica could have seen their fledgling empire broken by a similar dispute between the two likeliest claimants for Itzcoatl's throne — Motecuhzoma and Tlacaélel. Both were men of great ability and mature judgement in that field of action, held by the Mexica to be the supreme qualification leadership —

warfare. It could have sparked a disastrous civil war but did not. The two brothers had spent their lives in unusual harmony, serving Itzcoatl and the glory of their race. It was indeed an unusual harmony for such a large and aggressive royal kinship. When the period of mourning had ended, Tlacaélel addressed the royal council as the chief minister of the empire:

'Now the light that illuminated you is extinguished, the voice at whose sound all this kingdom moved is still, and the mirror in which all men saw themselves is darkened. Thus, illustrious warriors, it is not fitting that this kingdom be left in obscurity; may another sun rise to give it light. . . Who does it seem to you to be the best fitted to follow in the footsteps of our dead king? Who will preserve for us what has been won?'[37]

With great dignity and tact, Tlacaélel had removed himself from consideration and all but handed the turquoise diadem to his brother. There was a special bond between these two brothers born on the same day, that not even death would still. The chronicles give no hint of any friction but only speak of two personalities working in easy tandem. By giving up a throne, however, Tlacaélel did not relinquish power. As first minister upon whom his brother relied, the day-to-day running of the empire remained in his hands. His advice in council would invariably be decisive. Tlacaélel was evidently more interested in the reins of power than in its trappings. T. R. Fehrenbach caught the essence of the man:

'Tlacaélel was ruthlessly practical, with only one purpose: to increase the power of Tenochtitlan. His Toltec education gave him knowledge of things that went back to Teotihuacán — but it had not eradicated his true Mexica nature, barbarian, bellicose, parochial, with an island mentality and thoroughly tribal mind. His genius — and he had genius — lay in his ability to blend his knowledge and his qualities into empirical actions.'[38]

Motecuhzoma's name hieroglyph.

Despite having a brother and first minister with the talents of a Richelieu and a Cromwell, Motecuhzoma was no puppet. He was the other half of this unique pair of brothers who had been Itzcoatl's right and left hands. A man of strategic vision he would lead the Mexica in a far-reaching war of conquest outside the Valley of Mexico. His very names rattled with war; Motecuhzoma means 'The Angry Lord', and his additional name, Ilhuicamina, 'The Archer of the Skies.' To war was added the romance of his birth. His mother was the great beauty, Miyahuaxiuhtzin, daughter of the king of Cuauhnáhuac, with whom the Mexica king Huitzilíhuitl had been madly in love. Her father had kept her jealously safe from all suitors in a high-walled courtyard. Huitzilíhuitl tied a shining jewel to an arrow and shot it over the wall for his love. She swallowed the jewel and with its beauty quickened the life of the future Motecuhzoma.

The ceremonies of his coronation were far more resplendent than any the Mexica had seen before. From his election he climbed the pyramid of Huitzilopochtli's temple and there was arrayed in imperial robes and performed the rites of autosacrifice, piercing his thighs and earlobes with the sharpened bones of the ocelot and ram. His allies and vassals heaped his palace with fine gifts of jewels, weapons, shields, insignia, and delicate featherwork, and to the poor of Tenochtitlan, they were also generous. All of these gifts were as nothing to what Nezahualcoyotl brought. The Mexica had passed the danger of succession, but now they faced the danger of a breakdown in the Triple Alliance if Nezahualcoyotl chose to contest primacy of place. Itzcoatl had formerly designated the king of Texcoco as second in order of precedence, but he had become a successful conqueror in his own right and had made Texcoco a rich and powerful city. He came to Tenochtitlan upon his cousin's election and graciously acknowledged Motecuhzoma's elevation to the throne and the subordinate position of Texcoco in the alliance. It was an act of brilliant self-interest and a demonstration of the aphorism, 'Do what you must and see that you are thanked for it.' There was more to it than self-interest, though. Nezahualcoyotl was the third remarkable nephew of Itzcoatl, and the ties of family and affection were strong. He could not forget all that he owed his Mexica kin and that it had been Motecuhzoma who had saved his life by warning him at the court of Tezozomoc that he was in danger. He barely escaped the garotte in time.

Motecuhzoma was delighted with his cousin's allegiance. He recognised that the first years of his reign were needed for consolidation of Itzcoatl's conquests and for some unfinished business within the Valley of Mexico. Nezahualcoyotl had saved him from unnecessary strife, but the tension between the Mexica and Acolhua had become intense as each had successfully waged war both as alliance members and separately. Tlacaélel slyly suggested that Nezahualcoyotl's acknowledgement of his subordinate status was not enough and that too many disloyal vassals and meddlesome foreign lords would try to play the Acolhua against the Mexica to the ruin of both if the status of Texcoco was in doubt within the Triple Alliance. He emphasised, 'They must understand that we are capable of conquering the entire world.' He then proposed that a feigned and bloodless war be fought between Tenochtitlan and Texcoco so that the world would see the Mexica triumph by force of arms. Motecuhzoma ordered him to take the proposal to Nezahualcoyotl who agreed to the scheme. Only the most trusted captains in both armies were informed of the game. On the appointed day the armies faced each other and hurled nothing more dangerous than insults. On command the Acolhua turned and fled with the Mexica in a well-controlled pursuit. Nezahualcoyotl fired one of his own temples to signify surrender. With that both armies marched home while the captains and lords feasted. It had been a wonderful piece of realpolitik as theatre and had accomplished its objective.

Motecuhzoma devoted the first years of his reign to an intensive consolidation of power that would support the next phase of territorial expansion. The Mexica kingship now began to take on even more autocratic features as Motecuhzoma decreed that the tlatoani must appear in public on only the most important occasions and that only he might wear a golden diadem in Tenochtitlan. An exception was granted to great lords and captains who commanded armies in war since they represented the imperial dignity. The very palace became a sacred precinct in which only Motecuhzoma and Tlacaélel could wear sandals. In the city itself only great lords could wear similar gold embellished sandals. Even great captains and mighty warriors were limited to cheap footwear. The rest of the population was to go barefoot. Lip plugs, the mark of status, were assigned by rank as well. The finest of gold and jewels were restricted to great lords; mighty men of war were confined to plugs of bone and wood. Similarly, gold jewellery and the finest embroidered cotton clothing was restricted to the great lords. Everyone else had to wear garments of rough maguey fibre. Even the length of mantles for the commoners was not permitted to fall below the knee on pain of death. The one exception was granted to those who could show the scars of war wounds on their legs. 'Since the leg did not flee from the sword, it is just that it be rewarded and honored.'

The mention of rewards and honours is significant. Motecuhzoma had sharply drawn the lines between classes, but the lines were crossable by those ambitious enough to earn these rewards and honours. War and its loot fed these ambitions and supported a large and warlike nobility and swelled the ranks of those captains and warriors who sought the bubble of reputation.

'The battlefield is the place:
  Where one toasts the divine liquor in war,
Where are stained red the divine eagles,
  Where the jaguars howl,
Where all kinds of precious stones rain from
  ornaments
Where wave headdresses rich with fine
  plumes,
Where princes are smashed to bits.'[39]

Motecuhzoma did more than encourage ambitious valour, he bred its seed corn by estab-

lishing rigorous schools for all the boys of
Tenochtitlan with a uniform curriculum carefully supervised by the state. There were separate schools for the nobility and the commons.
The *calmecac* educated the leaders in war,
statecraft, and religion. The *telpochcalli* trained
the commons. The schools also served as a propaganda medium for Tlacaélel's imperial
mythology. They were uniquely successful in
producing a thoroughly indoctrinated fighting
force, inured to discipline and privation, and
eager for war. In this period of consolidation,
Motecuhzoma did not hesitate to follow Nezahualcoyotl's examples. He adopted his Texcocan cousin's law code, the first body of law
based on a fixed elements with prescribed punishments. He also freely sought Nezahualcoyotl's assistance in his many building projects,
for his cousin was famed as a builder. In the
most dramatic instance, the Lake of Texcoco
was flooding Tenochtitlan on too regular a
basis. Nezahualcoyotl designed a seven-mile
dike across the lake to be built of great stone
blocks and earth. The two monarchs inaugu-
rated the monumental project by carrying the
first stones as examples to their peoples.

THE CHALCA WAR:
MOTECUHZOMA SETTLES A SCORE

Another such project was the rebuilding of the
temple of Huitzilopochtli, and it was to be the
trigger of Motecuhzoma's first major war. The
Great Temple was rebuilt many times, each
time enlarged by superimposing a new casing
over the old structure. Motecuhzoma initiated a
particularly massive rebuilding effort and
demanded materials and labour from his allies
and vassals which they enthusiastically provided. The excavator of the Great Temple,
Eduardo Matos Moctezuma, considers that the,

'architecture and sculptures of this stage are
among the most spectacular known from the
Great Temple.'[40]

The rebuilding of the temple also offered a
splendid opportunity to settle unfinished business. Motecuhzoma had not forgotten the night
he spent in a wooden cage in Chalco almost
twenty years before. With seeming humility, in
1444 he requested from the Chalca great

stones from their mountains for the work on
the temple of Huitzilopochtli. For the Chalca to
fulfill it would be the submission of a vassal. To
refuse was an open affront to Huitzilopochtli
and the surest *casus belli* in Mesoamerica. The
Chalca overreached themselves in their confidence and chose war. A numerous people in a
confederation of many cities, they felt little fear
of the Triple Alliance and had ignored the pleas
of their neighbours in Xochimilco when the
Mexica had fallen upon them. They had even
gone so far as to murder two sons of Nezahualcoyotl and two sons of Motecuhzoma himself
while the young men were on a hunt. Their
dried bodies, like ghoulish candelabra, were
propped up holding torches in a royal audience
chamber.

Mexica reconnaissance discovered the whole
might of the Chalca confederation drawn up for
battle. The Triple Alliance army had stripped
the men of military age from their cities to meet
so large a number of Chalca. The Acolhua contingent was exceptionally strong and well-represented by Nezahualcoyotl's sons, all
seasoned in war. After the Mexica had marched
out of Tenochtitlan under the command of Tlacaélel, Motecuhzoma reflected quickly on the
great odds. The Triple Alliance would have an
enemy in their front and unsteady vassals in
their rear, ready to rise should the Chalca pre-
vail and successfully defy Motecuhzoma.

As the hosts faced each other, Tlacaélel
exhorted his men, for the Chalca were
renowned for their courage and prowess,
'Remember that those who stand opposite are
not lions that will tear you to pieces, nor
demons who will swallow you. Note well that
they are men like yourselves, and that you hold
in your hands the self-same weapons that they
bear.'[41] For two days the armies struggled in a
great but drawn battle. Then Tlacaélel switched
his tactics and for five days harassed the
Chalca with unremitting skirmishing that wore
them down. On the sixth day he attacked again
in full force, and now the Chalca broke and fled
the field. As the Mexica pursued, Chalca her-
alds asked for a five-day truce so that the final
battle could take place on the feast day of their
patron deity, Camaxtli. Then, they proclaimed,
they would smear his temple walls with Mexica
blood. It was just the sort of challenge the Mex-

ica could not refuse. Motecuhzoma vowed that it would be Chalca blood that dripped from the walls of Huitzilopochtli's temple. When the feast day dawned both armies attacked with new enthusiasm. Motecuhzoma had a trump this time. He armed all the youth of the city down to twelve years of age and dispatched them after Tlacaélel's army. He gambled that their appearance behind the struggling Mexica would give the appearance of a new army entering the battle. Motecuhzoma clearly understood the most important role of a very senior commander — to control the reserve and commit it at the critical moment. The Mexica already were pushing the Chalca back when the arrival of the army of boys snapped their already strained resolve. They fled with the Mexica in howling pursuit, killing Chalca in great numbers and seizing many prisoners. They were dragged back in triumph to Tenochtitlan, 300 seasoned warriors and 200 common soldiers to die on Huitzilopochtli's altar stone. For them Motecuhzoma had a special sacrifice. A huge brazier had been dug in the earth and filled with glowing embers. One after another the Chalca were thrown into it to flop hideously until they were dragged out by hooks attached to long poles and only then swiftly dispatched with the swift, practised slashes that tore out their hearts. So began the long, twenty-year war against the Chalca.

The next major round came about 1450 when the Mexica attacked Amecameca, one of the major Chalca cities. This time the Mexica appeared to have badly underestimated the Chalca as the army was commanded by neither Tlacaélel or Motecuhzoma. The Chalca summoned every fighting man, even boys, and encircled the Mexica army. Chalca numbers quickly engulfed the Mexica who were compressed into a circle. Disaster hovered over the Mexica as the Chalca threw themselves at the shrinking ring. For the Mexica it was truly a 'do or die' battle. They held on until darkness ended the battle. The Mexica survivors withdrew to lick their wounds, but there was no hiding the fact that only darkness had saved the Mexica from a massacre. So serious had the losses been that three of Motecuhzoma and Tlacaélel's brothers were found the next day on the field. They were found among heaps of Chalca. The bodies were brought before their brothers. Motecuhzoma was distraught over the loss of so many kinsmen and cried out:

'O valorous brothers of mine: happy are you who died proving your great personal courage. Go now in honor, wrapped in the precious stones and rich plumage of your heroic deeds, performed while fighting for your country and the honor of your brother!'[42]

Then he reproached Tlacaélel, in the only recorded friction between them, for being so mute and stoic at the sight of his dead brothers. It was a defining moment for the Mexica drive for empire.

'O mighty prince, I do not marvel at such deaths. That is how wars are fought! Remember Huitzilíhuitl the Elder, our lord and king, who died in Colhuacan before we were born; behold how he found eternal fame as a valiant man. The Aztec nation needs bold men such as those who lie before you. There will be more like them in Mexico. How long must we mourn them? If we stay here weeping we will not be able to accomplish more important matters.'[43]

The war went on. Armies would be defeated, kings lose their grip, but Tlacaélel would keep to the course, relentless and implacable — and the war went on. Tlacaélel could keep to such a course because the Mexica were instinctively like him, as shown by Ezhuahuacatl, a nephew who had been captured by the Chalca in the same battle. The young man was recognised by the Chalca as coming from the royal Eagle Clan. Perhaps they sought to placate the Mexica, but they asked the prince to be one of their kings. He asked, in turn, if the offer of freedom included the many other Mexica prisoners. It did not. He pretended to agree anyway and addressed the rest of the Mexica:

'Do you know, brethren, that the Chalca want to make me their king and lord? I would be willing if I knew that all of you would be given your freedom. But as this is not so, I will die with you since I did not come there to reign but to fight and perish like a man. I have already sold my life and with it bought the Chalca who are to serve my children and grandchildren and all their descendants. And all of you have done the same!'

He then asked the Chalca to build him a special platform atop a long tree trunk. From there, he told them, he would mock the other Mexica prisoners. Climbing to the swaying platform, he shouted to the Mexica to die like brave men. To the Chalca he threw his defiance. 'O Chalca, know that with my death I will have bought your lives and that you will serve my children and grandchildren! My royal blood will be paid for with yours!'[44] Then, like a warrior, throwing himself into the enemy ranks, he hurled himself from the platform to die on the stones below. Such was the Mexica spirit, the same spirit that burned most powerfully and purely in Tlacaélel himself. A collective shudder may have gone through the Chalca as the young prince dashed himself to death. The Mexica would never stop.

THE GREAT FAMINE

But they could be delayed. Nature chose this moment to present the Mexica with a crisis that they would barely surviv. With the most recent phase of the war against the Chalca in 1450, came unprecedented deep snow and sharp frosts in the Valley of Mexico. The severe cold devastated the Valley, killing not only many plants but trees as well. The frosts killed the young corn in the fields. There was no harvest that year, but stocks carefully laid up from fat years fed the peoples of Anáhuac. Frosts again killed the corn the following year. The next year drought withered the tender cobs. Now in the fourth year, there was no seed corn, and famine began to kill the weakened people in large numbers. Vultures which had not been known at such altitudes were attracted in large flocks by the endless supply of human carrion. Through the first three years of famine, Motecuhzoma had continued the work on the Great Temple, only reducing the ration of the vassal labourers to one meal a day. He had opened the granaries to feed the people, issuing a ration of one large tortilla a day to each person. By the fourth year, the granaries were empty. Many people had already fled the scorched Valley. Others had sold themselves into slavery to Totonac and Huaxtec merchants from the rich lowlands of the Gulf Coast who had brought heavy loads of corn and beans now that food was dear and slaves cheap. Many sold their

own children to save them, although the parents could ransom them some day for the price of their maintenance.

Those who remained became little more than walking skeletons, skin stretched over bones. When all hope was gone, Motecuhzoma assembled the Mexica, 'O my children, you know that I have done everything in my power and that the foodstuffs have been used up. It is the will now of the lord of the Heavens that each of you go his way to seek his own salvation.'[45] A great exodus followed, but many of the weak died along the way. In the fifth year (1455) the rains at last returned. The Valley burst into life in incredible abundance. The people began to return and resume their old lives. The corn grew, and in time the slave children were redeemed.

THE GREAT EXPANSION

The Mexica had tasted humiliation and near extinction in the great famine. Three years passed as they recovered their strength before they were ready to march again to a major conquest. It is no wonder that their eyes fixed on the rich coastal lowlands, known as the Hot Lands, of the Huaxtec confederation to the northeast. The Hot Lands had brimmed with assured abundance when Anáhuac had writhed in hunger. The Mexica could not forget the Huaxtec merchants with their loads of corn and beans come to buy starving Mexica. The Huaxteca were an ancient Maya-related people whose verdant land was considered a Garden of Eden by the Mexica. The Hot Lands were also the ultimate sources of so much that was prized as wealth by the Mexica — cotton, brilliant feathers, and jewels, and ocean products such as various prized shells, and exotic foods like chocolate and vanilla. Nezahualcoyotl had led his own Texcocan armies to conquests in that direction, and these cities would be perfect logistic stepping stones. Although the target area was eight days march from Tenochtitlan (155 km), the first five days would be in friendly territory.

The Huaxteca conveniently massacred Mexica merchants at this time. The misuse of merchants and ambassadors was to become a

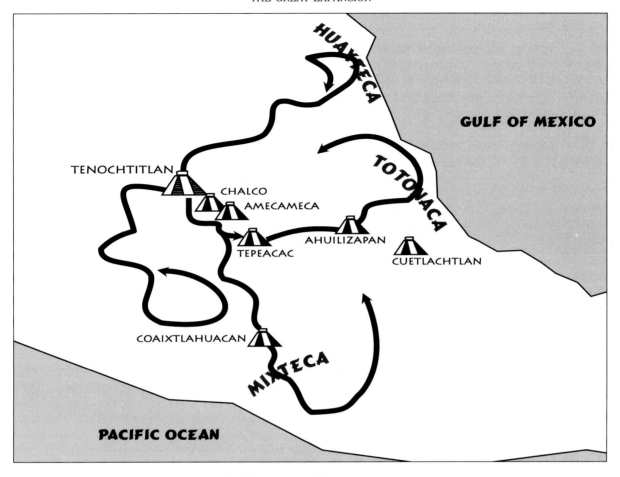

The Campaigns of Motecuhzoma I

favourite Mexica excuse for war. Of course, Mexica merchants were not free agents but tied closely to the state which they served as spies and provocateurs. It was not above the Mexica ruler to order merchants to commit such provocations that would lead to their own murder and hence provide a ready excuse for war.

The Mexica must have viewed the campaign with some trepidation. This would be the first time that they would campaign outside Anáhuac against people of different culture and language. The Huaxteca were also a warlike and numerous people. Their ancestors had once campaigned in Anáhuac itself in the time of Quetzalcoatl, to sack and burn brilliant Tollan itself. Now the Mexica, who claimed the imperial mantle of Tollan, would repay the visit. The night before the battle, an old captain reminded the Mexica of their duty in words saved by Durán that breathed the Mex-

ica warrior's code: 'You have arrived at a place where you may perish, like wild grass when it is set on fire. Contemplate your death and think of nothing else. . . . You have come here to conquer or die since this is your mission in life.'[46]

The Mexica warrior's code, like the Bushido of the Samurai that it so closely resembled, also left considerable room for cunning. That night 2,000 men of the Otomi and Cuachic knightly orders were assembled from all the contingents of the army — Mexica, allies, and vassals alike. Ordered to lie on the ground with their arms, they were covered with grass before the sun rose. Over 75 years later, the ferocious appearance and war cries of the Huaxteca remained fixed in Mexica memory. Noses were pierced with large plugs of crystal or precious stones, bodies and faces were painted with bright colours, hair festooned with feathers, the

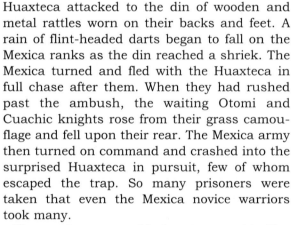

The tlatoani and the Eagle Council plan a campaign.

The tlatoani's war costumes.

Huaxteca attacked to the din of wooden and metal rattles worn on their backs and feet. A rain of flint-headed darts began to fall on the Mexica ranks as the din reached a shriek. The Mexica turned and fled with the Huaxteca in full chase after them. When they had rushed past the ambush, the waiting Otomi and Cuachic knights rose from their grass camouflage and fell upon their rear. The Mexica army then turned on command and crashed into the surprised Huaxteca in pursuit, few of whom escaped the trap. So many prisoners were taken that even the Mexica novice warriors took many.

These prisoners would play a new part in Tlacaélel's growing imperial cult — the sacrifice of the 'Skinning of Men', ironically and surely intentionally the special feast of the Flayed God, Xipe Totec, the special patron of the Huaxteca. Tlacaélel had caused a great round, flat-surfaced stone to be carved with scenes of the Mexica liberation from the yoke of Azcapotzalco. The Mexica warriors led the captives they had taken into the precinct of the Great Temple.

'When one showed himself strong, not acting like a woman, when one went with a man's fortitude; he bore himself like a man; he went speaking in a manly fashion; he went exerting himself; he went strong of heart and shouting with courage, not stumbling, but honoring and praising his city. He went with a firm heart, speaking as he went. "Here I come! You will speak of me there in my homeland."[47]

To the blare of conch shell trumpets and whistles and the roar of the crowd of warriors, the valiant Huaxtec was heaved upon the stone, tied around the waist with a rope, and given a sword edged with feathers instead of obsidian. On the stone he faced an eagle or jaguar knight armed with a stout shield and a real obsidian-edged sword. Despite the valour of the victim, the issue was seldom in doubt, though Durán recorded that a few Huaxteca were skilful enough to defeat two or three Mexica knights. The Mexica, however, fought only to wound, and when the crippling wound had been dealt, priests would leap upon the stone and cut out his heart. The captor of the prisoner was then rewarded with the flayed skin of the victim which he would wear in a cloud of putrefaction for twenty days until it rotted off him.

Tlacaélel had more than a domestic religious message in mind. The Mexica vassal lords and even enemy rulers were royally invited, feasted, showered with rich gifts, and then escorted to luxuriously appointed stands to watch the spectacle, and reflect on Mexica might. The show kept vassals and allies in their place and left their enemies increasingly intimidated. To his own people, delighted with such a rich conquest, he sternly announced, 'I wish you to have no illusions that our wars are at an end. We must continue to march onwards.'

The next march onwards in 1458 was to be to the south to the land of the Mixteca, 'The People of the Clouds' an ancient people renowned for their goldwork, fine pottery, and other crafts who had established great kingdoms in the wake of Teotihuacán's fall. Motecuhzoma's target was again a great source of wealth, the Mixtec confederation based on the city of Coaixtlahuacan ruled by its able king Atonal. Coaixtlahuacan was important because it was a centre of trade and dominated vital trade routes to the south. The Mixteca controlled the supply of the precious red cochineal dye made from the bodies of the insect coccus cacti. Atonal's kingdom was also the key to the entire Mixtec region to the south beyond.[48] Neither Motecuhzoma nor Tlacaélel accompanied this campaign, one of the first to have neither the First Speaker nor Snake Woman in direct command. Both were 60 years old, and the Mexica royal kin now had many seasoned commanders in their prime. Tlacaélel appointed a nobleman, Cuauhnochtli, to command in his place. The campaign against the Huaxteca had been merely a warm-up for this campaign, and, although Tlacaélel would not be leading it in person, the masterful organising hand of Motecuhzoma's first minister was everywhere. The scale and organisation of the campaign would be colossal by previous standards. An immense levy was placed on the fighting men of the Triple Alliance and their vassals — 200,000 men and 100,000 porters. The Mexica would remember that Tenochtitlan seemed empty when the army had left. The distances would be immense by any other standard. Ross Hassig estimated that the entire round trip journey would have taken 26 to 43 days for 823 km (510 miles). The horde of porters was needed to carry the 7,410,00 to 12,550,000 kilograms (16,336,000 to 27,018,000 pounds) of food necessary for the army, in addition to what would be supplied along the route by friendly sources.[49]

This hive of Mexica activity quickly came to the ears of Atonal as well as Huexotzinco and Tlaxcallan, the Mexica's bitterest enemies. They quickly patched together an alliance and dispatched large forces to bolster the Mixteca. Cuauhnochtli efficiently delivered his huge host to the plain in front of Coaixtlahuacan.

The ensuing battle was fierce and desperate, but despite their allies, the Mixteca were no match for the war-honed Mexica. Motecuhzoma's innovation of permanent military school systems for nobles and commoners had raised the professional level of the Mexica, man-for-man, well above the Mixteca. Constant campaigning had reinforced it. The allied army crumbled, and the Mixteca fled to their city with the Mexica on their heels. The women and children fled to the hills as the fighting swept through the city to the temple precinct which the Mexica finally captured and set on fire. The city was given over to a thorough sacking until its chief men offered their submission. With that out of the way, the Mexica got down to business, allowing the noncombatants to return and tribute to be set. Only Atonal's life was forfeit, and he was quickly strangled.

The next Mexica campaign took them back to the Gulf Coast to the south-east of their Huaxtec conquests to the land of the Totonaca. In a well-worn ploy, Mexica ambassadors were sent to the chief Totonac cities of Ahuilizapan and Cuetlachtlan, to ask for shells for Huitzilopochtli. The ambassadors were straight-away killed at the urging of visiting high-ranking Tlaxcallans who promised military aid if the Totonacs would stand up to the Mexica. The Tlaxcallans had hoped that heavy Mexica losses in the Mixtec campaign would weaken them against the Totonaca. They were mistaken, and the Totonaca were defeated without the promised Tlaxcallan help. Soon after the Mexica army had departed, the Totonaca regretted their submission and listened to Tlaxcallan recriminations for having surrendered and to more promises of military help. They murdered the Mexica tax-gatherers and instead gave gifts to the Tlaxcallans. When the tribute failed to arrive in Tenochtitlan, Tlacaélel sent ambassadors to inquire why. They were graciously received and shown to a room to rest. Outside the Totonaca set fire to a great pile of chili, the fumes of which filled the room, choking the Mexica to death. Vile desecrations of their bodies followed. A travelling merchant brought the news to Tenochtitlan. Motecuhzoma and Tlacaélel were enraged and ordered an immediate punitive expedition which promptly crushed the Totonaca again with

Otomi and Cuachic Knights.

great bloodshed. However enraged the two Mexica lords were, though, they had no intention of killing off too many taxpayers. Motecuhzoma had given his commander orders to be merciful if the Totonaca surrendered. This time, the long-suffering Totonac commons asserted themselves. They approached the Mexica general and stated that it was only their kings who wanted this war and that they were willing to surrender them immediately. The two royal prisoners were dragged back to Tenochtitlan. Motecuhzoma had reservations about executing fellow kings, a sentiment of which Tlacaélel quickly disabused him. They were rebels against the Mexica supreme deity and the ruler who represented him on earth. In addition, the common people had asked for justice. The throats of the Totonac lords were cut. As for the Tlaxcallans who had twice egged the Totonaca to war with the Mexica with false promises of aid, they surely now regretted their too clever game. For the conquest of the Totonaca had left them totally surrounded by Mexica-controlled territory.

It was now 1465, and Motecuhzoma returned to unfinished business — Chalco. The last serious campaign against Chalco had been before the great famine of the early 1450s; however, a low level of war, especially Flowery War, had continued even during the mighty wars of expansion. Now Chalco was almost surrounded by Mexica-controlled territory and itself was much smaller than at the beginning of Motecuhzoma's reign. He closed in for the kill. In 1464 the Mexica had stormed a hill dominating Amecameca, the second city of the Chalca confederation. The next year they returned, vowing never to return home until Chalco had been destroyed. To that end they built a permanent base camp in Chalco to which Motecuhzoma and Tlacaélel, both in their 67th years, repaired.

As the armies stood to arms through the night, Durán retells the Mexica account, that the cries of owls echoed eerily between the two camps. They seemed to call to each other and paralyse both armies with fear.

> 'Tiacan, tiacan! — Mighty, mighty!
> Nocne, nocne! — Alas, alas!
> Tetec, tetec! — Cut, cut!
> Yollo, yollo! — Hearts, hearts!
> Quetechpol chichil, quetechpol chichil! — Red throats, red throats!
> Chalca, Chalca! — O men of Chalco! O men of Chalco!'

Tlacaélel seized the balance of fear and strode to the king and his nobles:

'O Aztecs, listen to the owls, hear how they announce our victory! Some divine thing moves those birds to hoot in such a manner. It is not possible that they are doing it by themselves! Someone moves their beaks, announcing our triumph! It is fated, O Aztecs! Courage and strength! Let us not in our weakness lose what has been sent to us from above!'[50]

So frightened of the omen were the Chalca that the Lord of Amecameca sent three of his sons to Motecuhzoma to pretend treason in order to guide the Mexica through a pass and into ambush. So sure was Tlacaélel of victory now that he advised Motecuhzoma to brush aside the three princes, telling them to go or stay, it did not matter. The next day the final battle was joined in a ferocious crash of armies, the Mexica straining to seize the prize and the Chalca equally to stave off the end. Then the Chalca general was cut down, and the army, as Mesoamerican armies were wont, fled the field. The rout became a slaughter watched by the people of Amecameca from a mountainside above. They and the surviving warriors fled toward safety over the mountain to the friendly kingdom of Huexotzinco. Tlacaélel sent a captain to intercept them and promise safe conduct back to their homes, but 16,000 fled beyond the border. The rest accepted his terms and returned home. With the fall of Amecameca, the remnants of the Chalca confederation collapsed and passed into Mexica hands. The revenge of the man in the wooden cage had come to pass.

The following year, in 1466, Motecuhzoma was to oversee his final and least bloody conquest. In that year merchants of the Triple Alliance were murdered in the city of Tepeaca and their bodies thrown to wild beasts. This time the Mexica ambassador simply brought a sword and shield for the king of Tepeaca as a declaration of war. There would be no bargaining. By now Mexica reputation was enough to collapse an enemy's will to fight. The Mexica commanders were surprised when their scouts reported no evidence of any military preparation by the enemy. As the Triple Alliance army approached, Tepeaca simply surrendered. Its leaders were hustled to Tenochtitlan to adore Huitzilopochtli and to be told their place in the new order of things by Tlacaélel. Mindful of the fact that their land was a crossroads of travel and trade, he ordered them to take special care of travellers and especially of the merchants who traded with Soconusco and Guatemala 'since these are the ones that enrich and ennoble the earth.' They were also ordered to set up a major trade market. A governor was assigned to them, and they were dismissed to their homes. Tlacaélel's mercy, as shown repeatedly, had a hard-nosed basis — the preservation of tax-payers and the encouragement of wealth created by trade. Guatemala was a great source of riches, and he was determined to smooth the path to it. Of course, he did not neglect the columns of human tribute from Tepeaca, meant to feed Huitzilopochtli. Nothing would ever get in the way of that.

THE ARCHER OF THE SKIES DEPARTS

Huitzilíhuitl's sons could now look with great satisfaction at the splendour of their lives' work. Tribute and trade flowed in unheard of amounts from throughout the central plateau, rich Hotlands, and as far away as the land of the Mixtec Cloud People. Tenochtitlan was daily growing in size and splendour and had long outpaced any city in memory. It was 40 years since the two had led the men of the city to bring down Tezozomoc's empire. They had transformed the Mexica from vassals so poor they lacked cotton clothing and could only offer tribute of ducks and edible worms to become the heirs of Toltec splendour, the masters of mighty Tollan reborn.

For Motecuhzoma, the new splendour of Tenochtitlan was reflected in the soft glow of the sunset of his life. He knew that death was upon him, and like most men, sought to leave some bit of his mortality on the earth. This desire he would share with no one but his brother, the friend of his heart. Their wills had intertwined for four decades without anger. He had leaned upon Tlacaélel much as he himself had spun the strategy of empire. Now to his brother he confided that he wished to have statues of the two of them carved and placed in the gardens on the hill of Chapultepec. 'It will be a reward for our endeavors, and our sons and grandsons will see our images there, remember us and our great deeds and will struggle to imitate us.' As the heir to Toltec greatness, he was consciously imitating Quetzalcoatl who had also ordered that a likeness of himself be carved to preserve his memory. When the work was finished, the two old men left the city alone and unnoticed crossed the causeway to Chapultepec in the mask of grey dawn. They were not disappointed and marvelled at the quality of the work and the exact likenesses.

'Brother Tlacaélel, I am well pleased with these images! They will remain as a perpetual memorial to our greatness in the way we remember Quetzalcoatl. It is written that before the latter departed he left orders that his figure be carved in wood and in stone, to be adored by the common people. Yet we know that he was a man like us. Let us be glorified in the same way.'[51]

Upon their return, Motecuhzoma took Tlacaélel aside. He had a duty to settle. He said, 'If I die before you, I wish you to become the ruler of the land. From the beginning your deeds have made you worthy of this . . . only you are worthy of it. And if you die before I do, let one of your sons inherit the throne.' He was offering one last gift to his brother — the Turquoise Diadem. No other sons of Huitzilíhuitl remained alive, and Motecuhzoma's sons had all died without issue. Only a daughter remained.[52] To pass the throne to a brother was the Mexica rule. Tlacaélel, was loath to accept the throne, never more so than now as old age had settled equally upon himself. Perhaps to deflect the issue and in genuine affec-

tion for his brother, he instead suggested that Motecuhzoma erect one more monument to the glory of his deeds. He spoke of the plentiful waters of Cuauhnáhuac where Motecuhzoma's mother had been born, and encouraged him to make a garden there, channel the waters, and fill the grounds with the finest flowers and trees of the Hot Lands. Be remembered by the beauty of a garden to surpass all gardens, he suggested. The architects and masons diverted the water to the site and filled it with walks and arbours, and the gardeners from the Hot Lands carried countless plants and trees to nurse them in the fine air of Cuauhnáhuac. To their amazement, everything flourished more quickly in this new soil; the trees bloomed in three years instead of the expected eight. Motecuhzoma gave thanks to the Lord of All Created Things for this special sign of favour. Tlacaélel and he wept that they had lived to witness one last glorious moment.

It was indeed a final glory. Shortly after the blooming of his gardens in 1468, Motecuhzoma quickly sickened and died at the age of 70. The issue of the succession again arose, but Tlacaélel promised that he would assume the throne only after Motecuhzoma's grandsons had each succeeded him. With Motecuhzoma passed the first great phase in the rise of the Mexica. He was truly one of the world's great empire-builders, a master strategist, accomplished warrior, lawgiver, and a man with the good sense to employ his equally talented brother to the glory of their race.

Now that brother assembled all the nobles and lords to choose a new tlatoani. First he spoke Motecuhzoma's eulogy, the very prescription of Mexica kingship.

'The death of my brother is known to you! He was like one who carries a load on his back for a time. He carried the burden of being Lord of Mexico until the end of his days. He was like a slave subjected to his master, sheltering and defending this republic. What happened to him will happen to me and to all of us. We enjoy life, its pleasures and happiness. This is given to us for only a short time. All of my brothers are dead now and I am alone.'[53]

He was overcome with grief and openly cried before all of the great men of Tenochtitlan. The world was at his feet, but he could only cry, 'All

Mexica ambassadors were frequently sent with the express purpose of provoking a war by delivering unacceptable demands. This often resulted in their own deaths, an automatic just war cause for the Mexica. Mesoamerican ambassadors were not protected by any concept of immunity. (Drawing by Keith Henderson)

of my brothers are dead now and I am alone.' They tried to console him by offering him the Turquoise Diadem. Not for the last time, he refused the crown.

'O Aztecs, I thank you for the honor you wish to bestow upon me. But how can I be honored more than I have already been? What further sovereignty could I acquire than that which I have now? None of the past kings have acted without my opinion or counsel. But I am too old to carry the burden that you wish to place upon my back.'[54]

Instead, he ordered them to summon the kings of Texcoco and Tlacopan to confer with him to select the next tlatoani. The age of the founding triumvirate of Mexica greatness passed. Tlacaélel would survive as a living legend, an almost god-like figure, but history now passed to the grandsons of Motecuhzoma.

1. Ron Hassig, *Aztec Warfare: Imperial Expansion and Political Control*, University of Oklahoma Press, Norman and London, 1988, p. 142.
2. Domingo Chimalpain Cuauhtelhuanitzin, *Sixième et Septième (1358-1612)*, ed. Remi Simeon (Paris: 1889) p. 85; cited in Miguel León-Portilla, *Aztec Thought and Culture*, trans. Emory Davis, University of Oklahoma Press, Norman and London, 1990, p. 159.
3. Fray Diego Durán, *The Aztecs: The History of the Indies of New Spain*, trans. Doris Heyden and Fernando Horcasitas, Orion Press, New York, 1964, p. 50.
4. Durán, ibid., p. 52.
5. Durán, ibid., pp. 52-53.
6. Durán, ibid., p. 53.
7. Durán, ibid.
8. Durán, ibid., p. 54.
9. Durán, ibid., pp. 54-55.
10. Durán, ibid., p. 57.
11. Frances Gillmor, *Flute of the Smoking Mirror*, University of Arizona Press, Tuscon, 1949, pp. 74-77.
12. Gillmor, ibid., p. 77.
13. Nigel Davies, *The Aztecs*, University of Oklahoma Press, Norman and London, 1989, p. 73.
14. Durán, ibid., pp. 57-58.
15. Richard F. Townsend, *The Aztecs*, Thames and Hudson, London, 1993, p. 195. The position of Snake Woman evolved under Tlacaélel, who held the position from this point to his death about 1480, into an alter-ego of the king himself.
16. Durán, ibid., p. 58.
17. Durán, ibid., p. 58. Durán's account compresses the entire 114 day operation into one day. This first engagement which he describes as a victory is described elsewhere as an initial though temporary setback. The latter seems more likely since the Mexica were facing the bulk of the Tepaneca forces.
18. Mariano Veytia, Vol. II, *Historia Antigua de México*,

Editorial Leyenda, 1944 Mexico City p. 133; in
Davies, The Aztecs, ibid., p. 74.

19. Durán, ibid., p. 59.

20. Hassig, ibid., pp. 43, 147; Gillmor, ibid., p. 80.

21. Durán, ibid., p. 60. Durán credits Maxtla with hav
ing survived the fall of Azcapotzalco and assuming
the throne of Coyohuacan, contrary to most other
sources which depict him dying under Nezahualcoy
otl's sacrificial knife.

22. Durán, ibid., p. 77.

23. Durán, ibid., p. 77.

24. Hassig, p. 150.

25. Durán, ibid., pp. 77-78; Hassig, ibid. Hassig cites
sources in which Xochimilco was sacked, its temple
burned and its people fled to the hills. Durán's
account is plausible because Mesoamerican rules of
war spared a city from sack if it surrendered before
the assault. A ruined Xochimilco state, perhaps
could not have continued to manage the efficient pro
duction of foodstuffs, the secure supply of which
was, after all, one of the main Mexica objectives of
the war.

26. Nigel Davies, ibid., p. 85.

27. Hassig, ibid., pp. 155-156.

28. Durán, ibid., p. 84.

29. *Códice Matritense de la Real Academia de la Historia*
(Nahuatl texts of the Indian informants of Sahagún).
Facsimile edition of Vol. VIII by Francisco del Paso y
Troncoso, Hauser y Menet, 1907, Madrid, fol. 192, p.
v; quoted in León-Portilla, *Aztec Thought and Culture*,
p. 155.

30. Geoffrey W. Conrad and Arthur A. Demarest, *Religion
and Empire: The Dynamics of Aztec and Inca Expan
sionism*, Cambridge University Press, Cambridge,
1990, p. 38.

31. Chimalpain, *Sixième et Septième Relations (1368-
1612)*, Remi Simeon, Paris, 1889, quoted in León-
Portilla, ibid., p. 161.

32. Conversation with Scott Gentling, 22 August 1995.

33. Durán, ibid., p. 69.

34. Angel Maria Garaibay K., ed. *Viente Himnos Sacros
de los Nahuas*, p. 31; quoted in León-Portilla, ibid., p.
163.

35. Durán. Here I have preferred the translation of
Durán by Jack Emory Davis found in León-Portilla,
Aztec Thought and Culture, ibid., p. 163.

36. Ibid.

37. *Codex Ramírez*, Editorial Leyenda, Mexico City,
1944, quoted in Townsend, ibid., p. 87.

38. T. R. Fehrenbach, *Fire and Blood: A History of Mex
ico*, Da Capo Press, New York, 1995, p. 65.

39. Michael D. Coe, *Mexico: From the Olmec to the
Aztecs*, 4th edition, Thames and Hudson, London,
1994, p. 176.

40. Eduardo Matos Montezuma, *The Great Temple of the
Aztecs: Treasures of Tenochtitlan*, Thames and Hud
son, London, 1988, p. 73. The temple excavations
revealed a date glyph (4 Reed - 1431) that shows the
rebuilding initiated by Itzcoatl. Another (1 Rabbit -
1454) covers the reign of Motecuhzoma and indicates
that the reconstruction took at least ten years to
complete. This confirms chronicles which discuss the
feeding of workers on the temple during the famine of
the early 1450s.

41. Davies, ibid., p. 91.

42. Durán, ibid., p. 95.

43. Durán, ibid.

44. Durán, ibid., p. 96.

45. Durán, ibid., p. 147.

46. Durán, ibid., p. 107.

47. Sahagún, Bernadino de., *Historia General de las
cosas de Nueva España*, Editorial Porrúa, Mexico
City, 1956; this passage translated in Durán, ibid.,
endnote 61, p. 344.

48. Townsend, ibid., p. 90. Cochineal which produced
dyes from red to purple was to become, after the Con
quest, the world standard dye to be replaced only in
the last century by chemical dyes.

49. Hassig, ibid., p. 168.

50. Durán, ibid., pp. 96-97. Whatever the Mexica heard
in the night from the owls was bound to be momen
tous. The hooting of owls to the Náhuatl-speaking
cultures was so ominous as to put our superstition
of black cats in the pale. The vital thing in this
account is Tlacaélel's genius for seizing the main
chance. His boldness defined the nature of the omen
to be propitious for the Mexica and damning for the
Chalca. Alexander seized a similar moment on the
night before the Battle of Arbela when the moon suf
fered an eclipse that panicked his army. He had the
coolness to declare it a good omen — it was the Per
sian moon that was eclipsed by the Macedonian sun.

51. Durán, ibid., p. 149.

52. Durán (pp. 151, 185) states that the next three rulers
were sons of Motecuhzoma, but Ixtlilxochitl (vol. II, p.
260) contends that he was a grandson of Motecuh
zoma. The argument continues to
the present day. Ross Hassig (p. 176) follows Durán,
and Nigel Davies (pp. 125, 305) supports Ixtlilxochitl.

53. Durán, ibid., p. 151.

54. Durán, ibid., p. 151.

6

THE MIGHTY GRANDSONS OF MOTECUHZOMA I (1469–1502)

AXAYÁCATL THE SCOURGE (1469–1481)

With Motecuhzoma in his grave, Tlacaélel summoned Nezahualcoyotl of Texcoco and Totoquihuaztli of Tlacopan to join him in private to select the new tlatoani. By custom, Nezahualcoyotl had the right to announce the selection before the assembled lords and royal kin of the Eagle Clan. No one could have been more thunderstruck than the nineteen year-old young man to whom Nezahualcoyotl pointed his finger.

The Acolhua lord had chosen Axayácatl (Water Face), grandson of Motecuhzoma through his daughter, Huitzilxochtzin. His father was the prince, Tezozomoctzin, grandson of Itzcoatl, Motecuhzoma's own predecessor and uncle. It was a shrewd choice. Axayácatl united the lines of the first two rulers, and his selection 'stressed the elective nature of the monarchy', over any tendency to revert to primogeniture. Perhaps Tlacaélel and Nezahualcoyotl hoped to control such a young man, but in that case Tlacaélel could have promoted one of his own sons.[1] Already Axayácatl had, despite his nineteen years, proven an able warrior and had held important commands in his grandfather's wars such as the expedition to Tepeacac in 1466.[2] Perhaps it was this ability and its further potential that the old men had seen.

Axayácatl was dressed in the splendid robes and regalia of the tlatoani, seated on the low throne, presented with magnificent gifts and honoured with long and eloquent speeches. Election was only tentative for a new Mexica ruler. His coronation had to be ratified with a successful war which meant conquest, loot, and a train of captives for sacrifice. Although he had proven himself as a warrior and junior commander, these accomplishments must have paled before the overwhelming examples of his two grandfathers, the empire builders. Verses attributed to him express this trepidation:

Axayácatl's name hieroglyph.

'People never cease to take
    their leave, All depart,
The Princes, the Lords and
    the Nobles
Will leave us as orphans.
    Rejoice not, my lords,
Perchance may any one
    return?
May any come back
From the abode of the
    fleshless?
Will they come back to tell
    us something,
Motecuhzoma, Nezahual
    coyotl, Totoquihuatzin?
No, they will leave us as orphans,
    Be full of grief, O my lords.'[3]

Axayácatl's coronation war began almost immediately with an expedition to the Pacific coast region to the south-west. It was a distant area, but most of the march route was through the lands of tributaries who would assure the commissary of the army. The objective was the inland Zapotec city of Tehuantepec, a rich commercial centre far to the south-east. In the battle before the city, Axayácatl ordered his army to flee and ambushed the pursuing enemy with a force left in hiding. He then overran the city. It was a short march from there, but a momentous one, to the Pacific coast in which several more cities were subdued. For the first time, Mexica armies gazed upon the Pacific, and the rule of the revered speaker ran from sea to sea. He returned to Tenochtitlan to a splendid coronation.

In the dame year Axayácatl fought and won a flower war with Huexotzinco and Atlixco although the ruler of Tlacosan was killed. About this time, the Totonac region of Cuetlachtlan again revolted and was conquered, although this may be confused with Motecuhzoma's re-conquest of the region.

Axayácatl's first crisis followed in 1972 with the death of Nezahualcoyotl who had left his seven-year-old son, Nezahualpilli (Hungry Prince), as his heir. It was a decision almost designed to spark a war for the young prince had many mature and ambitious older brothers. Both Axayácatl and the king of Tlacopan ratified Nezahualpilli's succession, and almost immediately the young king's life was threatened by a plot of three of his uncles. Axayácatl and the Tlacopan king rushed to Texcoco to carry him to safety in Tenochtitlan. There Axayácatl crowned the boy in a sumptuous ceremony. So delicate were relations with Texcoco that Axayácatl was not able to punish the traitorous Texcocan princes but attempted to buy them off with lands and palaces. He had to tread warily. Texcoco was the second ranking member of the Triple Alliance and powerful in its own right. Direct action against the Texcocan princes could have led to a war that would have split the Triple Alliance into two powerful parts. Tenochtitlan's advantage would not be that great in such a conflict. Many of the Alliance's vassals in the Valley of Mexico would have rushed to Texcoco's aid. Patience was a better strategy. With Mexica help, Nezahualpilli was eventually able to assert his authority in his own kingdom. In

Mexica hieroglyph for a campaign.

doing so, he became increasingly dependent upon Tenochtitlan.

THE MEXICA CIVIL WAR

Axayácatl's great test was to come in 1473, immediately next door to Tenochtitlan itself. The Mexica had not settled only on the marshy island of Tenochtitlan when they had been expelled as miserable savages from the mainland. Other Mexica had settled a kilometre or so away on another island that was to become the city of Tlatelolco. Although not a founding member of the Triple Alliance, Tlatelolco had worked closely with Tenochtitlan in the rise of the Mexica people as the two island cities grew together. As an independent city it had waged wars and made conquests of its own, but its claim to renown was the acumen of its merchants rather than the cunning of its warriors. The merchants furthered the expansion of the empire in their own way, as much as the warriors of Tenochtitlan. They were the advance guard of the Mexica armies, gathering intelligence and negotiating trade that drew one area after another into the Mexica orbit. Their mistreatment was a ready excuse for war. By the beginning of Axayácatl's reign, they had made Tlatelolco the greatest market in all Mesoamerica and the source of incredible wealth.

By 1473 the relationship was rapidly souring. In that year a rowdy band of young nobles from Tenochtitlan had gone to Tlatelolco, looking for trouble and a good time. These Tenochca (Mexica inhabitants of Tenochtitlan) sought the attention of Tlatelolcan maidens. One thing led to another, and the former maidens rushed home crying that they had been ravished. Tlatelolco was enraged. This affair was just a spark on already dry tinder. The real source of discord was the growing domination of Tenochtitlan within the Mexica nation. It was a dangerous moment; the Tlatelolcan

Mexica priests and warriors on campaign. The devil on one priest's back is a post-Conquest Spanish comment.

ruler, Moquihuix, looked with disdain upon Axayácatl whom he regarded as a stripling. Moquihuix had already won distinguished honours on the battlefield at Cempoallan where he had saved the day for the Mexica. His distaste for the young tlatoani was fed by the loathing he openly displayed for his own wife, Axayácatl's sister, a woman of apparently few physical attractions. He treated her with open contempt, denying her cotton clothing which he gave to his more comely concubines. She slept wrapped in one tattered mantle in a bare corner of Moquihuix's palace. Her treatment was a public scandal that did not fail to enrage Axayácatl who was heard to remark that Moquihuix's concubines would be the ruin of his city.[4]

Moquihuix may have been emboldened by the recent death of Nezahualcoyotl who had exercised a stabilising effect by his prestige as one of the founders of the Triple Alliance. The ruler of Tlacopan had also died recently. To Moquihuix the time could not be better to throw off the overlordship of Tenochtitlan. His advisers urged caution. Tenochtitlan was by far the larger of the cities and the more devoted to war. So Moquihuix secretly searched for allies among the vassals and enemies of the Triple Alliance. He received positive replies from some of the Mexica vassals within the Valley of Mexico, but the major enemies of Tenochtitlan — Tlaxcallan, Cholollan, and Huexotzinco — refused outright.

He planned the attack for night, sending spies into Tenochtitlan the day before to see if Axayácatl had any warning. They found him playing ball with his young lords. It was Moquihuix, however, who had been deceived. A man as rash and indiscreet as himself had compromised his own secret long before. The attack had been openly spoken of in the great market of Tlatelolco. Axayácatl had been laying his own plans with much more cunning. He had just addressed his commanders:

'Let not the fame and glory of such valiant men as yourselves be obscured, but guard and defend the realm and nation of Mexico. See where you have to fight: it is not so far distant and you will not have to cross fords, bridges, rivers, mountains nor deep ditches and defences, since Tlatelolco is near by and the way is flat.'[5]

On Axayácatl's behalf the next morning, Tlacaélel sent a formal declaration of war to Moquihuix, a sword and shield and pitch to smear upon his face. It was a fair warning; by Mexica standards of war, a surprise attack was unchivalrous. Moquihuix bellowed that these emblems of death were better suited to Axayácatl and threw the envoy out of the room; his chief minister then killed him with a sword. The Tlatelolca threw the body within the city limits of Tenochtitlan, shouting their battle cry, 'Tlatelolco! Tlatelolco!' Nothing could have suited Axayácatl more. Moquihuix had just handed him a just war in Mesoamerican opinion. Tlacaélel climbed the Great Pyramid amid the din of drums and shell trumpets. Raising his sword and shield in the air, he cried out to the troops massed below:

'Sons and brothers do not be faint, justice is on our side! They have killed our ambassador without reason. . . Therefore cover yourselves with your shields, hold your swords tight, extend your arms strongly. From here I will watch and I will rejoice in your bravery!'[6]

The plaza resounded with deafening shouts, whistles, drums, and trumpets which must have been clearly audible in Tlatelolco. While Tlacaélel roused the spirit of the soldiery, Axayácatl was taking the practical measures to bring down Tlatelolco with one blow. He

blocked every approach to Tlatelolco to prevent the escape of the inhabitants and the arrival of their allies. He knew that the Tlatelolca planned to strike first and had planned for it.

Moquihuix had hoped to surprise Tenochtitlan with a night attack by canoe. The Tlatelolca had actually entered Tenochtitlan when the Tenochcas rushed out of hiding and attacked with demoralising surprise. The Tlatelolca fled back to their city with Axayácatl leading the pursuit, the head of the Tlatelolcan commander carried on a pole beside him. The battle raged through the city to the great market square where an alarmed Moquihuix unleashed his

Axayácatl the Scourge.

weapon of last resort, certainly one of the most bizarre in military history. To the utter shock of the Tenochca, squadrons of stark naked women and naked little boys with blackened faces rushed at them. The women were spurting milk from their breasts and the boys wailing. The Tenochca were momentarily so disconcerted that they fell back in confusion, but Axayácatl rallied them with a sharp order to capture the women and boys unharmed. With this speedily done, the Tenochca pressed the remaining Tlatelolca back until resistance had clustered around the base of the pyramid temple to Huitzilopochtli. Led by the tlatoani himself, the Tenochca fought their way to the top, step by narrow step, slippery with blood and bodies. At the top, Axayácatl met Moquihuix in single combat, cut him down, and threw his body down the steps.

The surviving Tlatelolca fled to the safety of the reeds in the canals and lake to escape. Only the humble intercession of a Tlatelolcan uncle of Axayácatl stopped the killing. The Tenochca ordered the Tlatelolca in the water to quack like water fowl. To the howls of the Tenochca, the Tlatelolca quacked so enthusiastically that they earned themselves the epithet of 'quackers', an insult that would last beyond the Spanish Conquest. Amid the quacking, Axayácatl settled the fate of Tlatelolco, ordering it sacked, the image of Huitzilopochtli carried away to Tenochtitlan, and the former temple filled with rubbish. The body of Moquihuix's chief minister was impaled at the entrance of Tlatelolco as a warning.

Axayácatl was not finished with the matter of Tlatelolco. The civil war had threatened the very security of the empire by suborning the loyalty of many vassals. This threat had been only narrowly averted. After the fall of Tlatelolco, contingents from Cuitláhuac, Mizquic, Mexicatzinco, and Huitzilopochco arrived to join Moquihuix, in what was surely one of the most flagrant cases of bad timing in military history. Axayácatl executed their kings immediately. He also killed the king of Xochimilco, not because he had aided the Tlatelolca but because he had not come to his aid quickly enough. Axayácatl, the Scourge, he was now called.

Tlatelolco itself essentially disappeared as a separate city by being incorporated into Tenochtitlan as two wards. Henceforth, they would worship Huitzilopochtli in Tenochtitlan, perhaps the greatest humiliation. In suing for peace, the city elders had promised rich tribute from the city's trade. This Axayácatl accepted but also made sure they provided campaign rations for the army in the form of beans and tortillas and the porters to carry them. Further humiliations confiscated Tlatelolco land, forced them to sweep the palaces of Tenochtitlan, and to provide slaves for sacrifice. When the first tribute payment came due in the traditional 80 days, the Tlatelolca provided no slaves and paltry excuses. At the apparent recommendation of Tlacaélel, Axayácatl ordered that they be forbidden the use of cotton garments and rich jewellery and fine feathers and even sandals. They were to dress in maguey fibre clothes like commoners and were forbidden even to visit the marketplace and ordered to stay indoors like women until the tribute had been paid. At the end of the next 80 days, the tribute was paid in full. Thereafter, the Tlatelolca vied to do great deeds in war and in the service of the state to regain the prestige of their city. Gradually the humiliations were removed, but the independence of the city was gone forever.

THE CONQUEST OF TOLOCAN

Two years later in 1475, the king of Tenantzinco begged Axayácatl's aid in the ongoing strife between his city and the city of Tolocan of the Matlatzinca people. Both cities lay to the west on the marches with the rising Tarascan empire centred in the modern Mexican state of Michoacán. At this time, Axayácatl was deeply involved with the creation of two great carved stones, magnificent symbols of imperial propaganda. On one was related the glorious deeds of the Mexica rulers and heroes in the creation of their empire. The second was the Stone of the Sun, the great, round calendar stone that centuries later was to become an emblem of modern Mexico. Tenantzinco's request came just as the setting for the first stone was being constructed. Tenantzinco's request suddenly offered Axayácatl a source of captives for the dedication. He was for war, encouraged by Tlacaélel who had always felt it necessary to add

The ruse ranked high in the Mesoamerican art of war. In the war against Tolocan in 1475, both sides attempted to use decoys to entice the other into an ambush. The Mexica decoys were more successful, and the tlatoani, Axayácatl, personally led the Mexica ambush force into the attack. (Drawing by Keith Henderson)

both Tolocan and Tenantzinco to the empire; they were also the last bit of old Tezozomoc's Tepanec empire not to be swept up by the Mexica. Barely 40 miles away, they would be a dangerous forward base should the Tarascans conquer them first. Conversely, they would make a splendid forward logistics base for further westward Mexica expansion.

Axayácatl sent the usual war-provoking message, a request for pine and cedar to decorate rooms in the Great Temple. Preparations for the war were underway before the Tolocan refusal even arrived. The Tolocans stole the first march and attacked Tenantzinco. That sent the Tenantzinco king scurrying back to Tenochtitlan to beg speed. Axayácatl ordered the Tenantzinco army to fall on Tolocan from the surrounding mountains at the signal of a great bonfire atop a mountain while the Triple Alliance army attacked directly through the

passes on the main road to Tolocan, thus trapping the enemy. Mindful of the dedication, he ordered that no Tolocan be killed but as many prisoners as possible were to be taken.

The night before the battle, Axayácatl ordered that a veteran captain address the army. He was still too self-conscious of his youth to harangue the army. The old warrior reminded the army that the enemy were neither jaguars nor eagles to be feared, but only men of the kind they had overcome so many times before. The battle itself almost never began because both sides attempted to use the same ruse on each other. It was the common trick of sending a large decoy force to lure the enemy's main body into an ambush. Axayácatl, though a hesitant public speaker, did not hesitate to put himself in the place of greatest personal danger — with the ambush force. He barely controlled his impatience as he lay covered with grass

watching both armies dangle their bait with little success. Finally, the Mexica contingent fled convincingly enough to the river in their rear to bring the Tolocan army in pursuit. At the right moment, Axayácatl leapt from cover and led the ambush force into the attack. The tlatoani was the first to crash into the Tolocan ranks in a frenzy of valour, remarkable even by Mexica standards. He took many prisoners in a few moments. The Tolocans staggered as the Mexica main force turned and struck their confused ranks. They gave way, with Axayácatl racing ahead of his army in pursuit, lost to the sight of his bodyguard.

As he ran after the Tolocans, he entered the very ambush ground they had set for the Mexica. He was resplendent in his glittering war costume and glowed in the rush of battle, a veritable young god. Every Tolocan eye in waiting would have seen him and thrilled at the thought of such a captive. From behind an agave plant, Tlilcuetzpal (Black Lizard), the war captain of the Tolocan host, threw himself upon Axayácatl. With a great swing of his sword, he tore open Axayácatl's thigh to the bone. That wound would have felled any ordinary man, but the young tlatoani was in his prime as a warrior, and his blood was coursing with adrenalin. He leapt upon Black Lizard and carried him to the ground. His bodyguard found them rolling on the ground in mortal combat, covered with dirt and blood. They would have killed the Tolocan instantly, but Axayácatl ordered them to take him prisoner. Black Lizard leaped to his feet, fought off the bodyguard, and slipped away into the surging melee all around them.

The battle now turned against the Tolocans who fled the field. The Mexica sacked their city and carried off the image of their god to Tenochtitlan. Humbling himself in the dust, the Tolocan king begged mercy of Axayácatl who lay on his litter while Mexica doctors bandaged his wound. The king of Tenantzinco was no less fearful having instigated the war that had almost led to a Mexica disaster and the capture and sacrifice of the revered speaker on the altar stone of Tolocan. The news of the near disaster and the tlatoani's personal brush with death had been a shock to Tenochtitlan; yet his

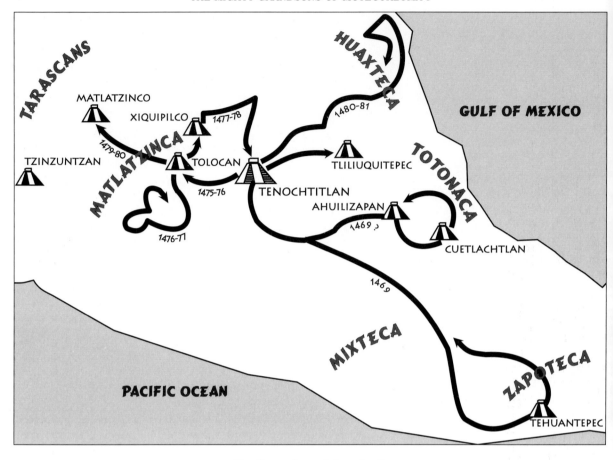

The Campaigns of Axayácatl

personal heroism had gilded the whole affair. His return with the army and an enormous train of prisoners was greeted with wild enthusiasm by the population. The way into the city was a succession of green triumphal arches with the road covered with foliage, all an enormous victory garland for the young tlatoani. The great wooden drums and the teponatzli[7] pulsated across the lake to welcome him and were joined by conch shell trumpets, whistles, and the shouts of the vast crowds.

He gave thanks immediately to Huitzilopochtli by drawing his own blood from his ears and thighs. Tlacaélel entreated him not to delay the upcoming feast of the Flayed God fearful he might die soon 'and I will not be able to take with me the memory of this happy event'. Snake Woman's obsession with blood sacrifice, long since pathological, was now an addiction that was consuming nations. Still, he could not forget to extract the full political advantage

from the bloodletting. Axayácatl asked him the best way to organise the feast, and Tlacaélel advised him to invite those kings from the Gulf Coast who had not yet been subdued by the Mexica. A refusal would be a convenient pretext for war. Tlacaélel for once was too clever by half. The two kings lavished the Mexica ambassadors with consideration and rushed to Tenochtitlan. There they were escorted to their seats of honour, booths decorated with every hue of flower and strewn with soft jaguar skins. They were showered with royal gifts: golden jewellery in the form of lip and nose plugs, pendants for the ears, necklaces, and richly embroidered mantles of fine cotton. To cool them during the sacrifice, they were given fans of fine featherwork, and bouquets of fragrant flowers and perfume to conceal the scent of blood. Amid all these comforts, they watched in horror, as one after another the Tolocan prisoners were tied to the gladiatorial stone to fight fully-armed Mexica warriors with feather-lined swords. The stream of prisoners seemed endless. So great was the killing that they feared to leave their flowery booths. If Tlacaélel had not been able to trick his war out of the visiting kings, he had sown a future victory by morally disarming them with the ruthless splendour of Tenochtitlan.

THE TARASCAN DISASTER

The mortar was barely dry around the great stone, when Axayácatl and Tlacaélel conferred on war with the Tarascans. The Stone of the Sun was nearing completion and required captives to inaugurate its emplacement as well. At the same time, Michoacán, 'Land of the Fish' had become an urgent problem. The Mexica expansion had eliminated or contained its most dangerous nearby rivals except for the Tarascans who were expanding in the direction of the Mexica empire. The war against Tolocan had been fought to deny that strategic area to the Tarascans. These people who called themselves the Purépeche, had their capital 300 kilometres west of Tenochtitlan at the city with the melodic name of Tzintzuntzan (City of the Hummingbird), on the shores of Lake Patzcuaro. The Tarascans were not part of the Náhuatl-speaking world of central Mexico; their language had many Quechua words, the imperial language of the Incas of Peru. If so, a splendid odyssey has been lost to history. The Mexica looked down on them as a strange and even bizarre culture, where both sexes shaved their heads and depilated their bodies. They were also unique in their rapid experimentation with copper and bronze tools and weapons, something the Mexica appeared to have failed to appreciate.[8] They also failed to appreciate the Tarascans' great skill as archers.

The first move was aimed at securing the southern and northern flanks of the advance by subduing more of the independent march kingdoms in 1476–1478. Tolocan was used as the forward logistics base. The chief objective on the northern flank was the town of Xiquipilco which only fell after much hard fighting that left 6,000 defenders dead and 11,060 captive. So bitter had been the resistance that

Axayácatl killed the defeated monarch, a serious departure from the usual practice. The following year, he assembled an army of 24,000 men from among the Mexica, allies and vassals; a force considered sufficient for the conquest of a large province or even Michoacán itself. The army marched directly on Tarascan territory by way of Tolocan. Already Axayácatl had placed a Mexica military governor in charge of the kingdom to ensure its reliability as the springboard of invasion. The Mexica penetration into Tarascan territory did not threaten the enemy heartland but merely pressed into its outermost conquests. Nevertheless, the Tarascans had not been taken by surprise. They had assembled a army of 40,000 men to bar the Mexicas' way. The Tarascan king, Tangaxoan I, a conqueror himself, commanded the host in person. Axayácatl was stunned at the report of his spies that emphasised both the enemy's numbers and the strength of their weapons. He was now at a place called Matlatzinco, on the shores of a lagoon, almost 170 kilometres from his base at Tolocan.

He quickly called a council of war. 'I have found out the Tarascans are forty thousand men, all of them robust, tall and brave. They have sixteen thousand more men than we! What shall we do?' It was a statement of common sense alarm. Unfortunately, Axayácatl was advised by a council that defied the military truism that 'councils of war never fight'. These were Mexica, men who had seen nothing but victory under Motecuhzoma. They counselled the young tlatoani not to fear mere numbers; the Mexica had never quailed at numbers before. Besides, if they were to retreat, Mexica prestige would surely suffer. Fight, they counselled, fight to triumph or die!

Axayácatl had been convinced; the next morning the army deployed for battle and advanced to find the Tarascans also arrayed for action, with their captains and lords in front of their regiments. The Mexica would remember their magnificent display, so lavishly decorated in gold that the morning sun's reflecting rays blinded them across the small deadly space between them. It was then that ambassadors arrived from Tangaxoan. Axayácatl surely was taken aback at their lack of respect. 'O great lord, who brought you here? Why have you come? Were you not happy in your own land? Was it perhaps the Matlatzinca whom you overcame a short time ago? Consider carefully, O lord, what you are to do! You have been deceived!'[9] Axayácatl could only answer in words of Mexica chivalry, that he had come to test their strength.

The Tarascans immediately seized the initiative and attacked. Their onslaught was so furious that the Mexica, who held the army's advance position of honour, wavered and began to break. Axayácatl then committed his Acolhua and Tepanec allies and the troops of his vassals. The reinforcements steadied the Mexica, but the fighting continued all day with Axayácatl's army barely able to hold its own. That night, a much chastised council met. The tlatoani could barely recognise the bold men in their finery who had urged him to fight the day before. Everyone was caked in dust mixed with sweat, their war costumes hacked and battered into ruin. The day's losses had been enormous, especially of the military orders of knights who had sworn not to retreat. The chronicles are silent, but perhaps the Mexica had suffered their first encounter with metal weapons. The tlatoani ordered that a special refreshing drink of maize meal and water be prepared for the whole army.

The next morning Axayácatl, bolstered with Matlatzinca reinforcements, attacked the Tarascans. It was a tactic of desperation, and they were completely overwhelmed by the Tarascans and driven back. Here it was that most of the surviving warriors from the knightly orders fell. Here also was captured one of the tlatoani's Eagle Council, Axayácatl's cousin. The Tarascans, realising the prisoner's importance, overran the Mexica camp to parade their prisoner and their insult. Had they pressed for the kill that day, not a single member of the Mexica army would have survived. Apparently Tarascan archery was taking a deadly toll. The Mexica must have exhausted their arrows and atlatl darts by this point and were reaping the consequences of trying to campaign at the end of a long line of communications. They could only fight with what they carried. The Tarascans, on the other hand, were in their own territory and close to sources of resupply. That night the

Temple of the Knights of the Sun where the gladiatorial sacrifices were held. (Drawing courtesy © Scott Gentling, photographed by David Wharton)

last council of war was held. The senior Mexica general openly stated the unthinkable: retreat. For the first time in 40 years, a Mexica army would abandon a field. The old warrior reminded everyone that the Chalca War had lasted many years and said, 'If you are still determined that we must all perish here, I will be the first to die, as the oldest among you. But if you feel that it is right that we should return, in order to reform our forces in Mexico-Tenochtitlan, then so let us do.'[10] Axayácatl assented, and the remnants of the army slipped away into the night, with the wounded carried on the backs of the porters. It was none too soon, for in the morning the Tarascans were in hot pursuit, harrying the survivors all the way back to Tolocan. With the danger finally passed, Axayácatl counted the survivors. Of his own Mexica, barely 200 were left. They had born the brunt of the fighting, their losses in experienced warriors and captains, many of them veterans of Motecuhzoma's campaigns, were staggering. Of their Acolhua and Tepanec allies, only 400 of each nation survived. The Xochimilca and Chalca contingents had been also reduced to 400 men each. Of the Otomis there were only 300. Of the men from the Hot Lands, almost none were left. Axayácatl had lost 91 out of every hundred men.

When the news reached Tenochtitlan, Tlacaélel called up warriors to guard the approaches to the city lest a suddenly emboldened enemy attack. He ordered drums and conch-shell trumpets to be played and doleful hymns sung in the temples. 'The entire city was filled with sorrow and lamentation, mourning and tears.' When the 200 survivors staggered into Tenochtitlan, they were met by a priestly delegation adorned with flowers as if they had returned in victory. It must have been a bitter sight for Axayácatl who quickly made his way to the temple of Huitzilopochtli to report his failure and to offer his own blood sacrifice from wounds he made in his own ears and thighs.

Meeting Tlacaélel, he burst into tears, 'Lord, it has been my fate to be unfortunate! Things that did not happen to my ancestors happen to me. What a terrible loss! What destruction the Tarascans have inflicted upon us!' Axayácatl was only 29, and his anguish was palpable. He had been the first of his noble lineage to fail and disastrously so. Tlacaélel was now 81. This was his first great defeat as well, and by urging the war he had had as much a hand in the outcome, perhaps more than the young man weeping before him. He poured what balm he could upon Axayácatl's pain:

'Son, do not be faint, let not your heart feel dismay! Have courage, your vassals did not die of their hearts, nor spinning like women, but on the battlefield, fighting for the greatness of your crown, and for the honor of their country. They won as much honor in their deaths as, in other times, they had gained in their victories! I give thanks to the Lord of All Created Things who has allowed me to see the deaths of so many of my brothers and nephews. But I do know why I have been spared!'[11]

The bitterest tears he had saved for himself. Then he ordered the ceremonies for the dead to begin. The extent of the losses was such that barely an extended family had no one to mourn. All of Tenochtitlan suffered through its grief together in a mass catharsis. The old men said to the women:

'O sisters, daughters, be strong, widen your hearts!
We have abandoned our sons, the jaguars, the eagles!
Do not think that we will see them again.
Do not imagine that this is
Like the times when your husband left your house sulking and angry
So that he would not return for three or four days;
Nor when he departed for his work, soon to return.
Understand that they have gone forever!'[12]

No survivor maimed on the field against the Tarascans was more crippled than the young tlatoani himself, though he bore no mark upon his body. His defeat desolated him. Still the wars continued. The Hauxteca murdered Mexica merchants and provoked a punative expedition in the 1480–81 Campaign season. That same period saw a flower war victory against Tliliuhquitepec which dragged 700 captives to Tenochtitlan for sacrifice. After the ceremony, Axayácatl was overcome by exhaustion and the stench of the sour blood. Fearing his illness was mortal, he begged Tlacaélel to carve his image in the rocks of Chapultepec alongside those of Motecuhzoma and Tlacaélel himself. In 1481 the work was finished. The tlatoani was now seriously ill but ordered himself carried by litter to the hill to see his likeness. He died in his litter on the return to Tenochtitlan, barely 31 years of age.

Axayácatl was surely one of the great tragic figures in Mexican history. He was indeed a valorous warrior, but more than valour was needed of an emperor. Try as he might to follow in the footsteps of Itzcoatl and Motecuhzoma, Axayácatl was too young and unseasoned. His predecessors had each been mature and experienced men when they came to the throne. They had long since passed the day when they risked the safety of the state by engaging in young men's heroics. They also had known how to employ Tlacaélel's genius. That genius, now of legendary power, had dominated if not smothered this young tlatoani's talent, rather than develop it. Unchecked by the cool shrewdness of a more experienced tlatoani, Tlacaélel's bold imperialism had become reckless when he had encouraged the Tarascan War. So crushing was the defeat that it would be over 30 years before the Mexica would seek another war with the Tarascans against whom they constructed their only fortified frontier.

Tlacaélel orchestrated a sumptuous funeral for him. This was his third imperial funeral, and each gave him the opportunity to adjust upward the splendour of Mexica power. In procession Axayácatl's fellow kings of the Triple Alliance addressed the corpse as if he were still alive to bid him farewell. The king of Tlacopan said, 'There you lie in the glittering house of fire of the Sun. Let your body take rest now, O my son!' They presented lavish gifts to the dead tlatoani to comfort him in the other world. The vassal kings followed in an endless succession. Besides the gifts of every sort, each major king brought four to five slaves to accompany Axayácatl to the other world. They were household slaves; prisoners of war were for the gods only. Beside the bier stood Tlacaélel, thanking each lord for his words and gifts. Even the rulers of enemy states, Tlax-callan, Huexotzinco, and Cholollan came secretly to pay their respects. Tlacaélel thanked them all eloquently at a rich banquet, and from the tlatoani's storerooms presented them in turn with fine mantles and loincloths. To the enemy lords he gave swords and shields.

When the enemies had departed, the funeral proceeded. A wooden statue in the image of the tlatoani was built in a green bower and dressed in the guise of the four gods whom he represented in life: Huitzilopochtli, Tlaloc, Yohualahua and Quet-zalcoatl. His wailing wives entered the bower to offer food they had prepared with their own hands. The great lords of Tenochtitlan followed with bundles of flowers, followed by men with bowls of burning incense. Then the slaves of the tlatoani, his hunchbacks and dwarfs, and the gift slaves of the kings were brought in richly dressed. The statue and the body were carried up the Great Pyramid by noble bearers and set in front of the temple of Huitzilopochtli upon its pyre and set alight. Axayácatl's ashes swirled upward into the sky in a spout of

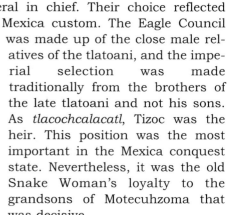

Tizoc's name hieroglyph.

sparks from the highest spot in the entire city. Once the fire had consumed the body, the ashes were poured through the slit of a teponatzli drum. The assembled slaves were admonished by the nobles to serve their master well in the other world. Then each was thrown down onto *teponatzli* and sacrificed. Finally the ashes, the hearts of his 50 to 60 slaves, gems, mantles and feathers were buried at the foot of Huitzilopochtli's statue.

TIZOC
THE POOR OCELOT WARRIORS GO WEEPING
(1481-1486)

Four days later, the Eagle Council met to pick a new revered speaker. Their choice was Tizoc (He Has Bled People), Axayácatl's older brother. Tizoc was also a member of the Eagle Council, the *tlacochcalacatl*, general in chief. Their choice reflected Mexica custom. The Eagle Council was made up of the close male relatives of the tlatoani, and the imperial selection was made traditionally from the brothers of the late tlatoani and not his sons. As *tlacochcalacatl*, Tizoc was the heir. This position was the most important in the Mexica conquest state. Nevertheless, it was the old Snake Woman's loyalty to the grandsons of Motecuhzoma that was decisive.

Tlacaélel, now a past-master at creating imperial spectacles, outdid himself. Neza-hualpilli arrived from Texcoco to formally designate the new Revered Speaker of the Mexica, as was the right of the kings of the Acolhua. Surrounded by all the other kings of the empire, Nezahualpilli placed a greenstone-studded diadem of gold upon Tizoc's head. The new tlatoani then had to steel himself to withstand the pain as Nezahualpilli drilled through the cartilage of his nose to place a long carved jade ornament through the incision. Gold and jade earrings he placed in Tizoc's ears and golden bands on his arms and anklets. Then Tizoc put onto his own feet the shoes of gold-decorated jaguar skin. He also dressed himself in a rich gold-embroidered mantle and loin-cloth. Nezahualpilli now led him to the Eagle Seat or Jaguar Seat, the throne called the *Cuauhicpalli,* adorned with eagle feathers and jaguar skins. Great lords carried him in a litter up the steps of the Great Temple before the statue of Huitzilopochtli where he performed a penance of autosacrifice, piercing his earlobes, shins, and calves with the sharp bone of a jaguar. Again he did penance before the Stone of the Sun, sacrificing many quail to let their blood pour down the drain in the stone. A third time he performed penance, in a darkened room called the 'blackness' of the temple surrounded by all the glowering images of the Mexica pantheon.

Tlacaélel had given Tizoc every advantage a first-rate propaganda spectacle can afford. To his distress he would quickly learn that he had wasted his time. The proof would be in Tizoc's coronation war. The Eagle Council discussed the choice of targets. Michoacán was suggested, then quickly dropped. Finally, the cities of Itzmiquilpan and Metztitlan over 200 kilometres to the north, were selected. The army's order-of-battle in this most important campaign should have raised questions from any keen observer. In addition to his Mexica contingent, the only other ones Tizoc selected from the core of the empire were the Chalca and Chinampaneca. Neither Texcoco nor Tlacopan sent troops. The other levies were from the regions only recently conquered by his late brother, the Matlatzincas, not the most reliable troops perhaps.

SINCE IT IS OUR DUTY

The first objective was Metztitlan, a state with many dependencies and a reputation for tenacity in war. It also had the advantage of geography. The Valley of Metztitlan is narrow and some 30 kilometres long, and the bordering mountains precluded any sort of manoeuvre by the Mexica. By this time, a veteran Mexica commander would have become increasingly nervous. Not only was a large part of the army probably less than reliable, but the new tlatoani was bringing them to battle at a place where Mexica advantages of manoeuvre and

numbers had been cancelled. Additionally, the Mexica army would be operating at the end of a long supply line and could not campaign for very long. The enemy had not been slow to grasp these essentials. They chose to offer resistance at the narrow valley entrance. Already they had been reinforced with Huaxteca from the Gulf Coast, a people only partially conquered in the reign of Motecuhzoma and eager for revenge.

Tizoc's management of the campaign to this point had been clumsy, especially for a new monarch whose future was riding on a clear-cut victory. The army of Metztitlan, on the other hand, had only to deny Tizoc a clean win. It could keep fighting a tenacious defensive battle all the way back up the valley, bleeding the Mexica until their logistics collapsed. Tizoc's handling of the battle itself was even more incompetent, not that he could have done much at that point after denying himself every advantage. He kept the Mexica contingent in the rear at the beginning of the battle when their traditional place had been the one of honour in the advance of the army. The Matlatzincas he placed in the van. If he had hoped to be clever and expend his unreliable new vassals first, he outsmarted himself. For a tlatoani to place such troops in the place of honour in a battle designed to prove his right to rule his proud People of the Sun, was to commit an incredible psychological blunder. These vassals also failed the test of combat and fell back. Then Tizoc committed the rest of his army to the fight, but again he held the Mexica back as the Chalca and Chinampaneca entered the fray. Tizoc was seemingly more interested in avoiding defeat than seizing victory.

By this time, his Mexica were probably beside themselves with fury at their inactivity. They were being denied the opportunity each man had waited for: to prove himself in combat and earn status and wealth. These were the very rewards that kept the fighting nobility, the seasoned warriors, and the ambitious commoners in support of a tlatoani. Finally, even the Mexica were thrown into the fight. Either the battle had deteriorated so badly for Tizoc by this point, or he was just inept. He threw the greenest Mexica elements into the most dangerous part of the battle. These were the eighteen- to twenty-year-old young warriors on their first campaign. Although seasoned warriors accompanied them, they were at a distinct disadvantage against a determined and more experienced enemy. In an act of incredible timidity, Tizoc now abandoned the field. The enemy had more than fought his army to a standstill. With the tlatoani absent from the field and the enemy still defiant and unwavering, the Mexica captains ordered a retreat. If Tizoc's performance in this vital campaign was any indication of his conduct in the Tarascan war where he served as *tlacochcalacatl*, it goes a long way to explain Axayácatl's defeat.

Tlacaélel was thunderstruck by the results of the campaign. The Mexica had lost 300 men while taking only 40 captives. The Tarascan disaster had had an element of heroism; this campaign had been merely pathetic. Tizoc was brazenly oblivious to the implications and was prepared to stand on a technicality that he had the minimum number of captives to ratify his coronation. Tlacaélel must have been grinding his teeth when he addressed the Eagle Council, 'Let us finish the solemn enthronement of our king since it is our duty.' The coronation was concluded with the usual great pomp and show, but in the minds of most must have been the realisation behind the façade of ceremony that for the first time a weak tlatoani sat in Tenochtitlan.

The rest of his reign was spent in putting down the inevitable revolts encouraged by such weakness. Apparently he did not take the field in these punitive expeditions except against Tolocan. Evidence of any real conquests is difficult to pin down. He spent his time in Tenochtitlan, devoting himself to work on the Great Temple and to adorning the city with palaces and gardens that outshone brilliant Texcoco itself. The more he devoted himself to such pursuits the more unstable the empire became. As time went on, he secluded himself in his palace, increasingly indifferent to his military duties. Ross Hassig captured the danger into which that empire was slipping:

'He lost the offensive and concentrated (to the extent that he did) on putting out brushfire revolts. The longer his reign continued, the more the Aztec empire eroded. Because the system was held together by threat of military reprisal, internal revolts were even more dangerous than failed campaigns, the former arose from a perception of Aztec weakness, while the latter were thrusts into unconquered and unknown areas and might require more than one effort to succeed. Tizoc forgot (or never realized) that the key to keeping the empire together was maintaining the appearance of power, which required constant attention...'[13]

At this point the empire was in an actual state of contraction. For such a conquest state to survive it had to be constantly expanding. The status quo was fatal. Part of the dynamism of expansion was the interest of the warrior nobility and warrior classes who depended on fresh conquest for prestige and wealth. With those cut off, Tizoc had alienated the very elements upon which his political survival depended. Surely, there were those reciting the prayer to Tezcatlipoca requesting the death of an unworthy ruler.

'. . . the rulership, the government, the realm, the honor, the glory — these give him perverseness, pride, trouble, make him crazed, make him besotted, make him drunk. . . .his words nowhere conform to his life, to his deeds. . . He seemeth to act in what manner he wisheth, to live in what manner he wisheth; to think in what manner he wisheth. . . . the poor eagle warriors, the poor ocelot warriors go weeping, go in sadness, seek thee, beg thee for thy freshness, thy tenderness, thy sweetness, thy fragrance — that which thou yieldeth not, that which thou has cherished. . . . perchance also thou wilt give him the great castigation — the paralysis, the blindness, the rottenness.'[14]

Happily for the Mexica, Tizoc died suddenly in the fifth year of his reign in 1486. As he was being carried from his palace, blood suddenly gushed from the mouth, and he died. The post-Conquest chronicles speak of regicide, though no convincing indictments are recorded. The question remains, then, who would have profited by his murder? Tlacaélel appears to have regretted his support of Tizoc. Perhaps the old imperialist's advice was particularly unwelcome to someone more interested in gardens than battlefields. Snake Woman was the ideological founder of the Mexica imperial idea. He had been there at the beginning; his companions had been heroes. Axayácatl had failed in battle, but his valour washed away defeat. Tizoc was a living insult to Tlacaélel and his life's work, and that life's work was clearly threatened as Mexica expansion slowed to a stop. By 1486 Tlacaélel was 88 years old but still lucid and respected. Would anyone else have dared to strike at a king except a man who was a king in everything but name?'[15]

AHUÍTZOTL, THE LION OF ANÁHUAC (1486–1502)

Tlacaélel threw his support to the last of Motecuhzoma's grandsons, Ahuítzotl (Otter), for the succession, but unexpectedly ran into strong opposition from the electors of the Eagle Clan. Under Ahuítzotl's brothers, the empire had faltered badly. And now Tlacaélel was nominating another young man, and this one so young that he was still in school and had not even been to war! So vehement was the opposition that Tlacaélel could not ram his selection through and had to refer the issue to Nezahualpilli, king of Texcoco, for advice.

Ahuítzotl's name hieroglyph.

Although Nezahualpilli was barely 31 he had acquired a growing reputation for statesmanship and wisdom. As ruler of the second power in the Triple Alliance, he had also inherited his father's role as the official nominator of the tlatoani. The messengers returned to the electors shouting, 'Long life to King Tlacaélel!' Nezahualpilli had recommended that Tlacaélel by tradition, as the brother of the great Motecuhzoma, should inherit. Ahuítzotl could work at his side, learn the arts of kingship, and succeed the ancient hero when he died. He thanked Nezahualpilli and the electors and said:

'I wish to ask you, what have I been during the eighty or ninety years since the war with Azcapotzalco? What position have I had? Have I been nothing? Why have I not put the diadem upon my head, why have I not worn the royal insignia? Have all the orders I have given been null and void? . . . If I could do these things, and I have been doing them for eighty or ninety years, I am then a king and you have held me as such. What more of king could I have been? And it will continue so until my death. Why are you disturbed, why are you troubled, over the election of my nephew Ahuítzotl? I will always be at his side to punish the evil-doer, no matter how high his position be. I will place him under the mat at my seat, under my seat and throne! I will honor the virtuous man, I will receive guests and strangers and honor rulers and monarchs. I will organize wars and command them. Be calm, my children, obey me, I am king and king I will remain until I die. I want the promise I made to my brother fulfilled. I want all my nephews to rule first and then, should you desire it, you may enthrone my sons. I will accept that in payment for the things I have done for my country and for your own persons.'[16]

In effect, Tlacaélel was promising to act as regent. With that reassurance, the lords of Tenochtitlan followed by great crowds of the people went to the *calmecac* school for highborn boys and, escorted teen-age Ahuítzotl to the palace and to the jaguar-skin covered throne of the tlatoani. There he was addressed by Nezahualpilli, who told him that it was time to put away the things of childhood,

'. . . now you must know and care for all things under the heavens. For this purpose you have at your side the mighty lord Tlacaélel. Follow his footsteps, observe how he rules and you will not err. He will watch over the way you govern so that you do not let the load that been given you fall upon the ground.'[17]

Tlacaélel now consulted with the great lords of the Eagle Council to decide against which nation to wage Ahuítzotl's coronation war.

Handy candidates were provided by the seven cities of the Mazahuacan region to the northwest of Tenochtitlan. Conquered by Axayácatl, they were now in rebellion. The contingents of the Triple Alliance army made a rendezvous at a place called Cilocan, fewer than 20 kilometres from the capital. It was an apprehensive army that watched the arrival of the young Ahuítzotl and his escort of nobles. The empire was plainly wobbling; the Tarascan defeat followed by Tizoc's impotent stewardship had clearly undermined the morale of the empire's fighting men and incited widespread rebellion. Now a boy was tlatoani. Tlacaélel may have been regent, but he was too old to command in the field.

The nobles dressed Ahuítzotl for battle and gave him his royal insignia. Young he was, but the army could see a certain bearing and boldness in the slight schoolboy figure almost overwhelmed by the magnificent war costume of a tlatoani. He addressed the army through a herald. The army listened and would wait to see. They did not have long.

The first city, Xiquipilco was stormed and sacked. A few other cities shared the same fate in rapid succession. Tlacaélel had put command of the army in the hands of competent generals. After the five cities had fallen though, it was clear the army's stamina was weakening as desertions increased. The chronicles are not clear on exactly what happened next, but the schoolboy-tlatoani suddenly asserted his own powerful personality. He ordered death for anyone, no matter how high born, who absented himself from the army. They were to be hunted down and killed, and every man was ordered to ensure that his companions were at their posts. Then he speeded up the tempo of operations by ignoring the day of rest after the last battle and pushing the army towards its next objective, Chiapan. In doing so they arrived outside the city without the enemy being aware of their presence. At the last minute, sentries gave the alarm and the men of Chiapan rushed to arms. Now clearly in command, Ahuítzotl pushed the Allied and vassal contingents from Texcoco, Tlacopan, Xochimilco, and Chalco immediately into the attack while he led his Mexica secretly through a gate opened by traitors. The temple complex was seized and set on fire. The defenders fled, and the city was sacked. Encouraged by the loot from Chiapan, the army's enthusiasm returned with such force that it attacked the army of Xilotepec directly from the march in a devouring rush that drove the enemy back into their own city. The Mexica followed them in and began to sack the place. The king surrendered to Ahuítzotl and begged him to stop the pillage. The young tlatoani assented, but his captains had to use force to drag the men from their new-found riches. After this victory, the army continued its march subduing more rebellious cities on a great loop route back to Tenochtitlan. Stamina was no longer a problem.

Tlacaélel organised a splendid triumphal entry, something Tenochtitlan had been denied for too many years. In addition to validating the choice of the electors, the campaign had been a demonstration of military prowess and determination not seen for years. Most of the benefit was internal, though. Invitations to the coronation had been sent to all allies and vassals, and they all arrived; it was a good measure of the imperial hold these states felt on themselves. Invitations had also been sent to all of the Mexica's major enemies with the express purpose of impressing them with Mexica power and glory. Their response would also be a measure of Mexica prestige. The rulers of Tlaxcallan and Tliliuhquitepec both said they could hold the same sort of festivals at home and spare themselves the trouble of a journey. Huexotzinco's king agreed to come but never showed up. Chollollan's king sent underlings in his place. In Yopitzinco the king could not be found, but a delegation of nobles was sent. The lord of Metztitlan who had humbled Tizoc replied to the messengers that they were lucky to escape with their lives. Tangaxoan I, the Tarascan king, was the most brutally dismissive.

'What do your masters think? Was it a whim to come and make war upon us, be defeated and flee having lost so many men? You must be mad! One day you wish war, and another day you wish peace. If I go there, what security will I have while I eat or drink among you after the way I treated you?'[18]

The most honeyed words of the Mexica ambassadors would not sway the Tarascan. Although he sent his congratulations to Ahuítzotl, he would not attend nor even allow members of his court to go in his place.

Tlacaélel and Ahuítzotl had no choice but to swallow the insults and put the best face they could on the coronation. The nobles from Cholollan and Yopitzinco were treated even more sumptuously than the kings of Texcoco and Tlacopan. Tlacaélel ordered that no effort be spared to show the grandeur of Tenochtitlan. The coronation would be an orgy of splendid display and gift-giving on a scale beyond anything that had gone before. The chief men of the city and the master builders, craftsmen, and artisans were pressed to create treasures and adorn the city. The streets of the jewellers, featherworkers, goldsmiths, potters, and even tobacconists and florists were hives of driven work. For four days the city feasted and revelled in its imperial spectacle. A thousand war captives were sacrificed, and the equivalent of a year's tribute was given away. Durán writes in amazement that no alcoholic drinks were present at the feast, though he does say that there was much foolishness after wild mushrooms were freely distributed.[19] All of this had been intended to overawe all the royal enemies of the

Mexica, but now it was spent on their allies and vassals, and the deliriously happy nobles from Cholollan and Yopitzinco.

Tlacaélel saw the emptiness of the show, though. Where once these kings would have flocked to Tenochtitlan at his invitation, now only a handful of their courtiers could be expected. There was much to repair. Some days later, he informed the tlatoani that the Huaxteca of the Gulf Coast had rebelled.

Ahuítzotl leaped at the opportunity to lead another campaign. There was now no question of his being a figurehead. He would command his armies in person in this campaign year of 1487–88. The tlatoani may have been eager to march off to war, but he was prudent enough to prepare carefully. He first ordered his allied and subject kings to accompany him on this campaign. That would keep them loyal and encourage the performance of their contingents. The mobilisation and approach march were both rapid and efficient; he was determined to deliver a surprise attack before his enemies could prepare. The first leg of the

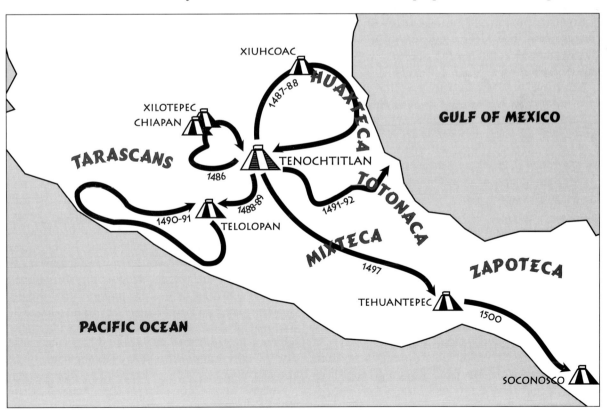

The Campaigns of Ahuítzotl, 1485–1500

march took the army 165 kilometres through friendly territory in five to nine days. The ruler of one vassal city offered his palace to Ahuítzotl for the remainder of the campaign if he wanted to leave the command to others. Ahuítzotl bristled at the suggestion that he leave his troops. 'It is not fitting for a good king and a brave captain to leave his own encampment.'[20]

This time he addressed the army himself. At an age when most young Mexica were perhaps on their first campaign, carefully mentored by seasoned warriors, Ahuítzotl was the supremely confident leader of the entire war host. The role fitted him perfectly; he had blossomed as a natural leader of men and was rapidly become a sagacious commander. Looking up at him was an army anticipating rich spoil with every confidence in this young man. The kings, everyone his elder in age and experience, were also equally under his moral influence. He was the Lion of Anáhuac, they started to whisper. He seemed to suddenly fill out the dazzling war costume of the Mexica king. Over his quilted cotton armour, he wore:

'The costly red spoonbill headdress set off with gold, having very many quetzal feathers flaring from it, and . . . borne upon his back, the skin drum upon a carrying frame, and decorated with gold.

'And they dressed him in red shirt, made of red spoonbill feathers, decorated with flint knives fashioned of gold; and his sapote skirt was made all of quetzal feathers.

'The shield was ringed with thin gold, and its pendants were made of precious feathers.

'He had a green stone necklace of round, large, green stone and fine turquoise combined.'[21]

If there had been any doubt in the army that the slackness of Tizoc's reign had lingered, he disabused them. There would be no hanging back by anyone, commoner or noble. Anyone failing to do his utmost would be stripped of all rank and honours. If he knew how to inspire men, he also knew how to discipline them.

The first objective was Xiuhcoac, chief city of the Huaxteca. Much of the Huaxtec lands had been conquered by his predecessors, but Xiuhcoac had not. His army was now a well-sharpened sword in his hand. A large reconnaissance in force of 1,200 men quietly overwhelmed the enemy's guard force on the edge of their cultivated lands. The main army arrived and was carefully hidden in ambush as a decoy force of 200 men moved toward the city itself. The Huaxtec army predictably rushed in pursuit of the decoy and right into Ahuítzotl's ambush and its own destruction with much slaughter and many captives. The city capitulated immediately. Ahuítzotl was loath to return home by the same route he had taken when there was more profitable fighting to be found on a different route. He led the army on another great circle of the Huaxtec lands, defeating local armies, and gathering in loot, captives, tribute, and submission. In all, his march route covered 350 kilometres and at one point skirted the Gulf Coast as he subdued fifteen towns and cities. As he headed for home, his army trailed an enormous train of captives. The Huaxtec men were pulled along by cords run through the pierced septums of their noses that had once held fine noseplugs. The women and children were secured with wooden yokes. A wailing dirge rose from this endless procession as it shuffled along, carefully tended by the Mexica. There is circumstantial evidence that many of the enemies of the Mexica had sent troops to help the Huaxteca for among the great mass of captives assembled in Tenochtitlan after the campaign were many from Huexotzinco, Tlaxcallan, Atlixco, Tliliuhquitepec and Chollollan.[22]

STREAMS OF BLOOD:
THE DEDICATION OF THE GREAT TEMPLE

Upon his triumphant return to Tenochtitlan, Ahuítzotl expressed his great desire to Tlacaélel of finishing the last rebuilding phase of the Great Temple of Huitzilopochtli begun by Tizoc. Its dedication would be the opportunity for a feast that would eclipse anything seen before in all the world. Tlacaélel wept in joy that the temple would now be finished before his own death. Seeing that he had pleased the old man, Ahuítzotl summoned his stewards and master builders to spare no effort to finish the structure.

He also sent embassies to the enemies of the Triple Alliance, begging them to attend the dedication as honoured guests. Barely a year had

A human sacrifice.

passed since these same kings had contemptuously refused to attend his coronation. Now they fell over themselves to honour the Mexica ambassadors and eagerly promised to come to Tenochtitlan. Ahuítzotl closely questioned his ambassadors upon their return. He must have been waiting in suspense to read the status of Mexica prestige in their replies. He could not have been more pleased. A healthy fear was drawing them all to Tenochtitlan. What a difference a year can make.

Now Ahuítzotl and the visiting royalty would play an extravagant game. The kings of Tlaxcallan, Cholollan, and Huexotzinco were met by their escorts on a forested road at the border. There they donned Mexica clothing so that they would not be recognised as they entered the city. They were cautioned not to speak and let their escorts reply to any questions from Mex-

ica passers-by. At the palace, they were shown to luxurious apartments. Every attention was shown to their comfort. Ahuítzotl personally greeted them when the rest of the delegations arrived at midnight. No one was allowed near the kings; they were waited upon by the very ambassadors that had delivered the invitations. These extraordinary precautions were taken to keep the presence of the enemy kings a secret from the Mexica common people. Mexica propaganda had woven an image of relentless war with their enemies; it was felt that the common people would not understand such friendly relations among royalty who shed common blood with such readiness.

The first day of the festival marking the dedication was given to an ostentatious display of Mexica riches. Ahuítzotl took his royal seat flanked by the kings of Texcoco and Tlacopan. The enemy kings were given honoured seats but in a position completely hidden from vulgar eyes. Nothing obstructed their vision, however, which was what Ahuítzotl had in mind. Now all the captives dragged to Tenochtitlan were assembled in full view. They were organised in long lines, each line made up of the captives taken by each city. Added to these multitudes were the many slaves that Ahuítzotl had ordered his allies and vassals to bring to swell the numbers of war prisoners. When they were assembled and counted, it was announced that they numbered 80,400. Next, came an endless relay of porters bearing a full year's tribute of the empire to deposit it in mountains before the tlatoani. Every 80 days, hundreds of thousands of porters entered the Valley of Mexico with the imperial tribute. Now the hours passed as the storerooms and warehouses in the capital were

Every 80 days hundreds of thousands of porters carried imperial tribute to Tenochtitlan.
(Drawing by Keith Henderson)

emptied to provide this spectacle. Ahuítzotl intended a greater audience for this display and had ordered that all of the neighbouring cities of Tenochtitlan send their entire populations on pain of death to swell the Mexica crowds. Perhaps as many as half a million people filled the city.

The next day these multitudes again swarmed through the city. Those that had come at dawn passed the endless files of prisoners being lined up from the temple precinct in the centre of the city to the three causeways and across them to the mainland. A fourth line ended at the city's edge along the lagoon. The three kings of the Triple Alliance dressed in a blinding array of gold and royal blue mantles and loincloths ascended the Great Pyramid in the company of Tlacaélel. The old Snake Woman was now 89 years old; surely he was carried up the long flight of narrow steps. At the top, each took his position as a royal sacrificer escorted by many priests: Ahuítzotl before the statue of Huitzilopochtli, the kings of Texcoco and Tlacopan to either side, and Tlacaélel before the Stone of the Sun itself. Assembled in the temple square below were the vassal kings and the massed Mexica nobility. Shielded by green bowers, the enemy kings were also watching.

Now the captives began to ascend the 100 steps of the pyramid itself.[23] The steps carried them 106 feet above the precinct floor. Soaring another 56 feet into the air were the twin temples to Huitzilopochtli and Tlaloc. At the top of the stairs, they were seized by priests and bent backward over the stones of sacrifice so that the chests arched upward. With a practice slash, each king sliced open the chest of his first victim to reach in and pull out the steaming, still-beating heart. Blood dripped down his arm as he offered it to the sun and the idols of the gods. Again and again the knives flashed amid red blood spray until the kings grew tired. They were readily replaced by relays of priests. The killing went on from dawn to dusk for four days. Imagine how much blood a body will bleed when cut like this: a gallon? Imagine more than 80,000 gallons of blood spurting out of 80,000 great wounds one after another to wash over the temple platform, run down the steps and over the sides. So fast were the sac-

The Great Temple after its final dedication by Ahuítzotl in 1487. (Drawing courtesy © Scott Gentling, photographed by David Wharton)

rifices conducted that there must have been a constant fountain-like spray of blood on the temple platform.[24] The aged Mexica nobles who dictated these accounts to Fray Durán, graphically described the scene:

'The streams of human blood that ran down the steps of the temple were so great that when they reached the bottom and cooled they formed fat clots, enough to terrify one. Many priests went about gathering this blood in large gourds, taking it to the different temples of the wards and smearing the walls, lintels and thresholds with it. They also smeared the idols and the rooms of the temple both inside and out, and the stench of the blood was so strong that it was unbearable. . . it had a sour and abominable smell, to the point that it became unendurable to the people of the city.'[25]

The dead were cast down the sides of the temple to be decapitated and dismembered by deft teams of butchers. Parts of the bodies were distributed to warriors who had captured prisoners, to be taken home and ritually cooked and eaten as a form of communion. Ahuítzotl ordered the existing skull rack in the temple precinct destroyed and a new one built to exhibit all the new skulls now so abundant. Still, the remaining mounds of human flesh presented an awkward problem that was temporarily solved by casting the headless corpses into the surrounding lagoon.[26] For once, the faultless Mexica sense of logistical organisation broke down. The bodies corrupted in the still waters and bred a pestilence that carried off many of the Mexica themselves.

On the fifth day Ahuítzotl bade farewell to his royal guests, loading them down with rich gifts. They left Tenochtitlan secretly by canoe at night. The boatmen were sworn to silence on pain of death. More than one of them must have glanced backward at the city disappearing in the gloom and shuddered. Ahuítzotl had executed a death-soaked propaganda tour-de-force. He had gathered his enemies in one place, overwhelmed them with the endless riches of the empire, then stunned them with the ruthlessness of the sacrifice, while all the time acting with a humbling open-handed noblesse-oblige to men ostensibly his equals in kingship. In five days he had morally disarmed them more thoroughly than had he beaten them all in the field. As they departed in silence, Tlacaélel remarked to Ahuítzotl that what they had seen here would long outlast the memory of the treasures that filled their canoes. 'Let our enemies go and tell their people what they have seen.'[27]

THE CONQUEROR

Conspicuous by his absence at the dedication was the ruler of Telolopan, about 160 kilometres south-west of Tenochtitlan in the modern state of Guerrero. Telolopan had become a Mexica tributary under Itzcoatl but had since reasserted its independence by refusing to attend the dedication. Ahuítzotl sent ambassadors the next year to ask the ruler to explain himself, but they found the route into the region blocked by a barricade of trees and cactus.

Ahuítzotl acted immediately. Forces were mobilised from the Triple Alliance and the Chalca and Xochimilca and advanced by different routes 125 kilometres to the city of Tetipac, two days from Telolopan.[28] Again Ahuítzotl commanded in person. He had a hand on the pulse of the army and actively encouraged the rank and file in their march. After concentrating his army at Tetipac, he discovered to his rage that the kings of Texcoco and Tlacopan had not accompanied their armies. He dressed down the two allied army commanders for the cowardice of their lords, 'threatening to reduce them to the status of subject cities and to deprive them of their foibles, their roses, and their perfumes.'[29] The clear subordination of these two cities within the Triple Alliance could not have been made more clear.

Ahuítzotl then advanced rapidly for two days and after a night march fell on Telolopan with such fury and slaughter that the city fell immediately. He levied a huge tribute that included 400 loads of cacao (40,000 pounds) every 80 days. The lords of Telolopan desperately tried to deflect the anger of Ahuítzotl from them. Slyly they told him that their rebellion had been incited by the neighbouring cities of Alahuitzlan and Oztoman. They would gladly help the Mexica subdue these treacherous neighbours.

Ahuítzotl needed no encouragement. In two days the army was again on the road, fully supplied by Telolopan. In another two days they were before the fortifications of Oztoman and demanding tribute. Oztoman, also a former tributary of the Mexica, refused, blaming the people of Telolopan for bringing this war to them by lying to the Mexica. Ahuítzotl attacked and quickly broke into the city and cried havoc. The entire adult population was put to the sword and the city levelled. Then he advanced eight kilometres on Alahuitzlan, a truly independent city, and demanded tribute. Even with the lesson of Oztoman so close by, the city defied Ahuítzotl and suffered the same fate. In the fighting there, an enemy captain had hacked his way through the Mexica ranks and then the royal bodyguard to throw himself upon the tlatoani himself. He unknowingly triggered a human fury as Ahuítzotl engaged him in single combat. With savage blows of his obsidian-edged sword, the tlatoani broke through the enemy's guard and shattered his skull in two places.

With 40,200 children in tow, Ahuítzotl returned in triumph to Tenochtitlan, his army loaded down with rich tribute and the entire wealth of two exterminated cities. Along the way he was greeted with great obeisance by his subjects. He had demonstrated the penalty of rebellion and the reborn efficiency of Mexica arms. Significantly, Ahuítzotl had commanded the army in person again. The Mexica had competent generals able to conduct campaigns without the presence of the tlatoani, especially against individual cities. But Ahuítzotl found that war was his vital element as much as did Alexander the Great and Charles XII, men to whom he rightfully should be compared in many ways. Like them, he was a genuine military genius, had an innate understanding of leadership, and was genuinely charismatic. Like them, he revelled in glory and pressed his armies to the edge of the world.

Upon his return to Anáhuac, Ahuítzotl distributed the captive children to the cities of the Triple Alliance and to his vassals to raise as their own. He also summoned the kings of Texcoco and Tlacopan to discuss what to do with these now empty but rich lands. Apparently, his anger at their absence on campaign had cooled. Instinctively, he turned to Nezahualpilli for advice on policy. He outlined his idea that 2,000 families were be sent from the empire to resettle the two new provinces: 400 from each of the Triple Alliance cities and 20 each from 40 vassal cities. Nezahualpilli congratulated him on the idea but recommended that 400 was too many from each of the three ruling cities. Instead, he suggested that the three cities supply only 200 families each, that the levy be spread over every ward, and that reliance should be placed on volunteers only. Ahuítzotl immediately saw the good sense of this recommendation and adopted it. Official word of the rich fields of cotton and orchards of cacao and fruit soon attracted more than enough volunteers. The lords of Telolopan had recommended that they would gladly help resettle the empty lands of their former neighbours. Instead, Ahuítzotl appropriated some of their lands for the new colonists who would also serve as garrison. The subject of military garrisons had also been on Ahuítzotl's mind for more than local security. The newly colonised provinces were on the marches of the Mexica and Tarascan empires. With their new and reliable populations, they served as natural and secure garrisons against Tarascan expansion.

During the 1490–91 campaign season, Ahuítzotl again campaigned in Guerrero, this time conquering a vast 240 kilometre stretch of the Pacific Coast that included Acapulco. Seven cities were conquered and many more simply submitted rather than test Mexica arms. Much of this conquest stretched north-west up the coast, curling around the Tarascan southern border. While Ahuítzotl took no action against the Tarascans, he clearly was beginning the long process of hemming in or surrounding a particularly hardy foe. Axayácatl's unfortunate experience was still too fresh in Mexica minds. In the 1491–92 campaign season, Ahuítzotl led his army toward the Gulf Coast to subdue rebellious cities of inland modern Veracruz state. His next major campaign took him far to the south in 1494, again to recover rebellious provinces originally conquered by Motecuhzoma, this time in the Huaxyacac region in the modern state of Oaxaca.

Oaxaca was rich, the major source of gold in Mexico. Its tribute yielded not only the precious metal, but precious cochineal dye as well as a large amount of finely worked mantles. It was also the home of the ancient Zapotec people, many of whom had been recently conquered by the Mixteca. A part of the Zapotec people had migrated further south to escape the Mixteca and founded the city of Tehuantepec, at the Pacific Ocean terminus of the isthmus of the same name. As a rich centre of trade, Tehuantepec had attracted the attention of Tenochtitlan. Such was the power behind the Mexica merchants who flocked there, that they were able to trade for the precious products of the area (gold, cacao, feathers, and precious stones) in exchange for products of the Valley of Mexico (mostly lagoon products of low value) at extortionary rates. Such situations were a ready source of sought-after wars for the Mexica as in this case when in 1496 the exasperated Zapotec murdered Mexica merchants and cut off further trade. Although many merchants had been slain, others had successfully fought their way out of danger with a great deal

The shadow of the Great Temple falls upon the Great Skull Rack. (Painting courtesy © Scott Gentling, photographed by David Wharton)

of the riches of the region; Mexica merchants were just as handy with a sword as barter. They arrived in Tenochtitlan bearing extraordinary treasures:

'. . . quetzal feather crests, shirts of blue cotinga or of trogonorus (black and green feathers); turquoise mosaic shields; golden, butterfly-shaped nose plates, which they had come wearing; and golden ear pendants which hung from their ears, each extending very wide, reaching their shoulders; and quetzal and troupial feather banners, bracelets for the upper arms with sprays of precious feathers.'[30]

The merchants presented all their treasures to Ahuítzotl who greeted them with great courtesy confirming their possession of all they had won and rewarding them with even greater largesse. 'None will refuse it to you, for it is truly your property, your array. For you went away to merit it.' He could afford to be generous. They had explored a land of great wealth and presented him with the pretext of a just war.

Ahuítzotl then ordered a massive mobilisation. Not only the usual Triple Alliance and empire core contingents were summoned but forces from many other vassals, such as those in the Hot Lands, and the Matlatzinco area on the Tarascan border. So great was the levy that in many places no adult men were to be seen. So fearful was the departure of their menfolk on a campaign to the end of the earth, that the women donned mourning and pledged not to wash their faces until news of victory was received, praying:

'O Great Lord of All Things, remember
  your servant
Who has gone to exalt your honour and
  the greatness of your name.
He will offer blood in the sacrifice which is
  war.
Behold, Lord, that he did not go out to
  work for me.
Or for his children! He did not abandon us
  to obtain things
To support his home, with his tump line
  on his head,
Or with his digging stick in his hand. He
  went for your sake,
In your name, to obtain glory for you.
  Therefore, O Lord,
Let your pious heart have pity on him,
  who with great labor
And affliction now goes through the mountains and valleys,
Hills and precipices, offering you the moisture from his brow,
His sweat. Give him victory in this war so
  that he may return
To rest in his home and so that my children and I may see
His countenance again and feel his presence.'[31]

Probably the most fearsome event in the year of every Mexica vassal state was the arrival of the imperial tribute-collectors from Tenochtitlan. By the reign of Ahuítzotl, a million bearers were bringing tribute every 80 days to Tenochtitlan. (Drawing by Keith Henderson)

Ahuítzotl realised that this campaign would be the most distant in Mexica history. The native accounts emphasise an extraordinary logistics effort to supply the army with campaign rations of toasted maize kernels, maize and bean flour, toasted tortillas, and sun-baked tamales as well as chili and ground cacao cakes all from the imperial stores and carried by porters. In addition each soldier carried as much of his own food as he could. The entire round trip distance to be travelled in the campaign was an unheard-of 1,900 kilometres, although only the final 300 kilometres would be into hostile territory. For an army entirely on foot, it was a breathtaking effort.[32] And Ahuítzotl had enticements to justify this long march. He declared that the return trip would be too long to justify encumbering the army with prisoners. Kill them all, was the order. He vowed to kill 2,000 of the enemy for every merchant that had been murdered. For the army, this meant unrestricted plunder of a fabulously wealthy city.

The journey to the Valley of Oaxaca exhausted the supplies the army had carried with it as had been expected. Ahuítzotl now ordered the local chiefs to resupply it and provide additional levies. Hearing this, the king of Tehuantepec threatened to take revenge on any of his fellow Zapotec in Oaxaca should they comply with the Mexica demands. Ahuítzotl was by far the more to be feared in Zapotec eyes, and they readily complied with his orders. True to his vow, he cut a bloody swath though lands of Tehuantepec, massacring one town after another, before reaching the capital, and giving each one over to pillage by the troops. Already he was repaying his army for its long march. When they reached Tehuantepec itself, its army was arrayed for battle, resplendent in brilliant feathers and gems, the riches of the region. The very sight of the enemy, dripping with loot, must have raised the enthusiasm of the Mexica even more. That and well-drilled discipline quickly broke the will of the warriors of Tehuantepec who found themselves being fed into the Mesoamerican version of a buzz saw. After the loss of several leaders, they broke and fled for the city with the Mexica in exultant pursuit. The Mexica stopped killing fugitives only long enough to strip the dead of their finery. Into the city the Mexica surged after their victims, butchering man, woman, and child as they broke into houses and palaces for loot.[33] Out of the rear of the city a panic-stricken mob of noncombatants must have fled, beginning as soon as the people watching from their rooftops witnessed the destruction of their army.

Ahuítzotl's concern now that Tehuantepec was beaten was less for slaughter than for the preservation of a city able to produce such treasures on a regular basis. When enemy lords came begging submission and offering rich tribute, Ahuítzotl ordered the killing stopped. But the troops were in a frenzy of bloodlust and pillage and ignored the orders. The consequences of the gruelling long march with treasure dangled at the end was having its effect. The Mexica captains now tried to physically force their men back into their ranks. The men ignored or forced them aside as they broke into houses or rushed baying down the blood-slippery streets after victims flushed from hiding places. Finally, even this frenzy abated, and the captains were able to restore order. But Ahuítzotl now had a simmering mutiny on his hands. The men were furious at being denied their promised loot. Although state booty was often distributed as rewards, it seldom equalled what could be obtained in the sack of a city by the troops themselves. They now vowed never to undergo the rigours of such a march again for such paltry rewards. Ahuítzotl placated them by announcing that he would make good their lost booty from his own purse. The lords of Tehuantepec had already given him fabulous gifts for stopping the massacre. All this and the imperial share of the booty and tribute he distributed to the army, keeping nothing for himself.

Upon his return to Tenochtitlan, Ahuítzotl gave thanks to Huitzilopochtli for his victory in a ceremony that would have rivalled any imperial procession in golden Byzantium. From the great doors of the palace to the entrance to the temple courtyard, priests formed two long lines. Black-clad and black-painted, all held incense burners upon which fragrant copal sizzled to drift away in clouds. Then came the tlatoani's imperial guard, every man noble born, praised in battle, and adorned in the richest jewellery. They wore in their hair the emblems of their knightly orders, blue or green feathers tied in a red ribbon. From this band hung tasselled cords down their backs, each tassel representing a valiant deed in battle. So awesome and sacred was the tlatoani that no man carried a weapon, only a staff. Then came the tlatoani himself, arrayed in the Toltec blue mantle and turquoise diadem, sporting quetzal feathers which he had adopted as his personal emblem now that he had conquered the city so rich in them. He wore golden armbands, anklets, ear-, nose-, and lip-plugs and long strings of gems. Following him were his pages, dwarfs and hunchbacks, who carried the most precious of the plunder from the south. They were also richly dressed in gold, feathers, mantles, and especially the skins of jaguars and ocelots, special booty from Tehuantepec.

As Ahuítzotl walked in procession, he was perfumed by the clouds of incense as if he were a god. Entering the temple precinct, he was greeted by a thunderous salute from massed conch-shell trumpets, drums, and flutes. The music followed him up the steps of the Great Pyramid, ending suddenly as he reached the top as every man abased himself. To those who watched Ahuítzotl this day, he must have seemed the incarnation of the Mexica nation itself: magnificent in his strength, warlike, valiant, ferocious, chivalrous, and the favoured of the gods. He was, at that moment, Huitzilopochtli on earth. Graciously he greeted the priests and dignitaries. He personally incensed the images of the gods with a golden censer. Then he sacrificed many quails, cutting off their heads and pouring their blood before the images, especially Huitzilopochtli's. He took a sharpened jaguar bone and knelt, Mesoamerican fashion before the god. He squatted and drew blood from his ears, arms, and shins. As the blood dripped down his body, he touched a finger to the pavement in front of the idol and then to his mouth, the ultimate reverence of the ceremony of 'The Eating of Holy Earth'.

Clouds of incense perfumed Ahuítzotl's victory procession to the Great Temple. (Drawing by Keith Henderson)

He rose, turned to the vast crowd below him and exclaimed in a loud voice his thanks to Huitzilopochtli, in words that were the essence of the Mexica imperial idea:

'O almighty, powerful Lord of All Created
  Things,
You who give us life, and whose vassals we
  are,
Lord of the Day and of the Night, of the
  Wind and the Water,
Whose strength keeps us alive! I give you
  infinite thanks

For having brought me back to your city of
  Mexico
With the victory which you granted me. I
  have returned
To the great city of Mexico-Tenochtitlan
  where our ancestors —
Chichimecs and Aztecs — with great pains
  found the
Blissful eagle seated upon the prickly pear
  cactus.
There the eagle ate and rested, next to the
  springs of
Blue and red water which were filled with

flying fish,
White snakes and white frogs. This won-
  drous thing appeared
Since you wanted to show us the great-
  ness of your power
And your will. You made us masters of the
  wealth we now
Possess and I give you infinite thanks, O
  Lord.
Since you did not frown upon my extreme
  youth
Or my lack of strength or the weakness of
  my chest,
You have subjected those remote and bar-
  barous nations
To my power. You did all of these things!
  All is yours!
All was won to give you honor and praise!
Therefore, O powerful and heroic
  Huitzilopochtli,
You have brought us back to this place
  which was only water
Before, which was enclosed by our ances-
  tors,
And where they built out city.'[34]

After the ceremony he caused all the wealth stored in the imperial treasure houses to be counted, and 'it was found to exceed the imagination'. Ahuítzotl was the perfect Mexica in every way. Not only must he be ever the bringer of victory to honour his divine benefactor, but he must constantly revel in the wealth and display of victory. Perhaps beneath even the Toltec blue robes of a tlatoani was the memory of a wretchedly poor Mexica barbarian driven from one miserable home to others ever worse until finally was found the miserable islands no other people would have. From this nothing the Mexica had built an empire, but the memory of that nothing still itched, and the wealth delivered by a million porters every 80 days could only sooth but not cure it.

THE DEATH OF TLACAÉLEL

Shortly thereafter in the same year, the great Tlacaélel grew ill and died at the hoary age of 96. If the Mexica empire could be said to be the work of any one man, it was Tlacaélel, the legendary Cihuacoatl, Snake Woman. In the last ten years he had faded away from public life. The annals speak little of him after the slaughter at the dedication of the Great Temple. Already he had been ancient when Ahuítzotl had come to the throne. It had been 72 years since the young warrior-priest had stood in the way of his panicked people and stopped them from begging mercy from their Tepanec overlords. Instead he had bearded the Tepanec king in his very hall and escaped with his life to stir the Mexica to fight. From that moment, he had become a great war leader, a role that would last for decades. More than that, he had been the intellect behind the creation of the Mexica imperial idea and its most skilled architect and administrator. Had he been alert enough to have heard Ahuítzotl exult that idea from the platform of the Great Temple upon which he had lavished so much attention? Now his eldest son succeeded him by order of the tlatoani. He was cremated and buried beneath the pavement of the Great Temple, next to the other kings of which he was surely the greatest. Another account said he was embalmed and carried into battle on a litter armed with sword and shield. So fearsome was the reputation of this empire-builder with a taste for human blood and flesh, that the very sight of him caused the enemy to flee.[35]

THE DROWNING OF TENOCHTITLAN

Now at the height of his success, Ahuítzotl looked to assure the well-being of Tenochtitlan itself. The rapidly growing city needed a greater supply of fresh water for its floating gardens and the daily needs of its population which now outstripped anything that Mesoamerica had seen. The dry season lowered the canals so low that canoes could not navigate them and imperilled the productivity of the floating gardens that ringed the city. He wanted to divert powerful springs near the city of Coyohuacan through an aqueduct directly to Tenochtitlan and sent to the city's ruler, Tzotzomatzin, with a pro forma request. Tzotzomatzin was willing to comply but warned Ahuítzotl that the flow of the springs was at times far more powerful than the tlatoani realised and was capable of flooding even so massive a city as Tenochtitlan.

Ahuítzotl flew into a rage. More used to the instant obedience of the campaign, he saw this loyal remonstration as a defiant insult. He ordered Tzotzomatzin's execution, brushing aside the horrified pleading of his own court that the ruler of Coyohuacan had only the tlatoani's best interest at heart. For some reason attributed to magic, the executioners failed in their first attempt. The second was accompanied by a threat to destroy the Coyohuacan. Tzotzomatzin then placed the noose around his own neck and warned that Ahuítzotl would be 'sorry that he did not listen to my advice.'

'This assassination, for such it was, caused consternation among Ahuítzotl's advisers; in particular, the ruler of Tacuba (Tlacopan) was distressed, since the victim was a close kinsman. It might be one thing occasionally to slay a remote provincial prince after a bitter war; it was quite another to kill the sovereign of a neighbouring city in cold blood. It virtually amounted to an offense against the gods, whom this ruler in his own sphere represented.'[36]

Ahuítzotl was oblivious both to the sacrilege and the seething outrage it provoked. The peoples of Texcoco and Tlacopan, the lesser members of the Triple Alliance, were particularly outraged. Ahuítzotl's anger had struck close to home; they could be next. Years of irritation at growing Mexica high-handedness in the affairs of the Alliance now mixed with a genuine sense of injustice to bring both states to the edge of rebellion. With Ahuítzotl's own reputation for murderous rage now established, men no longer would serve him with the truth, and the plotting went unreported. The plotters only waited for the right time to move.

Ahuítzotl was obsessed with the aqueduct. He ordered the project completed in the shortest time and committed to it all the resources of the state. Materials, skilled workmen, and masses of labourers poured into the Valley of Mexico, even loads of lime from the Hot Lands. Provinces vied with each other to finish their sections first. The springs at Coyohuacan were damned and all their waters collected in a reservoir. Then a vast stone bed was laid on which thick sections of fired clay pipe were fitted. The construction was a marvel of effi-ciency, completed in only eight days. So many labourers worked on the project that they were said to resemble ants on an ant heap.

When the work was finished and the structure had dried, Ahuítzotl ordered the waters unleashed in a brilliant aquatic festival. Dressed as the goddess of waters and springs, Chalchiuhtlicue, 'She of the Jade Skirt,' a man was escorted to the source of the water by a delegation of priests, naked save for their loincloths, blowing conch shells and flutes and carrying smoking censers of sweet copal incense. The man was dressed in blue (the colour of the waters) shirt and sandals, embroidered with blue and green gems, his skin painted blue and his face darkened with liquid rubber. His lip and ear plugs were of costly green stones and his bracelets of turquoise. He carried a bag of blue corn meal and rattles of turtle shells. At the water source, one of the priests sacrificed quail and let the blood mix with the surging water. Incense and liquid rubber were poured into the water as well, as the man implored the goddess to the music of the conch shells and flutes:

'O precious lady, welcome to your own
  road! From now on
You will follow this path and I, who repre-
  sent your image, have come here
To receive you, greet you and congratulate
  you for your arrival.
Behold, lady, today, you must arrive in
  your own city, Mexico-Tenochtitlan!'[37]

Then the man threw the blue corn meal into the water, sounded his rattles, and descended into the huge pipe to dance and leap amid the water. All along the route of the aqueduct, men and women joined in the festival — dancing, singing, and playing music. Old men brought tubs of fish and amphibians to toss into the pipe so that the creatures would be carried to Tenochtitlan to multiply. At the first culvert, four blue-painted six-year-old children were sacrificed over the pipe itself, and their hearts offered to the waters.

Waiting at the great outpouring of the aqueduct in Tenochtitlan itself, Ahuítzotl welcomed the water with a flowery speech as it shot out of the pipe. Then he threw into the stream frogs

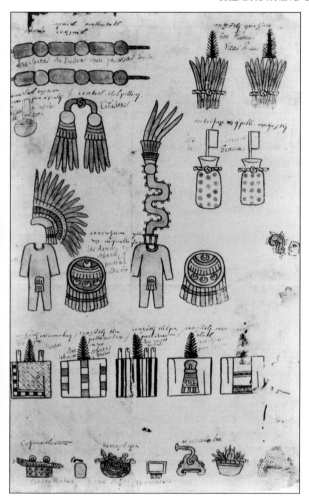

One of the Mexica tribute lists drawn immediately after the Conquest to provide a guide to the wealth of the empire for the Spaniards. This list includes beads of semiprecious stones, bunches of feathers, war costumes, and blankets. Such wealth was the foundation of the new empire created by Itzcoatl, Tlacaélel, and Motecuhzoma I.

and fish fashioned of gold and jewels. Crowds of the nobility followed his example with their own gifts. He exulted as the stream of gold and brilliant gems, flashing in the sun, were hurled into the powerful stream. As he had subdued nations, now he had subdued one of the elements of nature.

As the days passed, the levels of the canals rose, the floating gardens drank the sweet water as did the people as it filled the fountains and reservoirs of the city. A month passed, and the water continued to flow at the same heavy rate, but now the city's capacity had been reached. The water flowed over the canals, submerged the gardens, and began to flood the houses and buildings of the city as the level of the lagoon itself rose. In panic, Ahuítzotl ordered the building of a dam to keep the rising lagoon waters out of the city, but it failed. The tender young plants in the gardens were ruined, and the people began to evacuate the city. The leaders of the wards begged the tlatoani to stop the ruin of their city. For the first time in his life, Ahuítzotl panicked as the water reached the apron of the Great Pyramid itself. He begged advice from Nezahualpilli who was only too glad to give it:

'It is too late to be sorry and alarmed at your own perdition and that of the great city of Mexico. You could have considered and prevented this before. You are not fighting now against your enemies whom you could destroy or force to flee from your cities. You are fighting against water, a fierce element. How can you resist it? The great prince of Coyoacan (Coyohuacan), Tzotzomatzin, gave you good advice and not only would you not listen to his opinions, which he gave you like a loyal vassal, but you slew him. What did Tzotzomatzin do? In what did he sin? In what did he offend? Why did you deprive him of his life so pitilessly? Was he a traitor to the royal crown? Was he an adulterer or a thief?'[38]

Having reproached Ahuítzotl for his murder of Tzotzomatzin, Nezahualpilli then appraised him of the deeper consequences of his act:

'Recognize, most mighty lord, that you have offended and sinned against the gods, whose likeness this good ruler represented, and upon whose shoulders they had laid the burden of the government of his realm. And for that cause, the lord of creation now permits that this city should be destroyed and depopulated. How will it appear in the eyes of the enemies which surrounded us, when Mexico is emptied of its citizens and you and your lords are compelled to flee, as an eternal vengeance upon you and upon them? What will they say, save that what your ancestors built with so much sweat and labour, you have destroyed in forty days?'[39]

He then recommended that the dams channelling the waters at the source be broken and that rich offerings and sacrifices of more children be made to placate the goddess of the waters. Ahuítzotl rushed to comply. At the source of the streams, the assemblage of kings and nobles, led by Ahuítzotl, humiliated themselves before the goddess as divers carried the precious gifts to bury in the mud of the springs. The hearts of more children were thrown into the waters followed by stone images of the gods. Ahuítzotl ordered the dams broken so that the waters could return to their natural courses. Then he entered the city of Coyohuacan to beg forgiveness and to confirm Tzotzomatzin's legitimate son as rightful heir.

Whatever plots had been in play dissipated in the wake of the divine retribution visited upon Ahuítzotl and his subsequent public humiliation and atonement. The much-chastened tlatoani had a more immediate problem — to rebuild Tenochtitlan. Again he tasked the empire's vassals to deliver vast amounts of building materials and workmen. First the waters were drained away from the submerged city. Then the canals were deepened and planted on each side with willows and poplars. Embankments and other water control projects were built to drain off the water even if the canals overfilled. Many old buildings dating to the days of Mexica poverty had suffered major damage and were demolished and grandly rebuilt. Styles were new and original in many cases as might be expected now that architects and artists from many nations were on hand with the Mexica equivalent of carte blanche.

'. . . this time the nobles and others built to suit their fancy, using imported labour, each leader having a village or two assigned to him to help rebuild his house. And thus, they painted as they wished each in his own style, as was their own custom. And so Mexico became very fine and spectacular, with large and unusual houses, filled with great extensions of garden and splendid patios. . .'[40]

From this effort rose the brilliant city that Cortés was to see almost twenty years later.

A FINAL CAMPAIGN

The people of Tehuantepec had become the most loyal of vassals, thankful that Ahuítzotl had stopped the massacre of their city. In 1500 they took advantage of their status to demand the one thing they had every right to expect from the Mexica: protection. Their neighbours to the south in Soconosco, Xolotla, and Mazatlan, along the border with Guatemala, now considered them vulnerable after having been conquered. Bands of them had robbed travellers, sacked villages, and worst of all, murdered Mexica merchants.

Ahuítzotl may have been hesitant to campaign again so far south. The cost and effort of the last campaign had been enormous, driving his army to near mutiny. The only thing more expensive would be to let the world witness that the Mexica could or would not protect their vassals. Again he raised a great army, numbered at 200,000 men, and again the streets were empty of adult males. Chagrined that on the last expedition his two allied kings of Tlacopan and Texcoco had not joined him, he pointedly sent them the finest swords and shields. The king of Tlacopan begged to be excused that his age would not permit such a journey. It is not entirely clear, but Nezahualpilli of Texcoco also appeared to have escaped once more.

Again the army marched itself to exhaustion with the tlatoani sharing every mile, camping with his men, and refusing the comforts of nearby cities. This time Tehuantepec was merely the final friendly base. The enemy lay 350 kilometres further south; the entire round trip was a numbing 2,300 kilometres. Although Mexica arms prevailed in the storming of Soconosco, it seems they may have wavered in their exhaustion at the crucial moment. Only the spirited attack of the Tehuantepec levies appear to have saved the day. Again Ahuítzotl faced a breakdown in discipline when he ordered an end to the sack of a now valuable vassal. He prodded the native rulers to compensate the troops; this time there was no noble gesture in parting with his own royal booty. When the offending states had all submitted, the lords of Soconosco, eager to see the Mexica depart, suggested that even richer kingdoms lay just over the border in Guatemala. They even offered to send warriors to help him in their conquest. It was a bitter decision for Ahuítzotl to refuse. Like Alexander in India, his army would go no further. He excused himself by replying that these nations had done him no harm, and, more truthfully, that his men were played out.

Upon his return to Tenochtitlan, the tlatoani suddenly fell ill of a wasting disease that reduced him to a living skeleton of skin stretched over bones. Feeling death near, he ordered his image cut into the stone next to that of his grandfather and brother on Chapultepec. Ahuítzotl died in 1502, barely sixteen years into his reign.[41] Like Alexander he died a young man, in his early thirties. In many ways he marked an apogee of Mexica imperialism. He had rescued the empire from a near fatal falter under his brother Tizoc and carried its banners to the edge of fabled Guatemala far to the south. If he had committed murder in a rage, he had the good sense to repent and restore the balance of justice, something his successor would be incapable of. Ruining the Tenochtitlan of his fathers by his own misjudgment, he rebuilt it in fairytale splendour. He was everything the Mexica admired: successful in war, brave beyond a fault, pious, proud — and bloody. In his reign perhaps as many as half a million human beings perished.[42] His memory would survive the extinguishing of his world in the very word *ahuizote* in Mexican Spanish — someone violent, vindictive, and fierce.

1. Nigel Davies, *The Aztecs*, University of Oklahoma Press, Norman, OK, 1989, p. 125.
2. Frances Gillmor, *The King Danced in the Marketplace*, University of Arizona Press, Tuscon, 1964, pp. 10-11.
3. Miguel León-Portilla, *Trece Poetas del Mundo Aztecas*, Instituto de Investigaciones Históricas, Mexico City, Universitad Nacional Autónoma de México, 1967, pp. 145-147; quoted in Davies, ibid., p. 127.
4. Davies, ibid., p. 128.
5. Hernando Alvarado Tezozómoc, *Crónica Mexicana*, Editorial Leyenda, Mexico City, 1944, p. 194; quoted in Davies, ibid., p. 130.
6. Durán, ibid., p. 158.
7. The teponatzli was a drum made from a single hollowed out log with a single slit on one side and was struck with a soft instrument. Several exquisite examples, masterpieces of the wood carvers art, survive.
8. Eugene R. Craine and Reginald C. Reindorp, eds and trans, *The Chronicles of Michaoacán*, University of Oklahoma Press, Norman, 1970, pp. xiii-xiv; Davies, ibid., p. 146; Durán, ibid., p. 350, note 84. Perhaps there might be a connection between the possible Peruvian origin of the Tarascans who arrived in Michoacan about the time the Mexica arrived in the Valley of Mexico and their advanced knowledge of metallurgy. They apparently knew all of the metallurgy techniques of Peru.
9. Durán, ibid., p. 166.
10. Tezozomoc, *Crónica Mexicana*, ibid., p. 229; in Davies, p. 148.
11. Durán, ibid., p. 168. There is a remarkable echo in this speech of Pericles' oration for the first dead of the Peloponnesian War.
12. Durán, ibid., p. 172.
13. Hassig, ibid., p. 198.
14. Fray Bernadino De Sahagún, *General History of the Things of New Spain*, (Florentine Codex), *Book 6: Rhetoric and Moral Philosophy*, Part VII, The School of American Research and the University of Utah, Santa Fe, NM, 1969, pp. 25-27.
15. Hassig, ibid., pp. 198-199. Ross Hassig speculates that Tizoc's brother, Ahuítzotl, was just such a man. Hassig cites Torquemada 1975-83, 1:257 [bk. 2, chap. 63], and states that Ahuítzotl was *tlacochcala catl*, chief military officer of the state. The occupant of that position was essentially the heir apparent; however, that condition was based on the demonstration of military ability. Suppressing revolts hardly constituted an adequate demonstration. Tizoc's lack of aggressiveness was denying Ahuítzotl the opportunity to make his position as heir unassailable. Without that, other members of the Eagle Clan might have equally good claims to the Turquoise Diadem of the tlatoani. Ahuítzotl was a young man who saw the future slipping away. This account of Ahuítzotl at the time of Tizoc's death conflicts fundamentally with that of Durán (p. 185) whose Mexica informants clearly describe Ahuítzotl as still a schoolboy in the *calmecac* when he was chosen tlatoani by the electors. At first the electors wanted to reject the young man in place of a mature and experienced candidate, something they would hardly have done if Ahuítzotl was already serving as *tlacochcalacatl*, a position of supreme importance.
16. Durán, ibid., pp. 184-185.
17. Durán, ibid., pp. 185-186.
18. Durán, ibid., pp. 188-189.
19. Durán, ibid., p. 190. Hallucogenic mushrooms were apparently freely consumed at such festivals.
20. Tezozomoc, ibid., p. 294.
21. De Sahagún, ibid., *Book 8: Kings and Lords*, p. 33.

The drum tied to the back of commanders was used by them to signal commands.

22. Hassig, ibid., pp. 204-205. An alternate explanation is that these non-Huaxtec captives may have been taken in Flower Wars. Unfortunately, no breakdown by ethnic origin is provided.

23. Bernal Díaz del Castillo, *The Discovery and Conquest of Mexico*, Farrar, New York, Straus and Cudahy, 1956, p. 217; Díaz makes a point of the number of 114 steps. Conversation with Stuart Gentling reveals that the apron of the Great Temple contained 10 steps, the single vertical flight to the top of the pyra mid contained 100, and the small platform atop which the temple of Huitzilopochtli stood had another four.

24. The figure of 80,400 sacrificial victims has generated one of the great controversies of Mexican history. Many prominent historians scoff at the figure as being an administrative impossibility, simply from the perspective of body disposal. On the other hand, the Nazis also found that body disposal was a serious problem in the death camps; however, it was not a problem that was allowed to interfere with the killing. Durán (p. 199) insists that the figure of 80,400 is accurate, having checked numerous other Indian sources in 'written and painted manuscripts.' Given the Mexica penchant for propaganda, there is no telling if this original number was 'doctored' at the time of the event itself.

25. Durán, ibid., p. 199.

26. Tezozomoc, *Chrónica Mexicayótl*, in *Anales de Museo de Arqueologia, Historia y Etnografia*, epcoa 4, Vol. 5, 1927, p. 333; in Jonathan Kandell, *La Capital: The Biography of Mexico City*, Henry Holt and Company, New York, 1989, p. 54.

27. Tezozomoc, *Chrónica Mexicayótl*, ibid., p. 384.

28. The mobilisation of Chalca and Xochimilca contin gents with the forces of the Triple Alliance was becoming a regular feature of Mexica mobilisations. Both regions were among the early conquests of the Triple Alliance and were now part of the core of the empire. The Chalca, in particular, had been valiant enemies at one time and were seen as valuable aux iliaries. Their proximity to Tenochtitlan probably made them more easy to mobilise and their families more easily held as hostages.

29. Davies, ibid., p. 174, citing Tezozomoc as a source.

30. Sahagún, ibid., *Book 9 - The Merchants*, Part X, 1959, p. 3.

31. Durán, ibid., p. 203.

32. Hassig, ibid., pp. 216-217; Durán, ibid., pp. 202-203.

33. Davis, ibid., p. 183.

34. Durán, ibid., p. 207.

35. Durán, ibid., p. 208.

36. Davies, ibid., p. 193.

37. Durán, ibid., p. 212.

38. Durán, ibid., p. 215.

39. Durán, *Historia de Las Indias de Nueva España e Islas de la Tierra Firme*, Vol II, Editorial Porrúra, Mexico City, S.A., 1967, pp. 379-380; from Davies, p. 195. This Spanish language version of Durán, quoted and translated by Davies, has elements not included in the English language edition, used throughout this book. For example all of this paragraph, except for the first sentence, is missing from the English-language version.

40. Durán, Editorial Porrúra edition, ibid., p. 381; in Davies, p. 197.

41. An alternative explanation of the flooding of Tenochtitlan and the death of Ahuítzotl is found in Fray Juan de Torquemada, *Monarquía Indiana*, Vol I, Editorial Chavez Hayhoe, Mexico City, 1943-4, p. 193, cited in Davies, p. 206; and in Kandell, ibid., p. 55. By this account, a badly engineered dam burst and sent a flash flood through Tenochtitlan that drowned thousands of people. Ahuítzotl in his garden attempted to flee to the roof of his palace and struck his head on a stone lintel. Rescued by his servants, he lapsed into a three-year coma. Perhaps the pro longed coma explains the account of the wasting dis ease as his body slowly starved to death. Hassig (pp. 346-7) also suggests the last several campaigns of Ahuítzotl's reign were actually led by his nephew and *tlacochcalacatl* (general in chief), Motecuhzoma Xocoyotl (the Younger), the son of Axayácatl.

42. To arrive at 500,000 deaths, begin with perhaps 10,000 human sacrifices a year for fifteen years, totalling 150,000. Add to that the 80,400 sacrificed at the dedication of the Great Temple. The massacre of the two cities from which only 40,200 children survived would have accounted for perhaps another 80,000, totalling about 310,000 deaths. such as the general order to take no prisoners in the Tehuante pec campaign Add to these all the other successful wars of Ahuítzotl, and the total could easily have risen to 500,000.

7

MOTECUHZOMA II XOCOYOTL: THERE WAS DREAD IN THE WORLD (1502–1520)

The electors of the empire met to pick Ahuítzotl's successor the day after his ashes had been interred in the Great Temple. As was his right, Nezahualpilli addressed the assembled lords. First he spoke of the importance of the office they would soon fill.

'With your vote and consent we are to choose the luminary that is to give us light like one of the sun's rays. We are to choose a mirror in which we will be reflected, a mother who will hold us to her breasts, a father who will carry us on his shoulders and a prince who will rule over the Aztec nation. He will be the shelter and refuge of the poor, of widows and orphans, and he will have pity upon those who go about day and night in the wilderness working for their sustenance.'[1]

Then he spoke of the array of candidates, one of the great strengths of Mexica kingship. 'This is the one that you must elect, O mighty lords. Look about you, as there is much to see! You are surrounded by all the Aztec nobles . . . They are the jewels and precious stones which fell from the throats and wrists of those royal men.' Emphasising the elective nature of the monarchy, he explained that Axayácatl and Tizoc had left many bold and spirited sons, but if the council was still not sure of them, then they could choose from the many descendants of past kings. 'Extend your hands, point out your favorite, since anyone you indicate will be a strong wall against our enemies.'[2]

The king of Tlacopan spoke next, reminding the council of the need to elect a mature man.

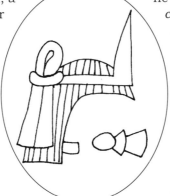

Motecuhzoma II's name hieroglyph.

The empire had expanded quickly, perhaps too quickly, under Ahuítzotl and could not afford another young and inexperienced tlatoani. Despite the hours of discussion and the many qualified candidates, there was a remarkable consensus on the right choice: Motecuhzoma Xocoyotl (the Younger) eighth son of Axayácatl, and great grandson of the first Motecuhzoma. At 34 years of age, he had served brilliantly as the *tlacochcalacatl*, general in chief, in Ahuítzotl's last campaigns.

Motecuhzoma was a bold and spirited commander, but he also had a reputation for piety. The messengers who sought him after his election, found him in the Shrine of the Eagles within the Sacred Square, in his own specially appointed room. Motecuhzoma had been educated as a priest of Huitzilopochtli and would have remained that had not an older brother, thought likely to succeed to the throne, been killed in the Flowery Wars with Huexotzinco.[3] Undoubtedly, he would have been happier had he remained in the priesthood. But at the moment of accession to the throne, he seemed to match the description of the perfect ruler recited in the lessons of the young.

'The ruler is a shelter – fierce, revered, famous, esteemed; well reputed, renowned.

'The good ruler is a protector; one who carries his subjects in his arms, who unites them, who brings them together. He rules, takes responsibilities, assumes burdens. He carries his subjects in his cape; he bears them in his arms. He governs; he is obeyed. To him as a shelter, as a refuge, there is recourse. . .'[4]

He thanked his electors with great modesty and with a reasoned eloquence for which he was famous,

'I would indeed be blind, most noble king, if I did not perceive that you have spoken thus, simply to do me honour; not withstanding the presence of so many fine and noble men in this kingdom, you have chosen me, the most inadequate of all for this calling. I possess few accomplishments required for such an arduous task, and know not what I may do, save to rely upon the Lord of Creation to favour me, and to beg all those present that they may give their support to these my supplications.'[5]

This modesty quickly slipped away in his first act. He summoned the Snake Woman (Cihuacoatl), his chief minister, and ordered him to dismiss all of the palace household of Ahuítzotl. He explained that his uncle had appointed too many commoners to these positions and 'that it was undignified and unworthy of a king to be served by lowly people. . . ' He was the representative of Huitzilopochtli, and only the finest blood was worthy of attending him. He also wished to teach the sons of the nobility the arts of government. The Cihuacoatl attempted to remonstrate, 'Great Lord, you are wise and powerful, and certainly you are able to do all that you will; but to me it seems that this may be taken amiss, because people will judge that you wish to denigrate former monarchs by undoing their works.'[6] Motecuhzoma was not dissuaded and ordered him to search out the finest of the young nobility to train in the imperial service. He was to exclude anyone born of a slave or illegitimate, even should it be the tlatoani's own brother. The Snake Woman dutifully found 100 suitable young men, going so far as to measure them all personally to arrive at a pleasing uniformity of height. The young men were instructed in their duties and threatened with death for even the most minor failings. Then Motecuhzoma summarily dismissed all the members of his household staff, followed by all the ward heads, royal officials, and captains of one hundred of common birth. Almost as an afterthought, he had them all killed.

Nigel Davies points to two obsessive motivations. Motecuhzoma was extremely sensitive to Ahuítzotl's immense popularity; a cold and rigid man, he must have seen his uncle's

Motecuhzoma as a young warrior. (Drawing by Keith Henderson)

charm and charisma as a constant reproach. He also had a stark class consciousness that completely overrode common sense,[7] best expressed in his own words:

'Because, just as precious stones appear out of place among poor and wretched ones, so those of royal blood seem ill-assorted among people of low extraction. And consequently, just as humble feathers do not look well alongside rich ones, so the plumes that came from great lords ill behove workers and their sons.'[8]

However artful his metaphors, the most telling expression of his class attitude was his massacre of the officials and officers of low birth. At one stroke he had destroyed much of an experienced and capable imperial administration to satisfy this prejudice. He was striking at his uncle's memory a second time, as the Cihuacoatl had hinted, because Ahuítzotl had advanced so many men on sheer merit. The warrior king Ahuítzotl had been happy to reward talent wherever he found it. Motecuhzoma had the pleasure of accepting into his service the sons of men whom Ahuítzotl had dismissed in favour of more capable commoners. Motecuhzoma even turned his class attitudes to language; he ordered that only the pure Náhuatl could be spoken in his presence.[9] Durán recorded another measure when he asked an old Mexica, decades after the death of Motecuhzoma, what the tlatoani had looked like. The old man recoiled, 'Father, I will not lie to you or tell you about things which I do not know. I never saw his face!' Motecuhzoma had decreed death to anyone who looked him in the face. The same act within his own household was an even greater offence for it was committed in the 'house of God'. The penalty was death by being shot with arrows or burned alive.[10]

His actions favouring the nobility may have been clear policy decisions playing one class off against another in order to buttress the power of the tlatoani. The rapid rise of commoners under Ahuítzotl's merit policy had disrupted the hierarchical structure of the state. While this argument is surely a part of the answer, it gives too little credence to Motecuhzoma's blatantly megalomaniacal nature and seething personal insecurity. His religious preoccupations were clearly leading to a merging of the person of the tlatoani with that of a deity. At the same time, his insecurity was evident in his demand to put his immediate environment under absolute control. Everywhere is his insistence on orderliness, routine, and formality. He killed without compunction for the most

Almost immediately after his enthronement, Motecuhzoma transformed himself from a man of reasoned good judgement to a pitiless autocrat. (Drawing by Keith Henderson)

minor disruptions of this closely-controlled world. His attacks on the legacy of his predecessor can be seen as a visceral reaction to a dynamic personality that seemed an enormous threat even from the grave.

Yet this same exactitude extended to the administration of justice. Motecuhzoma was merciless towards corrupt judges and was said to disguise himself to hear their verdicts. He was unusually severe in his own judgements. On one occasion when hunting he plucked a few ears of ripe maize from a peasant's garden and then entered the man's house, emptied by the terror of Motecuhzoma's name. He ordered the householder presented to him. When the man had kissed the earth in obeisance, he then straightened up and asked how the tlatoani himself was in possession of stolen corn. Shamed by the just reproof of man normally forbidden even to look upon him, Motecuhzoma removed his mantle, worth an entire village, and draped it around the shoulders of the peasant. The following day, he ordered the peasant brought to him before his court and said that this was the man who had taken his mantle. Calming the shouts of outrage, he explained, 'This miserable fellow has more courage and strength than all those here present, because he dared to tell me that I had broken my laws, and he spoke the truth.'[11]

THE CORONATION WAR

Motecuhzoma's coronation war was waged against the cities of Nopallan and Icpatepec to the south-west along the Pacific coast of Oaxaca. These cities had refused to pay tribute, thinking they could defy the Mexica as did Tlaxcallan. Before he departed, he summoned the lords of Tlatelolco and stated that just because his predecessors had remitted the tribute they owed, he would not. They were lucky he did not demand back tribute. They responded with such massive provisions for his campaign that he showed them special favours and allowed them to rebuild their temple to Huitzilopochtli. He never remitted their tribute nor anyone else's. One day into the march, Motecuhzoma ordered the Cihuacoatl to return to Tenochtitlan and execute all the tutors of his children and all the court ladies attendant upon his wives and concubines. Snake Woman returned with obvious misgivings but promptly complied with his orders. Motecuhzoma had sent spies back to the capital to ensure that this was done. In these two instances, he set the tone for his reign. He had brought the Tlatelolca to heel by demanding absolute submission; only then were they rewarded. He instilled fear with sudden and inexplicable executions, and tested the loyalty of his ministers; and he constantly checked to see if orders had been executed precisely. No remonstrations, delays or supplications were ever permitted.

Mexica scouts moving ahead of the army infiltrated Nopallan and Icpatepec at night to appraise their defences. Apparently these cities had erected significant fortifications, something unusual in Mesoamerican warfare. Moreover, the enemy chose not to contest the issue before their cities but to rely on their walls. Motecuhzoma ordered the construction of several hundred scaling ladders. Driven to excel the legendary Ahuítzotl, Motecuhzoma led the attack at Nopallan 'decked in plumes so resplendent that he appeared to be flying', and bounded up the first ladder himself and fought his way over the parapet.[12] The army followed him in a rush that flowed over the walls like a reverse waterfall, overwhelmed the enemy, and then thoroughly sacked the city. Motecuhzoma ordered the execution of everyone over the age of 50, stating that it had been the older people who had led the cities to rebellion.[13] As the lords of Nopallan abased themselves before him, he warned that he would punish any future rebellion with their extermination. The other cities in the rebellious area suffered the same fate.

Upon his return, Motecuhzoma rested at a pleasure garden outside the capital but ordered his entourage of kings and generals to proceed. He ordered Snake Woman to receive them with all the ceremony he had set out. When they had gone, he secretly boarded a canoe with six paddlers and entered the city at night. In hiding he watched that the ceremonies were carried out with commendable precision. Only then did he reveal himself.

To his coronation, Motecuhzoma invited all the kings of his enemies, and they all came, even the ruler of Michoacán. He entertained them lavishly but secretly, as had his predecessors. This time, though, not even the kings of Texcoco and Tlacopan, his theoretical equals in the Triple Alliance, were informed. The coronation was celebrated with a four-day feast, and each night there was a great dance in which the enemy kings participated. Before they emerged from their apartments, every light in the palace was put out, and they danced only to the shadowy glow of braziers. When they finished to disappear into their apartments, the torches were relit to make the palace glow like midday. On the fifth day, the sacrifice of prisoners in their thousands began. The final event was a mass hallucinogenic party as the thousands of dignitaries in attendance fed on mushrooms. After everyone had recovered, the enemy kings departed in secret and under escort, laden with rich gifts, designed for the fancy of each guest. Motecuhzoma thereafter invited his enemies to three great feasts a year. The Tlaxcallans invited him in turn, but he seldom attended in person.

HAMMERING OAXACA

The rich Mixtec region of Tototepec along the coast of Oaxaca had been under assault by the Mexica for several generations and had been much reduced in size. Motecuhzoma saw continued gains to be made after his coronation and directed his first campaigns there. On most of them, he led the army in person, determined to excel the reputation of Ahuítzotl as a commander and as a brave warrior.

His first target, however, was chosen more by greed than policy. In 1503 he heard of a small, rare *tlapalizquixochitl* tree, belonging to the Mixtec king of Tlachquiauhco. In a land already famous for its fruit trees, the king had imported this tree at great cost for its blossoms, of exquisite fragrance and incomparable beauty. Motecuhzoma determined to have it, despite that Tenochtitlan's cold climate was unsuited for such a tropical plant. Nothing of such beauty could exist without his possessing it. Motecuhzoma demanded it of Malinal, the king of Tlachquiauhco, who refused. That triggered the dispatch of an army from Tenochtitlan.

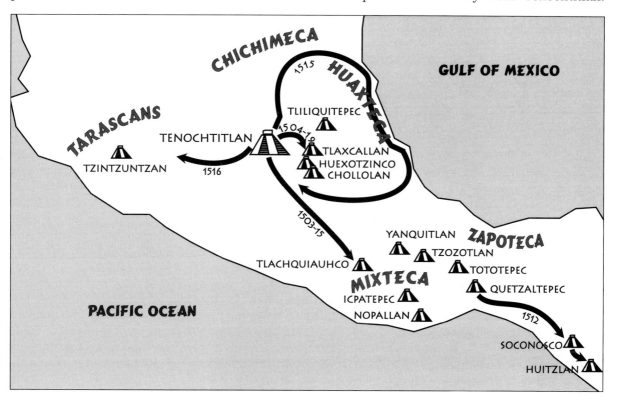

The Campaigns of Motecuhzoma II

Malinal and many of his people died defending their city which was annexed to the empire along with all its own subject towns. The tree died after it was uprooted.

Motecuhzoma restlessly looked to new opportunities for conquest in the region and was brought one by lapidaries and merchants of Tenochtitlan and Tlatelolco. These workers and dealers in precious stones appealed to him that the cost of the fine grinding sand and polishing emery from Tototepec and Quetzaltepec was far too high. Accordingly, he sent an embassy requesting the sand and emery for which he would be willing to pay, offering rich mantles. Ostensibly he was asking for an outright business transaction, but the people of the region saw it as it really was — a demand for tribute and promptly killed the ambassadors and closed its borders. Other merchants learned of the killings and brought word to the tlatoani. He sent other merchants in disguise to confirm the news.

He now mobilised a 400,000 man army for the 1505–1506 campaign season and marched directly on the two cities. Special commissary preparations were needed because of the 1,300 kilometre round trip distance. A final difficult approach march ended in the face of a river in full flood with the enemy cities safely on the other side. The force of the river disconcerted his soldiers; their frustration was not helped by the crowds of people from Tototepec and Quetzaltepec who gathered on the other side to jeer and taunt them. Motecuhzoma who 'was the enemy of lost time', was not impressed and immediately ordered balsa wood rafts and portable bridges built. The army crossed quickly at night and was breaking into Tototepec before the inhabitants knew they were there. Motecuhzoma cried havoc as his army rushed through the streets killing and burning until daylight when the men were ordered back into ranks. Aside from the 1,250 captives taken for sacrifice, only children nine years of age and younger had been spared on Motecuhzoma's orders. Quetzaltepec also fell.

The next year, 1507, much of the region was in revolt, emboldened by a severe Mexica defeat at the hands of Tlaxcallan. The cities of Yancuitlan and Tzotzollan went so far as to send challenges to Motecuhzoma. He gathered

200,000 men and rapidly marched them into the rebellious region. From the sleeping city, scouts snatched a prisoner for interrogation. The next day's attack struck the city's weaknesses and collapsed its defence. Motecuhzoma ordered its population put to the sword. The people of Tzotzollan were not slow to react and completely evacuated their city, fleeing so far that the Mexica scouts could find no trace of them.[14]

The army marched on Quetzaltepec which was again in arms against the Mexica. As usual scouts moved ahead to reconnoitre the city but could find no entry through its six sets of encircling walls. The city was now thoroughly alarmed and determined not to try the issue in open battle with the Mexica but to trust to its walls. Motecuhzoma faced a serious dilemma. Quetzaltepec was probably one of the best fortified sites in Mexico, a daunting prospect for an army unused to assaulting fortifications. Because of subsistence problems, Mesoamerican armies could not sustain long sieges. If he broke off the siege, the stronghold would remain a centre of rebellion. The solution was bold, decisive action. He ordered 200 scaling ladders built. Over three days the contingents from Tenochtitlan, Texcoco, and Tlacopan assaulted the city from three directions. Finally, under a hail of darts, arrows, and stones, assault parties scaled the walls and forced a breach through which the army poured. Only the women and children were spared. Motecuhzoma continued the march through the region, subduing many cities and dragging a growing train of prisoners. The city of Teuctepec alone yielded 2,800 sacrificial victims. Incredibly, the fighting men of Teuctepec left the protection of their four encircling walls to test the Mexica in open battle. The entire campaign stretched over 1,400 kilometres and 44 to 74 days.[15]

Another campaign was found in the Mixtec lands in the province of Amatlan in 1509, but so many men perished in a blizzard crossing a mountain range that too few remained to bring off a victory. The army's retreat only encouraged instability in an already volatile region.

In 1510 a series of heavenly apparitions appeared over Anáhuac. Their portents spread throughout the empire breeding rebellion. In

1511 Motecuhzoma had to send one army to the farthest reach of the empire, Soconusco, on the border of Guatemala. Tlachquiauhco, once sacked for its splendid tree, was wiped out, the 12,210 survivors of the city driven back to Tenochtitlan. Motecuhzoma's first conquest, Nopallan, was also reconquered yielding 140 more captives. The Mexica were successful wherever their armies confronted rebellion. By the campaign season of 1514–1515, most of these fires had been put out. New conquests were undertaken north up the Gulf Coast, gathering up the last of the Huaxteca into the empire and even attacking into the barbarous Chichimec lands further north. The obstinate kingdom of Metztitlan, which had defied his uncle, Tizoc, was fully encircled as well. The Mexica also achieved a strategic victory against the Tarascans under the command of the great Tlaxcallan captain, Tlahuicoli. Their army marched beyond Tolocan and fought a great battle on the Tarascan border. Although they did not retain the field, the Mexica took many captives and much booty. For Motecuhzoma, this battle must have been one of the sweetest of all; it restored Mexica prestige and furthered Ahuítzotl's gradual encirclement of Michoacán. Most importantly, it wiped away the defeat of his father, Axayácatl.

FLOWER WARS BECOME ARROW WARS

Victories in Oaxaca were paralleled by bitter frustrations in a series of Flowery Wars with the Mexica's traditional enemies nearer to home. Tlaxcallan, Huexotzinco, Cholollan, and Tiliuhquitepec had survived as independent states in the Puebla-Tlaxcalla Valley through their own strength and the Mexica's desire to keep them as companions in the Flowery Wars. In the years since Tlacaélel had founded the Flowery War, Mexica conquests had slowly encircled these states, especially Tlaxcallan. Motecuhzoma evidently believed this tradition had outlived its usefulness. Arrow wars for state conquest now replaced the Flowery Wars for personal prestige. Their very presence was an affront to his increasingly divine self-image as master of the world. In 1504 he attacked Tlaxcallan, beginning a conflict that would con-

tinue until the arrival of the Spaniards in 1519. The history of these wars remains confusing in detail, especially since Huexotzinco would change sides several times in that period.[16] Tlaxcallan turned back the first Mexica attack, whereupon Motecuhzoma dispatched an even larger force with no better results. These defeats encouraged the Mixtec revolts already discussed.

In one of those reversals of alliance, Motecuhzoma made war against Huexotzinco, Cholollan, and Atlixco in 1508. He called for volunteers, and the cream of the fighting men of the Triple Alliance rushed to join his expedition. Against all custom, he now sent 100,000, instead of the normal small contingent of warriors. To command the army, he picked his own younger brother, Tlacahuepan, who was joined by two more brothers. The three asked for omens, always a risky business for morale. They were all bad. Commending his family to Motecuhzoma's care, Tlacahuepan marched off.

Although, the army adhered to the etiquette of the Flowery Wars and committed only few hundred picked warriors to combat at any one time, the watching masses were clearly applying psychological pressure by displaying the might of the Alliance. Unfortunately for the Mexica, the watching masses were soon having their own morale depressed. Tlacahuepan first sent in 200 Mexica to meet a like number of men from Huexotzinco. The fighting quickly became a slaughter pen, as both sides forgot about taking prisoners. As the numbers of Mexica shrank, Tlacahuepan sent in a contingent from Texcoco. They too suffered heavily in the swirl of feathers and slashing obsidian, and were replaced by the men of Tlacopan. The Huexotzinca also rushed in replacements, and the corpses heaped the fighting ground, 'the men behaving like ferocious mountain lions drenched in blood.'

Tlacahuepan knew the moment had come for example. He embraced his brothers, 'Behold, my brothers, the time has come to show the valor of our persons! Let us go to the help of our friends!' With a shout, echoed by the battle cries of his men, he led the army into the attack. They crashed into the Huexotzinca with such force that many of the enemy were knocked down, but the Huexotzinca rebounded, held their ground, and called in reinforcements. Convinced that he was already a dead man, Tlacahuepan raged like a crazed lion among the Huexotzinca, driving so deep into their ranks that he quickly found himself cut off and surrounded. Battle madness overcame him. He hacked and slashed at everyone about him until he had left a ring of 50 Huexotzinca dead around him. When no one else would challenge him, he stood still for a moment, and the last of his frenzy drained away in utter exhaustion. 'Cease, O Huexotzinca! I see that I am yours and that I cannot defend myself. Let the combat end here! You see me here; now do what you will!' The Huexotzinca rushed to carry him off for sacrifice in their city, but he grabbed hold of the corpses demanding to be sacrificed among them. They obliged and tore his corpse to bits, every piece carried off as a relic.[17]

With their commander slain, the army recoiled. The Huexotzinca pressed hard on them, killed Tlacahuepan's brothers, and captured many lords and captains. As they returned to Huexotzinco in triumph, the Mexica crept silently into Tenochtitlan, leaving 8,200 dead on the field. They were met with mourning and lamentation and burned their weapons in shame. Then they reported to a tlatoani 'sunk in despair'. He ordered their wounds cared for and their nakedness clothed. His brothers he gave a splendid funeral. Motecuhzoma wept and complained that he did not know how he had offended the gods.

In 1515 Tlaxcallan and Huexotzinco had fallen out and now warred against each other. Tlaxcallan, now the stronger party, harried Huexotzinco so cruelly that its king and many of his people fled to Tenochtitlan for refuge where they were warmly welcomed by Motecuhzoma. He now attacked Tlaxcallan, but his army suffered a catastrophic defeat. Many were killed and captured, and all his chief captains were dragged back to Tlaxcallan as captives. Only 80 Tlaxcallan captives were taken. When this news reached him, Motecuhzoma leaped from his throne in fury and shouted:

'What is this you say? Do you know what you are saying? Are not the Aztecs filled with

The Tlaxcallan host fighting under its White Heron standard. (Drawing by Keith Henderson)

shame? Since when have you lost your vigor, your strength, like weak women? Are you just learning to take up the sword and the shield, the bow and the arrow? What has happened to all the skill acquired since the founding of this renowned city? How has it been lost to the point that I stand in shame before the entire world? Why did so many courageous lords and captains, seasoned in war, go to the battlefield? Is it possible that they have forgotten how to command their squadrons. . .? I can only believe that they were deliberately heedless in order to mock me!'[18]

The returning army was shown no honours nor even any signs of mourning. When its leaders arrived at the palace to make their report, its doors were slammed in their faces. Motecuhzoma ordered that they be publicly shamed. Royal judges went to their homes to strip them of their insignia and shear their hair. They were forbidden the right to wear cotton or wear sandals and even to enter the royal palace for a year.

The war against Tlaxcallan had yielded a single prize, however. Tlahuicoli, a famous Tlaxcallan captain of international renown, had been captured in the campaign. So impressed was he with Tlahuicoli's deeds and bearing, Motecuhzoma put him in command of an expedition against the Tarascans. Returning in victory, Tlahuicoli refused the freedom offered him by the tlatoani and demanded to be sacrificed on the gladiatorial stone. In the ensuing combat, he bashed out the brains of eight eagle and jaguar knights and wounded twenty more with his feather-edged sword, before he was cut down and his heart torn out by the Mexica high priest.

At the empire's core, the struggle for the throne of Texcoco nearly plunged the empire into civil war. Nezahualpilli left three legitimate sons but had failed to designate the heir. Motecuhzoma intervened and nominated Cacamatzin, the son of his sister. One of the other claimants, Ixtlilxochitl, refused to accept the tlatoani's high-handed interference, fled to the mountains, rallied support, seized the northern part of the kingdom, and successfully stood off the armies of Motecuhzoma and Cacamatzin. At this point, Motecuhzoma chose to cut his losses. A determined campaign to suppress

Ixtlilxochitl would have torn the Acolhua kingdom apart and fundamentally weakened a major component of the Triple Alliance. Instead, Motecuhzoma brokered a peace in which Cacamatzin was recognised as king but only of those cities he held. Ixtlilxochitl was recognised as the de facto ruler of the rest of the kingdom.

OMENS OF THE END OF THE WORLD

Already by 1509 the tight bonds Motecuhzoma had created to keep his world in place had frayed badly. Repeated campaigns in Oaxaca had not quelled the region's rebelliousness, and repeated defeats close at hand in the Flowery turned Arrow Wars were an open shame. One day, Nezahualpilli had arrived unexpectedly to seek a private meeting. Motecuhzoma was much surprised; it was not like a lord of the Triple Alliance to fail to formally announce his coming. Nezahualpilli's reputation as a seer made his words sink in with dread. He had been shown the future. 'You must be on guard, you must be warned, because I have discovered that in a very few years our cities will be ravaged and destroyed. We and our children will be killed and our vassals belittled. Of all these things you must not doubt.' As proof he had foretold that Motecuhzoma would never be victorious in his wars against Tlaxcallan, Huexotzinco, or Cholollan. 'I will add this: before many days have passed you will see signs in the sky which will appear as an omen of what I am saying.'[19]

One starry night about midnight a young priest of Huitzilopochtli awoke to relieve himself and saw a great comet that seemed to be approaching Tenochtitlan, 'bleeding fire like a wound in the eastern sky'. His shouts awakened the city, and all watched till dawn bleached it from the sky. The next night Motecuhzoma waited until midnight to see it. Its appearance filled him with such terror that he expected to die where he stood. Motecuhzoma cried out in despair asking if he, indeed, would be the one to witness the ruin of his ancestors' glory, 'all that the Mexicans had conquered by their strong right arm and by the valour and spirit that lies within their breasts?' Clearly the

Motecuhzoma II's superstitious nature quickly equated the arrival of the Spaniards in the year One Reed with the promise of Topiltzin Quetzalcoatl to return in the same year of the Mesoamerican 52-year calendar cycle. Here Motecuhzoma prays to Ehécatl, Quetzalcoatl's divine nature, in this brilliant composition by Keith Henderson.

warning had sunk to the bone; his first thought was of escape. 'What shall I do? Where shall I hide? Where can I seek cover? Oh, if only I could now turn to stone. . . before seeing that which I now await with dread.'[20] Nezahualpilli was not helpful, saying only that he had warned of this and adding that he himself would be lucky enough to die before all this came to pass. In panic, Motecuhzoma ordered all his soothsayers and astrologers to tell him the meaning of the comet. When they could not, he threw them into prison and let them die of hunger.

In 1515 Nezahualpilli died, and the omens came one after the other to crowd in upon Motecuhzoma's fears. Huitzilopochtli's temple atop its pyramid mysteriously burst into flame that not even a frantic bucket brigade could extinguish before it burnt completely. Then lightning, coming out of drizzling sky, destroyed the temple of the fire god in a seeming bolt from the sun. Following this, another comet, this one three-headed, ploughed across the sky from east to west hiding the sun. A sudden, inexplicable swell of Lake Texcoco surged through Tenochtitlan, destroying many of the poorer houses. Worst of all, a woman was heard at night, the time of greatest dread, wandering through all the districts of the city, wailing, 'O my children, you are lost; where shall I hide you?' This was seen as the goddess Cihuacoatl. The news of her shook Motecuhzoma to the core. Other omens, spawned by rumour flew about the city adding to the rising panic. Motecuhzoma summoned his new augurs, but they could answer no better than their predecessors. In blind rage he ordered them all killed, and their families as well. Even their homes were torn down to the foundations.

Legends have embroidered Motecuhzoma's increasing panic and confusion. In his pride, he had wanted to surpass his predecessors by the grandeur of his monuments and ordered that a great new sacrificial stone for the feast of the Skinning of Men be carved. After the stone was roughed out, its transportation to Tenochtitlan became a nightmare. At times it seemed to sink roots into the earth and could not be budged. At other times, many times the normal number of men were needed to drag it along. Then it spoke to the gangs, chiding them for their futility, for it would never arrive in Tenochtitlan because of Motecuhzoma's arrogance. 'Why does he want to take me? So tomorrow I can be cast down and held in contempt? Let him know that his reign has ended. Soon he will see what is to come upon him, and this will happen because he has wanted to be adored more than God Himself.' The stone then warned the workmen that harm would befall them should they try to move it, but their fear of Motecuhzoma was greater. Now the stone moved lightly until it reached a causeway bridge before Tenochtitlan. There it suddenly crashed through the tim-

bers and fell into the water dragging many of the workmen to their death. At Motecuhzoma's orders, divers searched for the stone but found nothing. Eventually the stone was found at its original site all covered with traces of the offerings and sacrifices with which it was covered when it fell into the water. Motecuhzoma travelled there, made offerings at the stone, and wept.

It is easy to see in this legend growing Mexica disquiet with Motecuhzoma. Perhaps a great stone was moved with difficulty only to crash through a bridge into the lake beyond recovery. Rumour would add the supernatural details and the proximate cause — Motecuhzoma's increasing identification of himself as a god, a great sacrilege. They would also have swept into the story the anger at his arrogance and cruelty. Many would have remembered the lessons of royal virtue taught in the schools.

'The bad ruler is a wild beast, a demon of the air, a demon, an ocelot, a wolf — infamous, deserving of being left alone, avoided, detested as a respecter of nothing, savage, revolting. He terrifies with his gaze; he makes the earth rumble; he implants, he spreads fear. He is wished dead.'[21]

The stories also embellished what was a distressingly visible panic in the tlatoani. Now thoroughly demoralised, Motecuhzoma prepared to flee Anáhuac to escape his fate. He had convinced himself that he could find refuge with Huemac, King of the Dead, in what he imagined to be a place of bliss. Sending messengers, he begged Huemac for refuge. Huemac tried to disabuse him of this fantasy and described the hideous torment of the dead. But the distraught tlatoani was insistent until the god agreed to see him. Secretly he prepared for his flight, and on the appointed night slipped out of the city in a canoe accompanied by his dwarfs, beckoned by a surreal light from Huemac's cave. At the same time, Huitzilopochtli awakened a priest and told him to intercept the tlatoani. Finding him seated and waiting for Huemac, the priest upbraids him for his cowardice. 'What is this, O mighty prince? . . . Where are you going? What would they say in Tlaxcalla? . . . Return, O Lord, to your throne and forget this folly because you dishonor us.' Then he stripped the feathers from Motecuhzoma's hair and pulled him to his feet. Shame-faced, he gazed back across the lake to see the light from the cave had gone out.[22]

FATE IN THREE PARTS

One of the bizarre stories was verifiably true. A Gulf Coast peasant had travelled to Tenochtitlan to tell Motecuhzoma of the great mountain he had seen floating on the sea. This was a Spanish ship of the Cordoba expedition of 1517. In 1518 ships of the Grijalva expedition were seen north of modern Veracruz. They were met by Motecuhzoma's local officials who presented gifts of rich mantles and received glass beads in return. These they brought to the tlatoani who suppressed information of the sightings, informing only the Eagle Council. In 1519 another fleet of ships was sighted off the Yucatán coast outside the empire. Neverthe-

The round Temple of Quetzalcoatl built by Motecuhzoma, with the Temple of Yupi Tepec behind. (Drawing courtesy © Scott Gentling, photographed by David Wharton)

less, Motecuhzoma's spies quickly brought him reports of horses, huge man-killing dogs, and cannon. They sailed north-west up the coast as relays of messengers sped to Tenochtitlan to report their progress as observed by men perched high in trees.

Apparently at this point, Motecuhzoma assumed that it was Quetzalcoatl, Lord of Great Tollan, returning from the east. It was the fateful year Ce Acatl (One Reed), the year of Quetzalcoatl's birth and of his departure across the sea in the repeating 52-year cycle of the Mesoamerican calendar. Also, major events of years under the Reed sign were to originate in the east. Already before 1519 Motecuhzoma had had a growing fascination with the cult of Quetzalcoatl. Hugh Thomas speculates that Motecuhzoma suspected that the Mexica may have erred badly by tying their fate to Huitzilopochtli and that Quetzalcoatl, the patron of Anáhuac, might have been a better choice. Shortly after his ascension to the throne, in 1502, he built a new temple to Quetzalcoatl near the Great Temple dedicated to Huitzilopochtli and Tlaloc. The temple was round, an unusual shape, since as god of the winds in one of his guises, Quetzalcoatl's currents would find easier passage around it.[23]

With this assumption, Motecuhzoma supplied the third part of his tripartite fate. The first two were already on the ships sailing along the coast. One was the Spaniard, Hernan Cortés, leader of the expedition, and one of history's bold Renaissance men — warrior of great physical and moral courage, dreamer of chivalrous adventures, and crusader. As important, he was an educated man with a keen insight into human nature that made him both a master war leader and master diplomat. The second was the Indian woman, Malinal, known as Doña Marina, the Náhuatl and Maya-speaking interpreter, given as a gift by the Maya in Yucatán. With her tongue and quick mind, she supplied to Cortés a subtle understanding of the intricacies of this new world. Motecuhzoma's assumption was the fatal third piece. For by believing Cortés to be Quetzalcoatl, Motecuhzoma utterly disarmed himself. Quetzalcoatl, as the founder of the golden age of Toltec Tollan, was the founder of Mexica imperial legitimacy; Tlacaélel's propaganda had claimed that the Mexica were simply

Malinal, called by the Spaniards Marina, the woman who changed the course of history. (Drawing by Keith Henderson)

'...They knew that, according to the signs...
If he comes on 1-Crocodile, he strikes the old men, the old women;
'If he comes on 1-Jaguar, 1-Deer, 1-Flower, he strikes at children;
'If he comes on 1-Reed, he strikes at kings...'[24]

Nevertheless, it is difficult to believe that any of his predecessors, especially, the cold-blooded Tlacaélel, would have hesitated to wipe out these invaders, superstition or not. But for Motecuhzoma, the superstitions wove a deadly enchantment.

His dread was not so deep, though, that it smothered his curiosity to ascertain exactly who these strangers were. Accordingly, he sent a delegation to the coast. They bore Cortés two gifts. The first consisted of rich presents of gold and featherwork that included the ceremonial costume of Quetzalcoatl in which they dressed Cortés. The ambassadors were to closely observe him to pick up any clues that would confirm his identity as Quetzalcoatl. Especially he was to observe if the leader ate the food presented to him. 'If he and drinks he is surely Quetzalcoatl as this will show that he is familiar with the foods of this land, that he ate them once and has come back to savor them again.' The second gift was of priceless intelligence to Cortés. It was the incredible message:

'Also tell him to allow me to die. Tell him that, after my death, he will be welcome to come here and take possession of his kingdom, as it is his. We know that he left it to be guarded by my ancestors, and I have always considered that my domain was only lent to me. Let him permit me to end my days here. Then let him return to enjoy what is his!'[25]

The Spaniards ate the Indian food with relish, and Cortés presented gifts for Motecuhzoma — a string of beads and some hardtack. The messengers rushed back to Tenochtitlan to find Motecuhzoma waiting with such apprehension that he had been unable to sleep or eat, moaning to himself, 'What will befall us? Who indeed standeth [in command]? Alas, until now, I. In great torment is my heart; as if it were washed in chili water it indeed burneth, it smarteth. Where in truth [may we go], O our lord?' Because the ambassadors had wit-

the rightful heirs of Toltec glory. That argument was now turned upon the them with deadly effect. The originator of that glory had now returned to reclaim his domain from his Mexica caretakers. In Motecuhzoma, the assumption was doubly crippling. It struck not only a ruler already predisposed to believe it by a series of terrifying omens and prophesied defeats but also a man whose rigid nature, priestly education, and innate fatalism combined to dismiss any notion to struggle with destiny. Ancient prophecies of the end of Mexica rule only increased his torment.

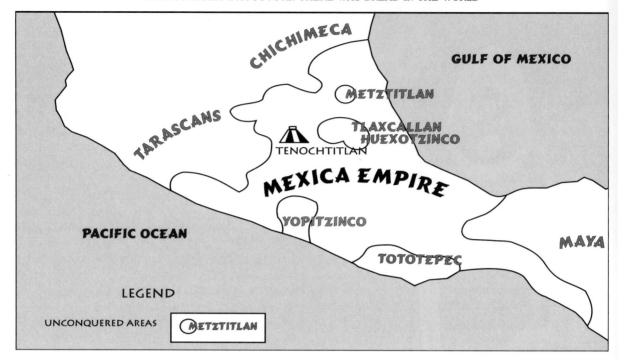

The Mexica Empire in 1519

nessed great events, he had two slaves sacrificed before them and sprinkled them with blood.[26] He questioned them on every detail, and the descriptions of the great ship, the white and black men, the huge war dogs, and the report of the cannon only fed his dread. The beads he treated reverently and had buried in the temple of Huitzilopochtli. He tasted the hardtack and said it tasted like tufa stone and then ordered it placed in a costly vessel, wrapped in rich mantles, and sent to Tollan to be buried in the temple of Quetzalcoatl. His ambassador further reported what Motecuhzoma feared most, that this possible Quetzalcoatl desired to come to Tenochtitlan to meet the tlatoani in person. 'And when Moctezuma so heard, he was much terrified. It was as if he fainted away. His heart saddened; his heart failed him.'[27]

He was now in the grip of such anxiety that he gathered his imperial council to advise him. They convened in the House of the Eagle Knights — Cacamatzin, king of Texcoco, and Totquihuatzin, king of Tlacopan; and his chief minister, Cihuacoatl, and his four chief ministers, which included his brother Cuitláhuac. This brother was blunt in opposing a soft line on the strangers. Cacamatzin, however, keyed on his uncle's apparent desire and suggested that it was unworthy to refuse to receive the ambassador of a great king. In the end, Motecuhzoma decided that everything, short of war, was to be done to ensure that the strangers did not come to Tenochtitlan. It was a fatal compromise. He then sent more embassies loaded with food and the finest gifts, including the great gold and silver wheels. He also dispatched a crowd of sorcerers to see if magic would drive the Spaniards away but to no avail. The ambassadors also bore the repeated message not to come to Tenochtitlan because the journey was too arduous and dangerous. Motecuhzoma had not reckoned that the very richness of the gifts would inspire the Spaniards to defy the hardships and dangers to reach the source of such wealth.

By this time Motecuhzoma had essentially surrendered to what he considered the inevitable. He was particularly terrified of the reports that the Spaniards asked continually what he looked like. He thanked his ambassador and said, 'my fate has been ordained and the Lord of All Created Things is venting his ire against me. Let his will be done since I cannot flee.' He could see what lay ahead. 'I beg a favour of you: after the gods have come and I have received death at their hands, and I know that they will kill me, I beg you to take charge of my children. . . . In the belief that I have surrendered the nation to the strangers, the Aztecs will take vengeance on my wives and children.'[28] He moved out of his great palace and returned to his princely mansion. Finally, he resolved to meet his fate with dignity, as Sahagún relates. '[Moctezuma] only awaited the Spaniards; he made himself resolute; he put forth great effort; he quieted, he controlled his heart; he submitted himself entirely to whatever he was to see, at which he was to marvel.'[29]

While messengers sped back and forth to the coast from Tenochtitlan, Cortés entered the Totonac city of Cempoallan and easily convinced its chief to renounce his Mexica allegiance. As Motecuhzoma agonised over the divine nature of the newcomer, Cortés had already begun to chip away at the weak joints holding the empire together. He also lost no opportunity to confuse Motecuhzoma. When five of his tax-collectors or *calpixques* entered the city and pointedly ignored the Spaniards, Cortés encouraged the terrified Totonacs to arrest them later. Then he met with them in two groups, telling each that he opposed the arrest and was seeing to their release out of the great respect he had for their master.

In early August Cortés marched inland having informed the Mexica ambassadors that he was coming to see Motecuhzoma. Spies reported every step the Spaniards took. Now the deeds of Cortés began to resemble a god's. He marched into the heart of Tlaxcallan and defeated its armies in open battle, a feat at which the Mexica had repeatedly failed. He marched into Cholollan, the sacred city of Quetzalcoatl, with his new Tlaxcallan allies and conducted a massacre that horrified all of Anáhuac. Motecuhzoma's panic had spread to the population. Tenochtitlan became a city on the edge of hysteria as this mysterious, divine doom approached. 'It was just as if the earth had moved; just as if the earth had rebelled; just as if all revolved before one's eyes. There was terror.' The Indian memory of the coming of the Spaniards still carries the ring of impending doom.

'And when there had been death in Cholulla, then [the Spaniards] started forth in order to come to Mexico. They came grouped, they came assembled, they came raising dust. Their iron lances, their halberds seemed to glisten, and the iron swords were wavy, like a water [course]. Their cuirasses, their helmets seemed to resound. And some came all in iron; they came turned into iron; they came gleaming. Hence they went causing great astonishment; hence they went causing great fear; hence they were regarded with fear; hence they were dreaded.'

'And their dogs came leading; they came preceding them. They kept coming at their head; they remained coming at their head. They came panting; their foam came dripping [from their mouths].'[30]

A final stirring against his fate caused Motecuhzoma to send a delegation to meet Cortés just beyond the Valley of Mexico, with one of his lords impersonating him with golden presents, asking futilely for the Spaniards not to enter Anáhuac. Alerted by Marina, the Spaniards saw through the trick and dismissed the false tlatoani. One final time he sent out his sorcerers to bar his way with enchantments, and once more they failed. The Indian sources described how these sorcerers encountered a drunken man on the road who told them their effort was in vain. He pointed back to the Valley where they could see Tenochtitlan in a sea of fire with the temples roaring like high torches above the general conflagration as the noise of war echoed across the Valley. In terror they fled back to Motecuhzoma.[31]

THE MEETING OF TWO WORLDS

As Motecuhzoma followed the inexorable progress of Cortés, he summoned the kings of Texcoco and Tlacopan to his palace to be with him when he welcomed the *teules* — the god-favoured ones. He moaned as he said,

'O mighty lords, it is fitting that the three of us be here to receive the gods and therefore I wish to find solace with you. I wish to greet you now and also bid farewell to you. How little we have enjoyed our realms which our ancestors bequeathed to us! They — mighty lords and

Motecuhzoma II had nearly had a hysterical break-down in fear of Cortés' arrival, but composed himself as he arrived in a magnificent litter carried by eight members of his court. (Drawing by Keith Henderson)

kings — went away in peace and harmony, free of sorrow and sadness! Woe to us! Why do we deserve this? How did we offend the gods? How did this come to pass? Whence came this calamity, this anguish? Why did this not happen in the times of our ancestors? There is only one remedy: you must make your hearts strong in order to bear what is about to happen. They are at our gates!'[32]

Now in fear of the corporal gods marching in iron to him, he lost his reverence for the etherial gods. In front of the kings, the court, and even a large number of commoners, he bitterly reproached the gods for allowing this to happen to him. Had he not served them well, he cried through tears of rage? To the people massed listening in terror, he howled that he was afraid and begged the gods to spare the poor, the orphans and widows, the children and aged. He

sacrificed and bled himself to show his innocence. Then returning to the palace he bade farewell to his wives, concubines, and children.

If Motecuhzoma had finally resolved to submit to fate and come face to face with Cortés, he at least was determined to do so in style. If for nothing else, traditions of Mexican hospitality demanded it. As the Spaniards marched up the causeway to Tenochtitlan from Ixtlapalapan, Motecuhzoma came to meet them in all the magnificent state of the tlatoani of the Mexica. A contingent of 1,000 nobles had been sent ahead to greet Cortés at the double-towered, merloned fort at Acachinanco, commanding the intersection of two causeways. This was the point where returning victorious armies were greeted, also the spot named Macuitlapilco (the tail end of the file of prisoners) where the file of victims of Ahuítzotl's mass sacrifice of 1487 had extended. Upon Cortés' approach each of them touched the earth with his right hand, kissed it, bowed, and passed on in the same order in which he had come. This took an hour and was something to see.'[33]

At a wooden bridge near the entrance to the city, a place called Xoloc, Motecuhzoma's procession met the Spanish column. No one could tell that the slight, serene figure sitting in his litter borne by eight noblemen had been in a state of hysteria only a short while before. Now he was completely composed, as coolly under control as when he had led his armies into battle as a young man. His litter was a glittering rainbow, decked with flowers. The Spaniards saw, 'the royal palanquin blazing with burnished gold. It was borne on the shoulders of nobles, and over it a canopy of gaudy featherwork, powdered with jewels, and fringed with silver, was supported by four attendants.'[34] He was accompanied by 200 barefoot lords, all more richly dressed than the first contingent met at the fort. They marched in two columns hugging the sides of the road with eyes downcast. He had eyes for none of them; his gaze was fixed ahead of him on the flashing steel armour and weapons of the Spanish and on their horses, trying to pick out the god himself.

At an appropriate distance he dismounted his litter and approached the man who could be no other than the god. Prescott described Motecuhzoma at this moment.

Right: Motecuhzoma II approaches the sacred precinct at Xoloc to meet the dreaded strangers. (Drawing by Keith Henderson)

Below: The procession of 200 lords of Motecuhzoma's court preceded his litter to his meeting with Cortés at Xoloc on the edge of the city. (Drawing by Keith Henderson)

'Montezuma wore the girdle and ample square cloak, tilmatli, of his nation. It was made of the finest cotton, with the embroidered ends gathered in a knot around his neck. His feet were defended by sandals having soles of gold, and the leathern thongs which bound them to his ankles were embossed with the same metal. Both the cloak and sandals were sprinkled with pearls and precious stones, among which the emerald and the chalchiuitl — a greenstone of higher estimation than any other among the Aztecs — were conspicuous. On his head he wore no other ornament than a panache of plumes of the royal green, which

The meeting of two worlds. Motecuhzoma II and Cortés, the tlatoani was escorted by his brother Cuitláhuac, Lord of Ixtlapalapan, and his nephew Cacamatzin, Lord of Texcoco. (Drawing by Keith Henderson)

floated down his back, the badge of military rather than regal rank.

'He was at this time about forty years of age. His person was tall and thin, but not ill made. His hair, which was black and straight, was not very long; to wear it short was considered unbecoming persons of rank. His beard was thin; his complexion somewhat paler than is often found in his dusky, or rather copper-coloured race. His features, though serious in their expression, did not wear the look of melancholy, indeed, of dejection, which characterizes his portrait, and which may well have settled on him at a later period. He moved with

The first lengthy conversation between Motecuhzoma and Cortés.

dignity, and his whole demeanour, tempered by an expression of benignity not to have been anticipated from the reports circulated of his character, was worthy of a great prince.'35

As he walked forward under his glittering canopy, his arms were supported lightly by his brother, Cuitláhuac and his nephew, Cacamatzin. Cortés had dismounted when he had seen Motecuhzoma descend from his litter, threw his reins to a page, and walked forward to meet him accompanied by his own captains.

Motecuhzoma watched as the shining god, who topped him by more than a head, strode ahead of his captains and opened wide his arms to embrace him. He did not flinch from this contact, but Cuitláhuac and Cacamatzin moved forward to restrain Cortés from the sacrilege of touching the tlatoani. Unperturbed, Cortés grasped Motecuhzoma by the hand in greeting. It was Cortés who spoke first, 'Is this not thou? Art thou not he? Art thou Moctezuma?' Motecuhzoma replied, 'Indeed, yes; I am he.' As all his lords and attendants kissed the earth in respect of the god, Motecuhzoma presented him a priceless featherwork flower, and personally placed around his neck, as a distinct honour, a golden, jewel-studded necklace and a garland of flowers. Cortés returned the gift, placing a necklace of perfumed crystals and pearls around Motecuhzoma's neck. He was much pleased by the gift and in the style of a great prince unwilling to receive a gift without giving a greater one in return. Motecuhzoma summoned a servant and, as a sign of great honour, personally hung around Cortés' neck two heavy gold necklaces, hanging with golden pendants in the shape of shrimps. Then taking him by the hand, he led him to the shrine of the goddess Toci, Our Grandmother, and motioned him to sit on one of the two royal seats placed there. The two men talked through Cortés' interpreters as thousands waited in absolute silence broken only by the sound of the water lapping against the causeway walls. There Motecuhzoma poured out his heart in a speech that must have thunderstruck the Spaniard.

'O our lord, thou hast suffered fatigue, thou has endured weariness. Thou has come to arrive on earth. Thou has come to govern thy city of Mexico; thou hast come to descend upon thy mat, upon thy seat, which for moment I have watched for thee, which I have guarded for thee. For thy governors are departed — the rulers Itzcoatl, Moctezuma the Elder, Axaya-catl, Tizoc, and Ahuitzotl, who yet a very short time ago had come to stand guard for thee, who had come to govern the city of Mexico. Under their protection thy common folk came. Do they yet perchance know it in their absence? O that one of them might witness, might marvel at what to me now hath befallen, at what I see in my sleep; I do not merely dream that I see thee, that I look into thy face. I have been afflicted for some time. I have gazed at the unknown place whence thou hast come — from among the clouds, from among the mists. And so this. The rulers departed maintaining that thou wouldst come to visit thy city, that thou wouldst come to descend upon thy mat, upon thy seat. And now it hath been fulfilled; thou has come; thou hast endured fatigue, thou hast endured weari-ness. Peace be with thee. Rest thyself. Visit thy palace. Rest thy body. May peace be with our lords.'[36]

For his part, Cortés was frank when he replied that he came as the representative of his king to persuade Motecuhzoma to accept him as his sovereign and to accept the Catholic faith.

Motecuhzoma now led the Spanish through the city in his litter to the palace of Axayácatl. The procession was led by dancers and merry-makers and saluted by delegations of black-painted priests shaking censers of fragrant copal and by the old warriors, now retired from war, in their jaguar and eagle costumes, carry-ing their shields and staffs. The procession passed magnificent buildings, mansions of the nobility, lining the street into the centre of the city, their parapets dripping with flowers from rooftop gardens. Everywhere along the street and from the rooftops, vast crowds had gath-ered to see the strangers. Their wonder stiff-ened into snarls of rage after the Spaniards passed as they watched the 6,000 Tlaxcallan allies march arrogantly through the city they hated, bearing arms. They knew they had thrown a mortal insult into the faces of the Mexica — carrying weapons into Tenochtitlan was absolutely forbidden.

Motecuhzoma was waiting in the courtyard of the palace to greet Cortés, saying, 'This is your palace, Malinche,[37] and your brethren.' He encouraged them to rest after their long jour-ney, then withdrew to allow the Spaniards to eat a princely meal from his own kitchens. He returned that afternoon and was met with great deference by Cortés. After the usual courtesies, the two got down to their first serious discus-sion. Despite his fatalism, Motecuhzoma was still desperately trying to make sense of the Spaniards. Surrounded in respectful silence by Mexica nobles and Spanish captains, he spent hours carefully asking questions about the country from where they came, of their sover-eign, and especially of the reasons for their presence in his empire. Were they of the same people that had been seen over the past two years off his coasts? He showed a special inter-est, as might have been expected, of the rank of his visitors. Were they related to their sover-eign? Cortés deftly parried these probes. As to their presence here, why, they had wanted to meet such a famous monarch and introduce him to the faith of the True Cross. As to their relationship to the sovereign, they were kins-men of each other and vassals of their king. Cortés had the uncanny ability to give answers that raised more questions than they settled. His answers can only have left Motecuhzoma more disquieted.

After distributing more largesse to every Spaniard, a habit that was quickly earning him the rank and file's affection, he ceremoniously withdrew. This affection would survive to be reflected in the Spanish accounts of the Con-quest, making of Motecuhzoma a sympathetic and tragic figure. The Conquistador, Bernal Díaz del Castillo, wrote, 'His face was some-what long, but cheerful, and he had good eyes and showed in his appearance both tenderness and, when necessary, gravity.'[38] It was totally at odds with the feelings of his own people who would have been stunned at the use of the word, 'tenderness' to describe him. What Díaz and the rest saw as tenderness was more likely a fear-induced attempt to ingratiate himself in order to stave off the dreaded fate they brought with them. Still, he oscillated between fatalism and cunning. The advice of his councillors had been divided, and those who were not as impressed with the strangers continued to urge a harder approach, especially the priesthood. These men had long ago concluded the Spaniards were not divine creatures.

Playing on Motecuhzoma's mind was the tormenting possibility that the strangers were not gods or emissaries of Quetzalcoatl after all. Yet if they were not divine, they were not entirely human. The word loosely translated as gods, *teules*, had many shades of meaning. One of them was god-favoured and invincible, much like the heroes of ancient Greece. Motecuhzoma would test them — at a distance. Perhaps as early as Cortés' entry into Tenochtitlan, he had given orders to kill a few Spaniards near Veracruz. The head of a Spaniard was duly brought to him. When it was lifted from the jar in which it had been brought by swift runner, Motecuhzoma 'turned from it with a shudder, and commanded that it should be taken from the city, and not offered at the shrine of any of his gods.'[39] Heads he had seen in plenty, but this one was of unusual size and fierceness with a great mop of curly hair. If he had looked for an answer, he had received instead an omen of dread in a pair of dead blue eyes.

Nevertheless, during the first week after Cortés' arrival, he played the humble and munificent host. The day after their arrival, Cortés played a courtesy call on Motecuhzoma in his vast palace of red tufa and marble. Over the entrance was the tlatoani's coat of arms, an eagle bearing an ocelot in its talons. Prescott's description of the palace is worth recalling.

'In the courts through which the Spaniards passed fountains of crystal water were playing, fed from the copious reservoir on the distant hill of Chapoltepec, and supplying in their turn more than a hundred baths in the interior of the palace. Crowds of Aztec nobles were sauntering up and down in these squares, and in the outer halls, loitering away their hours in attendance on the court. The apartments were of immense size, though not lofty. The ceilings were of various sorts of odoriferous wood ingeniously carved; the floors covered with mats of the palm leaf. The walls were hung with cotton richly stained, with the skins of wild animals, or gorgeous draperies of feather-work wrought in the imitation of birds, insects, and flowers, with the nice art and glowing radiance of colours that might compare with the tapestries of Flanders. Clouds of incense rolled up from the censers, and diffused intoxicating odours through the apartments.'[40]

From the end of his audience hall, he advanced to greet them with more informality and friendliness than any Indian of whatever rank had been accorded. Cortés promptly undertook to preach the Christian religion, point by theological point; 'the interpretation was conveyed through the silver tones of Marina, as inseparable from him on these occasions as his shadow.' Cortés was utterly sincere in his attempt to convert the man before him, but he was oblivious to that man's equally sin-

Motecuhzoma II ordered the killing of a few Spaniards near Veracruz about the time Cortés entered the city. Here he reacts in horror as the ferocious-looking head of one of the dead Spaniards is shown to him. (Drawing by Keith Henderson)

Motecuhzoma shows Cortés the splendours of Tenochtitlan from atop the Great Pyramid. (Drawing by Keith Henderson)

cere belief. Treading on the heels of the Spaniard's faith, however, was an unfortunate Spanish sense of legalism. As he finished his homily, Cortés addressed his Spanish companions, 'With this we have done our duty considering it is our first attempt.'[41] Motecuhzoma had listened politely but now quickly put an end to the theological lesson, '. . .we have worshipped our own gods, and thought they were good, and no doubt yours are, so do not trouble to speak to us any more about them at present.' He went on to say that his past efforts to keep them from visiting him had been based on childish stories that had terrified his vassals — that they were angry gods. He could see that they were men like any other. Laughing, he said that the Tlaxcallans surely lied to him that he was a sort of god and that his city was made of gold. Opening his robes, he showed them his bare chest and grasped his own arms, 'Behold now, Señor Malinche, my body is of flesh and bone like yours . . .' Perhaps it was after this he sent the order to kill Spaniards at Veracruz.

On the fourth day, the Spaniards asked to see the great market at Tlatelolco and the Great Temple. Motecuhzoma awaited them on the platform of the temple. He sent six priests and two nobles to help Cortés up the 100 steep steps of the pyramid. The Conquistador contemptuously waved them off and strode up unaided. At the top Motecuhzoma emerged from the temple to greet them, saying politely that they must be tired from the climb. Cortés replied, that Spaniards were never tired of anything. This utter and complete self-confidence surely did nothing for Motecuhzoma's peace of mind. For seventeen years no man had ever been as bold in his presence. Nevertheless, he took Cortés by the hand and with a sweep of his arm showed him the panorama of great Tenochtitlan, the brilliant jewel of the Americas in its lake blue setting. If Cortés had not realised the extent of the Mexica heartland, he could not have escaped it in this breathtaking moment. His men who had travelled across Europe and even to Constantinople whispered that nothing they had seen compared with the shining city in the lake. 60,000 houses spread across the water, with temples rising in white picked out with polychrome brilliance, grand palaces, the network of canals and bridges, squares, gardens, markets, adding colour and relief to the mass. The white stucco surfaces were polished to the reflective brilliance of enamel. The roof of Huitzilopochtli's temple was faced with polished obsidian that flashed in the sun. Across the lake the shoreline was crowded with more white cities and beyond were fields of gold and green, more cities, and then the wooded, snow-capped mountains and volcanoes. And the Mexica coursed through their city in numbers that set most of the Spaniards to tremble at the odds.

Cortés then asked to see the inside of the temples, and after viewing the great images of Huitzilopochtli and Tezcatlipoca and the blood encrusted walls and floors, he boldly asked if he could place a cross on the roof of the temple and a statue of the Virgin Mary to show that 'these idols of yours are not gods, but evil things that are called devils. . .' Motecuhzoma allowed himself a display of controlled anger that was nothing like the outrage of the two black-clad priests with him. Cortés had touched the one thing he would not surrender.

'If I had known that you would have said such defamatory things I would not have shown you my gods, we consider them to be very good, for they give us health and rains and good seed times and seasons and as many victories as we desire, and we are obliged to worship them and make sacrifices, and I pray you not to say another word to their dishonour.'[42]

Clearly, Cortés knew he had gone too far at that moment and suggested everyone depart. The tlatoani dismissed him, saying he had to stay and offer penance and sacrifice for the sin done in allowing the Spaniards to climb the Temple, see the gods, and insult them. Cortés descended with a little of the starch taken out of his confidence.

Right: The kidnapping of the tlatoani. Informed of the murder of the Spaniards, Cortés seized Motecuhzoma II in his own palace and carried him off to the Spanish compound in the Palace of Axayácatl. (Drawing by Keith Henderson)

THE SEIZURE OF THE TLATOANI

On the sixth day, Tlaxcallan messengers slipped into the Spanish compound with letters reporting the murder of the Spaniards near Veracruz. Already Cortés' captains had demanded he seize Motecuhzoma to prevent his turning upon them. The size and splendour of Tenochtitlan had left them sleepless in fear of just such an event, equally shared by Cortés himself. Then with a boldness that underwrote his every deed, Cortés coolly announced a visit to the tlatoani.

With Marina and 30 men he was welcomed into Motecuhzoma's presence. After a few pleasantries, Cortés began to berate his host for a series of conspiracies that led all the way back to the coast and especially for his murder of a Spaniard. There was no choice but to accompany the Spaniards back to their own compound where he would be treated as well as in his palace, 'but if you cry out or make any

disturbance you will immediately be killed, by these my captains, whom I have brought solely for this purpose.' These words staggered him. His first thought was to deny any treachery. He pulled off a signet and gave it to a messenger ordering the officer responsible for the death of the Spaniard to report to him immediately. Then remembering who he was, he tried to stand on his dignity, saying such a demand could not be given to one such as he. Cortés found his every argument parried by a better one; this was the man who had charmed the electors of the Eagle Clan with his well-reasoned words. Unfortunately, this time his skill was wasted on the grim captains. After half an hour, one of them broke in and told Cortés to either drag him off or stab him on the spot. His growl and body language cut through all the blather. Motecuhzoma asked Marina what they meant. Now this iron woman with the silver voice, became a player herself. In his own language, she made it deadly clear that he had no

choice but to come now or die. She sweetened the choice by saying that all would be made clear once he was in the Spanish compound. Now he was truly unnerved. Desperately, he offered his children in his place. 'Señor Malinche, if this is what you desire, I have a son and two legitimate daughters, take them as hostages, and do not put this affront upon me, what will my chieftains say if they see me taken off as prisoner?' Cortés was obdurate. He must come. More talk. Finally his spirit shrank to the size of his whisper in which he consented to go. Then the Spanish rattle of iron melted into sweet words of consideration, even caresses for the ruined king.

The man who whispered his own moral death was not the young tlatoani who was first over the wall at Nopallan in the glory of his coronation war. There is a telling Spanish saying, 'He was a brave man that day.' Courage waxes and wanes in each man, but weariness and fear devour physical courage, and Motecuhzoma's

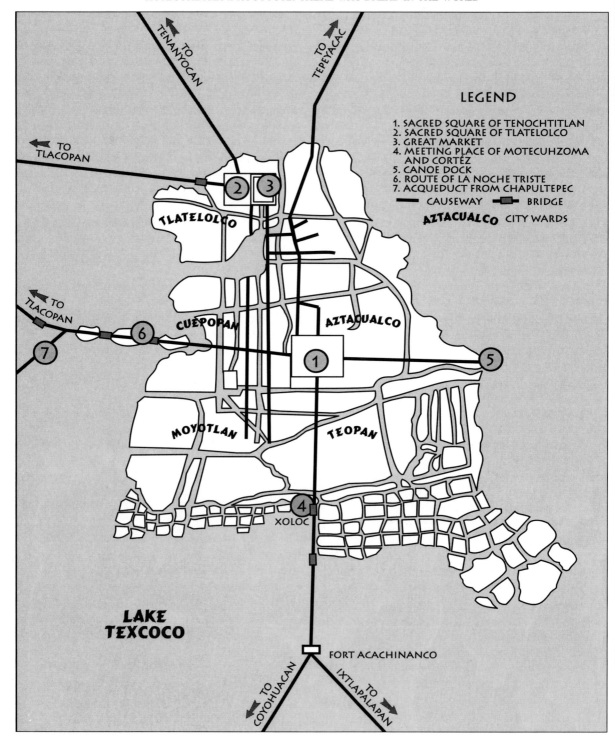

LEGEND

1. SACRED SQUARE OF TENOCHTITLAN
2. SACRED SQUARE OF TLATELOLCO
3. GREAT MARKET
4. MEETING PLACE OF MOTECUHZOMA
   AND CORTÉZ
5. CANOE DOCK
6. ROUTE OF LA NOCHE TRISTE
7. ACQUEDUCT FROM CHAPULTEPEC

━━━━ CAUSEWAY   ━◼━ BRIDGE

AZTACUALCO CITY WARDS

TO TENANYOCAN

TO TEPEYACAC

TO TLACOPAN

TLATELOLCO

TO TLACOPAN

CUÉPOPAN

AZTACUALCO

MOYOTLAN

TEOPAN

XOLOC

LAKE TEXCOCO

FORT ACACHINANCO

TO COYOHUACAN

TO IXTLAPALAPAN

Tenochtitlan in 1519

fears had been a long time simmering. Still, courage comes easier when you are the champion of your host in the glare of the sun. Now surrounded by his enemies, the fear had eaten him through. There was no courage left. It was a fear of his own special making. Within him was a doubt of himself that all the godlike trappings, all the rigid control, and all the haughtiness could not heal. And in this place, fear found a rich breeding ground. Had he been a different man, he might have died well then and there. Surely every one of his predecessors, even Tizoc, would. Old Tlacaélel would have taken a few of the Spaniards into hell with him. Nezahualcoyotl's father had thrown his life away in the flashing whirl of obsidian swords when surrounded by his enemies and offered a similar ignoble surrender. Some men do not doubt themselves. It was Motecuhzoma's irony that his entire rule was built upon a doubt. The man who set such a store by his exalted majesty failed that very majesty at the test. That was his own bitter irony; for Anáhuac, it would be a tragedy beyond all measure.

The word of his abduction had run through the palace and into the streets where crowds seemed to form out of nowhere. The Spaniards had wasted no time in summoning his litter. The stunned nobles who carried it can not have hurried, and even now Motecuhzoma could have rescued at least his reputation and shouted to his subjects to come to his aid. But he preferred the sham of a now empty pride and calmly told the crowds he was going with the Spaniards of his own free will. So passed his last chance to die well. Sahagún's Indian informants remembered the great confusion of the minutes when he was carried across the square. Spanish cannons thundered over the crowds stirring their terror.

'As if in confusion there was going off to one side, there was scattering from one's sight, a jumping in all directions. It was as if one had lost one's breath; it was as if for the time there was stupefaction, as if one was affected by mushrooms, as if something unknown were shown one. Fear prevailed. It was as if everyone had swallowed his heart. Even before it had grown dark, there was terror, there was astonishment, there was apprehension, there was the a stunning of the people.'[43]

THE TAMING OF MOTECUHZOMA

Within the palace of his father, he was allowed to pick his own gilded cage, the suite of rooms that pleased him most. To there was transferred such of his royal household as he wished. Within this cage he picked up the reins

of government, now increasingly directed by Cortés. Two weeks later arrived the lord Quauhpopoca, his son, and fifteen captains, whom the tlatoani had summoned at Cortés' demand. Motecuhzoma received him coldly and referred him to Cortés for questioning. When asked if he was Motecuhzoma's subject, Quauhpopoca replied, 'And what other sovereign could I serve?' He readily confessed to killing Spaniards and loyally did not implicate that sovereign and went so far, as Cortés himself wrote, to deny Motecuhzoma's responsibility.[44] Now it was up to Motecuhzoma to defend the actions of a faithful subordinate. It was a moment when character mattered. When the sentence of death was read out to the entire party, Motecuhzoma remained silent. Then and only then did, Quauhpopoca and his followers cry out that they had only been following the tlatoani's orders. It did not save them. They were burned at the stake in front of Motecuhzoma's palace, weapons carried from the Sacred Square's gatehouse armouries piled high around them in place of faggots.

The burning of Quauhpopoca. (Drawing by Keith Henderson)

Motecuhzoma was chained to prevent his interference with the execution of Quauhpopoca, an entirely unnecessary precaution. (Drawing by Keith Henderson)

Motecuhzoma's silence had bought him nothing but more ignominy. Cortés came to him before the execution to put him in chains while the sentence was being carried out so that the tlatoani could not interfere. Cortés could be excused out of fear of Motecuhzoma's duplicity, a prudent concern. Yet, if Motecuhzoma, would not stir to defend his own majesty and the sovereignty of his race, could he be expected to risk everything for a servant he had already abandoned? Still, he angrily wept at the state to which he had fallen, grieving for the outraged appearance of majesty when the substance had gone. Even Cortés recognised a broken and pliant man. After the execution he personally removed the fetters and told him that he loved him much and that he was free to return to his own palace. He had set his Spanish interpreter, Aguilar, to tell Motecuhzoma that though he, Cortés, wanted to release him, his captains and soldiers would not permit it. Díaz recounted Motecuhzoma's attempt to rationalise his only choice.

'He answered with great courtesy, that he thanked him for it (but he well knew that Cortés' speech was mere words), and that now at present it was better for him to stay there a prisoner, for there was danger, as his chieftains were numerous, and his nephews and relations came every day to him to say that it would be a good thing to attack and free him from prison, that as soon as they saw him outside they might drive him to it. He did not wish to see revolutions in his city, but if he did not comply with their wishes possibly they would want to set up another Prince in his place. And so he was putting those thoughts out of their heads by saying that Huichilobos (Huitzilopochtli) had sent him word that he should remain a prisoner. . . When he heard this reply, Cortés threw his arms around him and embraced him and said: "It is not in vain Señor Montezuma that I care for you as I care for myself."[45]

And well he might, for, as Díaz put it well, 'The great Montezuma had been tamed.' None knew this better than Motecuhzoma himself who felt the awe and obedience of his people begin to shrink away from him. In response he clung more closely to his captors to preserve the appearance of his majesty. They were happy to oblige with elaborate courtesy and

The Spaniards loot the Mexica treasury and melt down the gold and silver.

deference. Now Cortés began a wide-ranging survey of the empire, sending out teams of observers accompanied by members of the tlatoani's court. The wealth-producing potential of each province was recorded, and all gold and silver ordered turned over. At the same time, Cortés was breaking down the system of vassalage that held the empire together, replacing it with a more direct allegiance to the Spanish throne. Their hunger for gold drove them to drag Motecuhzoma almost literally by the hand through the city to point out its treasure houses which they looted and ransacked. They ripped the gold and silver from every object, trampling the exquisite feather work underfoot, tossing it to their Tlaxcallan henchmen, and even burning it in piles.

As the empire had suffered the same fate as the city's treasure houses, Motecuhzoma's hold on his subjects was fraying badly. His capture had left the Mexica and their vassals in a state of political paralysis. Seventeen years of Motecuhzoma's autocratic rule had conditioned an already collective society to immediate and unquestioned obedience, but daily humiliation was more than this race of conquerors could bear. Their bitterness ate away at this unquestioned obedience. Soon supplies to the Spanish compound had begun to fall off. As Motecuhzoma's own personal treasure was torn apart and stripped of its precious metal, Marina summoned all the Mexica noblemen in the palace from a vantage on the wall and ordered them to bring food, fodder, and firewood to their compound.

The first lord to offer open defiance surprisingly was Cacamatzin, King of Texcoco. This king with the reputation of being Motecuhzoma's creature was, in fact, a bold patriot. He was the first great lord to dismiss his uncle's authority. The man whose elevation was seen as the final subjugation of Acolhua independence now reasserted that independence openly. In response to the orders of both Motecuhzoma and Cortés, he replied that 'if we required anything from him we should go and get it, and that there we should see what sort of man he was and what service he was obliged to render.'[46] He was also mobilising an army. Motecuhzoma attempted to persuade him to visit him. Cacamatzin's reply was worthy of his ancestors, calling Motecuhzoma a chicken for having allowed himself to be captured, and 'that, when he did visit his capital, it would be to rescue it, as well as the emperor himself, and their common gods, from bondage. He should come, not with his hand in his bosom, but on his sword, — to drive out the detested strangers who had brought such dishonour to their country.'[47]

Motecuhzoma surrenders the sovereignty of the Mexica to the King of Spain. (Drawing by Keith Henderson)

Motecuhzoma eagerly offered a solution when Cortés asked his advice. To openly move to seize such a great lord would unleash a bloody and destructive war. Rather, Motecuhzoma suggested, let us seize him by cunning and deception. He had many servants beholden to him in Texcoco. Cacamatzin was lured to one of his palaces at Texcoco that stood half over the water of the lake. There men hidden in canoes under the palace seized him and swiftly transported him across the lake straight into the Spanish compound. He was taken first to Motecuhzoma. The young man's courage had not deserted him, and he berated his uncle for his cowardice. In anger, Motecuhzoma turned him over to Cortés who promptly clapped him in irons. The lords who had supported him, including the king of Tlacopan and his own brother, Cuitláhuac, were seized one by one to join him in chains.

Now Cortés held all three kings of the Triple Alliance. Minor Tlacopan was in no position to lead. It is tempting to speculate what subsequent course history might have taken had Cacamatzin raised the banner of open revolt and marched on Tenochtitlan. Might the Mexica have gone over to him in a rush and elected a new tlatoani? Motecuhzoma's authority was quickly decaying. It would not have survived such a dramatic catalyst of change as a warrior king in the mould of Nezahualcoyotl and Motecuhzoma I. But Motecuhzoma's collaboration cut off that channel of history. Instead, he seemed to adjust to his situation. Cortés even allowed him to offer sacrifices on the Templo Mayor and to go hunting and sailing on one of the new Spanish brigs, although in the company of 200 Spaniards with orders to kill him if he attempted to escape or raise a revolt. They never had to. He returned happily each day to his cage.

With Cacamatzin safely in hand, Cortés decided to squeeze another concession from Motecuhzoma — his formal oath of allegiance to Charles V, king of Spain. He readily acquiesced and ordered all his vassal kings and lords to assemble to witness his oath. When all the lords were met, Cortés arrived. Motecuhzoma spoke of the Quetzalcoatl legends that foretold the god's return to resume his rule over his subjects in this land. Cortés was his representative, and the time had come to restore his rule. He implored them, tears running down his face as he choked out the words,

'You have been faithful vassals of mine during the many years that I have sat on the throne of my fathers. I now expect that you will show me this last act of obedience by acknowledging the great king beyond the waters to be your lord, also, and that you will pay him tribute in the same manner as you have hitherto done to me.'[48]

Such was the drama and pathos of the scene that even the hardbitten Spaniards wept with him.

THE GODS HAVE THEIR SAY

Motecuhzoma had surrendered all the things of earthly value — power, wealth, and even the sovereignty of his people, almost gladly. Now Cortés pressed him again for the things of the spirit. Perhaps he felt that this too would follow. Accompanied by his captains, he demanded an end to human sacrifice and the removal of the idols from Huitzilopochtli's temple. The temple was to be rededicated to the Virgin Mary and a cross erected on its roof. Motecuhzoma was horrified.

'Oh, Malinche, how can you wish to destroy the city entirely! for the gods are very angry with us, and I do not know that they will stop even at your lives. What I pray you to do for the present is to be patient, and I will send to summon all the priests and I will see their reply.'

Taking Motecuhzoma aside, he suggested that if some accord were not reached, the captains would take matters into their own hands and throw the idols down. After prolonged, tense negotiations, the priests agreed to make room in the temple for an altar and a cross. With this victory, all the Spaniards ascended the temple steps and heard mass in the section of the temple, cleaned of blood, and reserved for the Virgin. In the adjoining rooms, the images of the gods still stood wreathed in incense and fed on hearts. It was not an accommodation meant to last.

Almost immediately, the Mexica priests spread the word that Huitzilopochtli and Tezcatlipoca were abandoning Anáhuac having suffered an intolerable insult by the placement of the shrine and cross. They would remain only if the strangers were killed. The priests and nobles had been coming with great frequency to confer with Motecuhzoma who now summoned Cortés to him. With more firmness than he had ever shown in the Conquistador's presence, he turned on Cortés his own ploy of blaming others for pushing him to do what he did not wish. Of course, he was distressed that the gods had told him to destroy the Spaniards. 'This, Señor Malinche, I say that you should not fail to do, for it is to your interest, if not you will be killed, remember it is a question of your lives.'[49] Cortés countered that they could not leave if they wanted to — they had no ships. He suggested that Motecuhzoma give him carpenters to build them which he readily did. Cortés secretly ordered the work to be hindered at every point to buy time. Now the Spaniards slept lightly in their armour.

Above left and above right: The Toxcatl massacre.

History was about to be diverted by another character walking onto the stage. Panfilo de Narváez had arrived with 1,300 men near Cempoallan with the express orders from the governor of Cuba to arrest Cortés. He was even able to communicate his mission to Motecuhzoma who did not inform Cortés. Motecuhzoma's spirits rose. He seemed to shake out of his fatalism. Perhaps the gods had sent these new strangers to help drive out the first.

Cortés was sure that was Narváez's intention. Informing Motecuhzoma that he must leave immediately to identify this new expedition, he left Pedro Alvarado in command of 120 Spaniards. It was a fatal choice. A giant, blond and blue-eyed, ferocious in war, and charming; the Mexica called him Tonitiuh — the Sun. It was one of Cortés' few serious mistakes. Alvarado's judgement was rash, and the man was a killer.

MASSACRE AND WAR

Motecuhzoma was visibly saddened at Cortés's imminent departure and even offered him 100,000 warriors and 30,000 bearers to help him against Narváez. Cortés charged him with the protection of the remaining Spaniards, the shrine of the Virgin, and the property and authority of the King of Spain. He had come to feel kindly for the man whom he had bullied out of his throne.

Before Cortés departed, Motecuhzoma asked of him and received permission to hold the most important of all Mexica festivals, the Toxcatl festival of renewal, dedicated to Tezcatlipoca and Huitzilopochtli. Motecuhzoma repeated this request to Alvarado who also approved it with the provision that no human sacrifice attend it and that no arms be carried. Then Alvarado panicked. Egged on by the malicious words of the Tlaxcallans, he saw a Mexica plot to murder them all in every preparation for the festival.

The morning of the dance, the flower of the Mexica nobility and its most seasoned young warriors streamed into the Sacred Square completely unarmed, eager to show themselves and their most sacred of dances to the Spaniards. The dance commenced in the large open square in front of the Great Temple and the Temple of Tezcatlipoca. Bound by the south gate, calpulli buildings, the skull rack, and a few other temples, the area was easily sealed off. Durán states that Cortés had earlier requested Motecuhzoma to summon the cream of the Mexica nobility and the most courageous men to show themselves at the festival.[50] As many as 800 of the young seasoned warriors danced to the music of the huehuetl and teponatzli drums, flutes, fifes, and conch shell horns, as several thousand more clapped and sang in accompaniment. The seasoned warriors were the elite of the Mexica; each had taken four or more prisoners in hand-to-hand combat and wore the most prized of all military

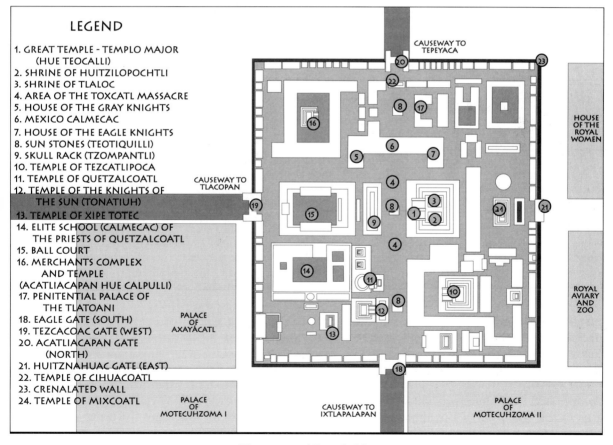

LEGEND

1. GREAT TEMPLE - TEMPLO MAJOR (HUE TEOCALLI)
2. SHRINE OF HUITZILOPOCHTLI
3. SHRINE OF TLALOC
4. AREA OF THE TOXCATL MASSACRE
5. HOUSE OF THE GRAY KNIGHTS
6. MEXICO CALMECAC
7. HOUSE OF THE EAGLE KNIGHTS
8. SUN STONES (TEOTIQUILLI)
9. SKULL RACK (TZOMPANTLI)
10. TEMPLE OF TEZCATLIPOCA
11. TEMPLE OF QUETZALCOATL
12. TEMPLE OF THE KNIGHTS OF THE SUN (TONATIUH)
13. TEMPLE OF XIPE TOTEC
14. ELITE SCHOOL (CALMECAC) OF THE PRIESTS OF QUETZALCOATL
15. BALL COURT
16. MERCHANTS COMPLEX AND TEMPLE (ACATLIACAPAN HUE CALPULLI)
17. PENITENTIAL PALACE OF THE TLATOANI
18. EAGLE GATE (SOUTH)
19. TEZCACOAC GATE (WEST)
20. ACATLIACAPAN GATE (NORTH)
21. HUITZNAHUAC GATE (EAST)
22. TEMPLE OF CIHUACOATL
23. CRENALATED WALL
24. TEMPLE OF MIXCOATL

CAUSEWAY TO TEPEYACA

CAUSEWAY TO TLACOPAN

HOUSE OF THE ROYAL WOMEN

ROYAL AVIARY AND ZOO

PALACE OF AXAYÁCATL

PALACE OF MOTECUHZOMA I

CAUSEWAY TO IXTLAPALAPAN

PALACE OF MOTECUHZOMA II

The centre of Tenochtitlan

insignia, the 'long lip-plugs and the headbands with eagle-feather tassels'.[51] For brief moments as the dance line snaked through the square, a shimmering snake of colour and movement, 'the singing resounded like waves breaking', and the full splendour of Mexica glory unfolded. The Mexica had not paid much attention to the Spaniards and Tlaxcallans assembling at the gate and around the dance area, closing off escape. As the dance reached a crescendo of ecstasy, the Mexica did not hear Alvarado shout, *'Mueran!'* ('Let them die!'). The first to die was the young dancer who led the great procession. The next to die were the priest drummers. A Spaniard leaped forward and sliced off the old man's hands at the great drum, and as he staggered back stunned, his stumps spurting blood, the next blow sent his head to tumble onto the flagstones. Now the slaughter became general as the Spaniards and Tlaxcallans converged on the dancers. Sahagún records it vividly.

'Then they all pierced the people with iron lances and they struck them each with iron swords. Of some they slashed open their backs: then their entrails gushed out. Of some they cut their heads; their heads were absolutely pulverized. And some they struck on the shoulder; they split openings . . . Of some they struck repeatedly the shanks; of some . . the thighs; of some . . . the belly; then their entrails gushed forth. And when in vain one would run he would only drag his intestines like something raw as he tried to escape. Nowhere could he go.'[52]

When they had butchered the dancers, they turned on the crowd. Some bravely, futilely tried to defend themselves with pine staves. Most died. Durán wrote, 'The dreadful screams and lamentations in that patio! And no one there to aid them!'[53] Some climbed over the walls, others feigned death in the heaps of corpses, while others fled to hide in the surrounding temple buildings where the Spaniards pursued them. Blood pooled across the polished flagstones of the square raising a great stench. While this was going on, other Spaniards killed almost all of Motecuhzoma's attendants and most of the imprisoned lords.

The Mexica had suffered a national calamity. Alvarado had massacred much of the military

and political leadership of the empire in one bloody hour. Most of the experienced military commanders at all levels, from leaders of armies to the seasoned warriors whose experience steadied the ranks, were dead. The few bloodied survivors fled out of the now unguarded gates and over the walls to disperse into the city with their tale of horror. A priest shouted the alarm. 'O brave warriors, O Mexicans, hasten here! Let there be arraying — the devices, the shields, the arrows! Come! Hasten here! Already they have died, they have perished, they have been annihilated, O Mexicans, O brave warriors!'[54]

The city now erupted in a wild, roaring frenzy; men rushed to the armouries to arm themselves as the few surviving leaders sounded the tocsin. Alvarado's men had cut their way to the top of the Great Temple and murdered all the priests. As they tried to make their way back to their compound, they met the unorganised fury of the Mexica who rushed upon them freshly armed. Other men had rushed to the temple,

Opposite page:
A priest calls the
Mexica to arms.
Right: The Mexica
relentlessly attacked
the Palace of Axayá-
catl soon after
Cortés' return.

littered with its dead priests, to beat the great throbbing drums to rouse the city. The Spaniards fought desperately through the hacking press back to the compound, pursued by sheets of missiles so thick, 'it was as if a mass of deep yellow reeds spread over the Spaniards.'[55]

Alvarado stormed into Motecuhzoma's rooms, his head streaming blood from a sling stone. He shouted for the tlatoani to see what his people had done to him, as the blood of Motecuhzoma's attendants still lay fresh on the floor. Motecuhzoma would not cringe. 'Alvarado, if you had not begun it, my men would not have done this. You have ruined yourselves and me also.'[56] Alvarado's attention was quickly turned to the mass of Mexica warriors attempting to storm the compound. The situation became so desperate, even with the help of several thousand Tlaxcallans, that Alvarado rushed back to Motecuhzoma and put a knife to his chest, ordering him to call off the storm. He climbed to the roof and spoke, saying to his people that

they were unequal to the Spaniards and to cease fighting. 'Let the arrow and shield be stilled', he said. Slowly the angry crowds of warriors broke up and left the square. Motecuhzoma had used the last of his authority. From that day onwards, he was no longer the tlatoani. As the days passed, the Spaniards could hear the keening and lamentation of a city in mourning. Sporadic fighting continued here and there, but no more assaults struck the compound. But the bridges over the canals were taken up, and it was death for a Mexica to deliver food to the compound. With Motecuhzoma a discredited ruler and most of the candidates who could have replaced him murdered, the situation hung in limbo.

Perhaps what had forced Motecuhzoma to climb to the roof that day was his recent knowledge that Cortés had defeated Narváez and was returning with both armies under his command. Outside of Texcoco, Motecuhzoma's envoys related Alvarado's outrage to the Conquistador. When he entered the city it was

deathly silent with not an inhabitant to be seen. The fury that he could not turn on Alvarado, a man needed in the coming fighting, he turned on Motecuhzoma, snubbing him when the Mexica tried to greet him in the courtyard upon his return. He had learned on his expedition that Motecuhzoma had communicated secretly with Narváez to effect

Motecuhzoma II is attacked by his own people for suggesting that they put down their arms and return to their homes because the Spaniards are more than a match for them. Their traditional awe of the tlatoani did not survive this final humiliation. (Drawing by Keith Henderson)

Cortés'arrest and his own liberation. He was even in a worse mind when Motecuhzoma requested Cortés to call upon him. He shouted, 'Go to, for a dog, who will not even keep open a market, and does not order food to be given us.' According to Díaz, his captains immediately remonstrated with him, exclaiming, 'Señor, moderate your anger and reflect how much good and honour this king of these countries has done us, who is so good that had it not been for him we should all of us be dead, and they would have eaten us, and remember that he has even given you his daughters.'[57]

Cortés did not have much time to worry about Motecuhzoma. His erstwhile subjects had suddenly appeared in vast numbers to assault the compound. The next days passed in ferocious fighting stopped only by the coming of night. The Spaniards fell into even more desperate straits as Mexica assault parties fought for lodgements on the walls while other parties sapped their foundations or smashed at the gates with improvised battering rams. Cortés clearly saw that it was only a matter of time before the Mexica overwhelmed them. He needed peace desperately and was willing to sue for it. He sent first to Motecuhzoma to ask him to address his people again from the roof and order them to desist. The messengers found him overwhelmed with grief and furious at his treatment. He said, 'What more does Malinche want of me? I neither wish to live nor to listen to him, to such a pass has my fate brought me because of him.' He then said he would not go to the roof and did not want to see Cortés or hear his lies again. Two of the Spanish leaders went to Motecuhzoma to beg him to help. Although cooped up in the compound, he had retained his sources of information. 'I believe that I shall not obtain any result towards ending this war, for they have already raised up another Lord and have made up their minds not to let you leave this place alive, therefore I believe that all of you will have to die.'[58] Desperately, they tried to convince him that they wanted to leave and would do so only if he could calm the Mexica to allow them to go. Reluctantly he agreed and climbed again to the roof. Perhaps he understood the nature of this last appearance because he clothed himself in the full regalia of the tlatoani. Attendants draped the blue and white checked mantle over his shoulders, held

by a brilliant green chalchiuitl stone. Greenstone gems sparkled from his golden jewellery, and golden-soled sandals were placed on his feet. Finally he placed on his head the imperial Toltec diadem of turquoise.

Thus attired and preceded by the golden wand of office and guarded by a group of shield-bearing Spaniards, he walked along the battlements. The noise of battle among the Mexica quickly died as he was recognised. Many of his warriors instinctively kissed earth or averted their gaze. The rest watched in expectant silence. His calm voice carried across the packed square.

'Why do I see my people here in arms against the palace of my fathers? Is it that you think your sovereign a prisoner, and wish to release him? If so, you have acted rightly. But you are mistaken. I am no prisoner. The strangers are my guests. I remain with them only from choice, and can leave them when I list. Have you come to drive them from the city? That is unnecessary. They will depart of their own accord, if you will open a way for them. Return to your homes, then. Lay down your arms. Show your obedience to me who have a right to it. The white men shall go back to their own land; and all shall be well again within the walls of Tenochtitlan.'[59]

Four Mexica captains came forward and spoke to him below the wall to tell him that they had elected his brother, Cuitláhuac, as the new tlatoani. They had pledged to Huitzilopochtli to fight the war to a finish. In these few moments, the import of Motecuhzoma's speech had sunk into the mass of his listeners. Rage shot through the vast crowd. The last tatters of respect for the tlatoani evaporated, replaced by contempt for the man who had repeatedly betrayed his nation. The mass snarled in hate, throwing once unthinkable insults up to the man on the battlements. 'Base Aztec, woman, coward, the white men have made you a woman, — fit only to weave and spin!' Then the snarls turned to action. Hands that held bows, stones, atlatls now used them. Motecuhzoma's bodyguard had dropped their shields at the crowd's initial silence and was now unprepared for the rain of missiles that fell on the party on the wall. Motecuhzoma was struck with three stones and fell to the parapet. He was quickly rushed to his apartments. Only one stone, which struck him in the head, caused serious injury, but the anger in the stone was more deadly than the substance. He simply wanted to die now. From absolute monarch, he had allowed himself to become the prisoner of an enemy, then his puppet, and finally his ally in battle against his own people. This realisation, which he had kept at bay for a long time now crushed him more utterly than the stone. As Prescott wrote so fittingly, 'He had survived his honor.' Cortés and others came to encourage him in his recovery, but he remained silent and brooding. Soon after they returned to the fighting, Motecuhzoma died.

His body was carried out by six nobles and two priests remaining in Spanish captivity, to relate how Motecuhzoma had died. This is a Spanish description of events. The Indian accounts consistently claim he was murdered by the Spanish. Durán's Indian informants insisted, even under his persistent questioning, that Motecuhzoma had survived his stoning, and in fact, the wound was almost healed. After the Spaniards had fled the city, the Mexica had entered Motecuhzoma's apartment to do him great harm in their hatred. They found him still shackled with five stab wounds in his body and the last members of his suite similarly murdered around him. In one last bloody act, for all he had done for them, the Spaniards had killed him before they fled the palace.[60]

The traditional funeral of a tlatoani was ignored as his body was simply cremated. As Sahagún wrote, 'the fire crackled, seeming to flare up, to send up many tongues of flame; many tongues of flame, many sprigs of flame seemed to rise. And Moctezuma's body seemed to lie sizzling, and it smelled foul as it burned'. And the people cried out in their anger, cursing him even in death:

'This blockhead! He terrorized the world; there was dread in the world, there was astonishment. This man! If anyone offended him only a little, he at once disposed of him. Many he punished for imagined [faults] which were not real, which were only a fabrication of words.'[61]

His subjects in their vengeance sought out his wives and children and killed all they could find. Surely they thought of the description of the bad ruler. And its last line — 'He is wished dead' had surely come to pass.

1. Fray Diego Durán, *The Aztecs: The History of the Indies of New Spain*, trans. Doris Heyden and Fernando Norcasitas, Orion Press, New York, 1964, p. 220.
2. Durán, ibid.
3. T. R. Fehrenbach, *Fire and Blood: A History of Mexico*, Da Capo Press, New York, 1995.
4. Fray Bernadino de Sahagún, *The Florentine Codex, Book 10 - The People*, Part XI, University of Utah Press, Salt Lake City, UT, 1961, p. 15.
5. *Codex Ramírez*, Editorial Leyenda, Mexico City, 1944, p. 97; quoted in Nigel Davies, *The Aztecs*, University of Oklahoma Press, Norman and London, 1989, p. 209.
6. *Codex Ramírez*, ibid., pp. 97-98.
7. Nigel Davies, *The Aztecs*, University of Oklahoma Press, Norman and London, 1989, pp. 97-98.
8. *Historia de Las Indias de Neuva España e Islas de la Tierra Firma* Durán, Vol. II, Editorial Porrúra, Mexico City, 1967, p. 404; quoted in Davies, p. 215.
9. Davies, ibid., pp. 215-216.
10. Durán, ibid., p. 224.
11. Tezozómoc, Hernando Alvarado, *Crónica Mexicana*, Editorial Leyenda, Mexico City, 1944, p. 402; in Davies, p. 213.
12. Davies, ibid., p. 217.
13. Durán, ibid. p. 228.
14. Durán, ibid., p. 237. Durán describes Cihuacoatl as the commander in this campaign or at least the part that marched on Tzotzollan. In any case, Motecuhzoma would rarely command his armies in person in the future.
15. Hassig, ibid., p. 230.
16. Durán is not helpful in presenting a clear sequence of these wars. The accounts of two different campaigns, in each of which three close relatives are killed, apparently is referring to a single operation. See accounts beginning on pages 231 and 237.
17. Durán, ibid., p. 232.
18. Durán, ibid., p. 242.
19. Durán, ibid. pp. 241.
20. Durán (Editorial Porrúra), ibid., p. 467.
21. Sahagún, *Book 10 - The People*, ibid.
22. Durán, ibid. p. 258.
23. Hugh Thomas, *Conquest: Montezuma, Cortés, and the Fall of Old Mexico*, Simon and Schuster, New York, 1993, p. 184.
24. *Codex Chimalpopoca*, trans J. Bierhorst in *Four Masterworks of American Indian Literature*, New York, 1974, p. 37; in Thomas, ibid., p. 184.
25. Durán, ibid., p. 264.

26. Sahagún, Book 12, *The Conquest of Mexico*, ibid., pp. 17-18.
27. Sahagún, Book 12, ibid., p. 20.
28. Durán, ibid., p. 275.
29. Sahagún, Book 12, ibid., p. 26.
30. Sahagún, Book 12, ibid., p. 30.
31. Thomas, ibid., p. 270. Thomas suggests that the sorcerers were experiencing the hallucegenic effects of eating sacred mushrooms.
32. Durán, ibid., p. 287.
33. Francisco López Gómora, *Cortés: The Life of the Conqueror by His Secretary*, trans. and ed. Lesley Byrd Simpson, University of California Press, Berekely, Los Angeles, London, 1964, p. 138. Gómora claims 3,000 nobles were in this ceremony against 1,000 claimed by Cortés. The latter seems more likely given that both stated the ceremony took one hour.
34. W. H. Prescott, *The Conquest of Mexico*, Vol. I, Chatto and Windus, London, 1922, p. 336.
35. Prescott, ibid., pp. 336-337.
36. Sahagún, Book 12, ibid., p. 44. The sources are divided about when Motecuhzoma delivered this speech. The Indian sources of Sahagún and Durán place it at the bridge, but Cortés places it later in the day after they had been shown to their quarters in the palace of Axayácatl. I have relied on the Indian sources here, suspecting that Motecuhzoma was probably anxious to relate what weighed so heavily upon him and would have done so on the causeway when the two sat to speak.
37. 'Malinche' meant 'Master of Malinal', the name of Cortés' Náhuatl-speaker interpreter. Cortés named her Doña Marina, but history has awarded her the name of 'Malinche' in modern Mexico, a vile epithet for betrayer.
38. Bernal Díaz del Castillo, *The Discovery and Conquest of Mexico*, Farrar, Straus and Cudahy, New York, 1956, p. 208.
39. Prescott, ibid., p. 393.
40. Prescott, ibid., Vol. I, p. 344.
41. Díaz, ibid., p. 206.
42. Díaz, ibid., p. 221.
43. Sahagún, ibid., p. 47.
44. Cortés, ibid., p. 90.
45. Díaz, ibid., p. 232.
46. Cortés, ibid., p. 97.
47. Prescott, ibid., Vol. I, p. 413.
48. Prescott, ibid., Vol. II, p. 3.
49. Díaz, ibid., p. 252.
50. Durán, ibid., p. 297. Durán states that Cortés did so to set the Mexica up for the massacre. Given Cortés' rage at Alvarado upon his return, this appears doubtful.
51. Inga Clendinnen, *The Aztecs*, Cambridge University Press, Cambridge, 1991, p. 115.
52. Sahagún, ibid., Vol. XII, p. 55.
53. Durán, ibid., p. 298.
54. Sahagún, ibid., p. 56.
55. Sahagún, ibid.
56. Thomas, ibid., p. 391.
57. Díaz, ibid., p. 299.
58. Díaz, ibid., p. 309.
59. Prescott, ibid., Vol. II, p. 81.
60. Durán, ibid., p. 305.
61. Sahagún, ibid., pp. 65-66.

8

O MEXICA, COURAGE!
(1520–1525)

CUITLÁHUAC:
THE MEXICA FIND A WARLORD (1520)

It was a gloriously beautiful morning in April of 1520. A buzz of excitement ran throughout Tenochtitlan as the city was about to celebrate the first day of the Toxcatl festival in honour of Huitzilopochtli and Tezcatlipoca. Within Axayácatl's Palace, the captive Mexica lords sensed something altogether different. The Spaniards and their Tlaxcallan creatures were palpably nervous and fully armed. In the morning most of them left the compound to attend the festival. The remaining Spaniards were even more tense. These captive lords, perhaps 20 to 30 had all been arrested in January for plotting with Caca-

Obsidian-edged sword and Mexica shield with device.

matzin, king of Texcoco, and second city of the Triple Alliance, to destroy the Spaniards. Motecuhzoma himself had permitted and even helped the Spaniards arrest them and done nothing while they were all shackled to the same long, heavy ship's chain. With Cacamatzin was also the king of Tlacopan, the third city of the Triple Alliance. Even Cuitláhuac,[1] the tlatoani's own brother and likely heir as captain general - *Tlacochcalcatl*, had not been immune.

They may have been talking about previous Toxcatls where they had danced to ecstasy for Huitzilopochtli, when the Spaniards burst in upon them with drawn daggers and swords. The defenceless lords died quickly, all except Cacamatzin who fought so furiously that the Spaniards had to stab him 47 times.[2] Only a few were spared including Cuitláhuac and the

Cihuacoatl, the empire's chief minister. At the same time Motecuhzoma witnessed the slaughter of most of his own household and attendant nobles.[3] In the nearby Sacred Square thousands of Mexica nobles and war leaders were being butchered.

For Cuitláhuac, lord of Ixtlapalapan, and eleventh son of Axayácatl, these horrendous moments were only the culmination of months of mounting Mexica humiliation, the long, drawn-out surrender of everything his father and the other empire builders of his house had achieved. As a favoured brother of the tlatoani and possible heir, he had had an important place on the Eagle Council. He had been a close observer of his brother's increasing irrational and desperate fatalism as it overwhelmed his judgement from as early as 1510 when the first of the dire omens appeared. Both brothers were part of a superstitious culture, to be sure, but Cuitláhuac had kept his wits about him. If anything, he, and not Motecuhzoma, resembled their ancestors, men of shrewd, clear-headed judgement and direct action. The strangers were clearly a band of criminal predators. At the council meeting when Motecuhzoma asked for advice Cuitláhuac summed up the opinion of the majority, 'My advice is not to allow into your house someone who will put you out of it.' His cousin, Cacamatzin, had argued against him, wishing to curry favour by supporting the tlatoani's evident desire. Now Cacamatzin's torn body lay in its own blood. In the end, the council recommended that the strangers be

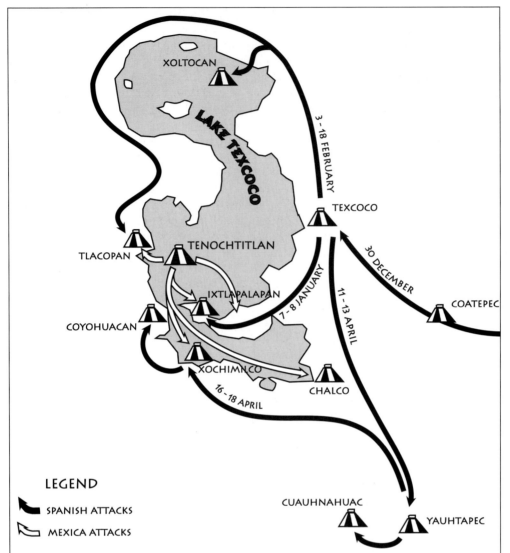

Battles preceding the siege of Tenochtitlan, 1520–1521

kept out of Tenochtitlan by every means short of an outright attack. Cuitláhuac was even dispatched at one point to intercept Alvarado and Vásquez de Tapia, who had been sent ahead by Cortés to visit Tenochtitlan, to tell them that Motecuhzoma was ill and to proceed no further.

But the Spaniards kept coming, and Motecuhzoma caved in to the inevitability of their arrival. Accordingly, when Cortés was approaching Tenochtitlan, Cuitláhuac, greeted him cordially at his own city of Ixtlapalapan, described by Cortés as a city of 12–15,000 thousand inhabitants, 'built by the side of a great salt lake, half of it on the water and the other half on dry land.' After presenting him rich presents of gold, clothing, and slave girls, Cuitláhuac offered him the hospitality of his magnificent palaces. Cortés described them in a letter to the king that they 'although yet unfinished, are as good as the best in Spain; that is, in respect of size and workmanship both in their masonry and woodwork and their floors, and furnishings for every sort of household task. . .'[4] Cortés' initial description was filled out later in the words of his secretary, Francisco López de Gómara,

'Cuitláhuac lodged the Spaniards in his house, or rather in several large palaces all of stone and woodwork, very well carved, with rooms on two floors and excellent service. The rooms were hung with many cotton drapes, rich after their fashion. The palaces were in the midst of cool gardens of flowers and fragrant trees, many paths lined with canes and covered with roses and herbs, and many ponds of sweet water. There was also a beautiful grove of fruit trees and greenery, in it a large shelter built of stone and mortar, measuring some 400 paces to the side and 1,600 roundabout, with a number of staircases leading down to the water and even to the land. The ponds were filled with all kinds of fishes, and many herons, ducks, gulls, and other birds swarmed there, at times covering the surface. . .'[5]

Cuitláhuac excused himself after seeing his guests to travel the few leagues to Tenochtitlan to attend his brother before he received Cortés. Motecuhzoma's descent into hysteria hours before the meeting must have appalled him. His meeting with the Spaniards had done nothing to change his mind of his original opinion, but the tlatoani was beyond reason at this point. Cuitláhuac was at his now-composed brother's side when he went to meet Cortés on the causeway. As the tlatoani stepped from his litter, Cuitláhuac and Cacamatzin each took an arm to formally escort him. They dropped back slightly as the two leaders approached. Then the stranger opened his arms and moved forward to embrace Motecuhzoma; the two princes reacted automatically to the sacrilegious impertinence and rushed forward to stop Cortés. After the meeting, Cuitláhuac escorted the Spaniards to their quarters in the Palace of Axayácatl.

Now the Mexica had found a warlord – Cuitláhuac, Keeper of the Kingdom.

In the days that followed as Motecuhzoma slipped into his fate-besotted surrender, the Mexica leadership moved in the other direction. Cacamatzin swung quickly around to Cuitláhuac's opinion of the Spaniards and the danger they posed. With his separate power base out of immediate Spanish reach, he renounced the subservience he had so lately given his uncle and fomented a plot to destroy the strangers. Almost all the leading men of the Mexica joined him, including Cuitláhuac. But with his fall, they were all implicated, arrested, and chained to the long ship's cable in the Palace of Axayácatl. The long months from January to April ate at Cuitláhuac's pride and at his loyalty to his brother. Like Cassandra, he had clearly identified the future and not been believed.

Cuitláhuac's clearsightedness was little comfort to him now. Death had barely passed him by but still hovered near. The news of the slaughter in the Sacred Square convinced him that desperate measures were needed. His brother, who had seemed to serve the Spaniards against his own people, was an obstacle that had to be shoved aside. Even now as the aroused warriors of the city hurled themselves against the compound's walls in their fury, the tlatoani was again pleading with them to return to their homes. The bile must have risen in Cuitláhuac's throat as once more his brother whined that the Mexica were no match for the Spaniards.

THE FIRST BATTLE OF TENOCHTITLAN, 1520

Cortés' chief concern upon his return on 24 June was to reopen the market which had shut with the Toxcatl massacre and siege. Alvarado and his force of 120 Spaniards and most of the 6,000 Tlaxcallans who entered the city in November, had already been short of food. Now Cortés had brought an additional 1,300 Spaniards and 2,000 Tlaxcallans. Motecuhzoma said it was beyond his tattered powers at this point, but one of his chief men might be able to arrange it if released. Cortés said to pick anyone, and Motecuhzoma suggested Cuitláhuac. Almost absent-mindedly Cortés agreed. Cuitláhuac walked out of the palace gate on 25 June never to return.

He immediately filled the desperate Mexica need for leadership. As *Tlacochcalcatl*, he was the expected heir. As *Tlacochcalcatl* – an experienced warrior and commander of the Mexica host - he was also the best man to lead the Mexica on the eve of battle. The Mexica at last had a bold and determined leader, a warlord. Already they had been preparing for war, but Cuitláhuac now supplied three vital elements: the firm unity of command that quickly brought order and efficiency to the preparations; the plan of operations to destroy the criminals in the Palace of Axayácatl; and the political direction and will to fight to the finish. There would be no negotiations.

Cuitláhuac's plan of operation was relatively simple: unremitting assaults on the palace compound to grind the Spaniards and Tlaxcallans down while hunger and thirst did its work inside. Vast numbers of Mexica and their allies fought in relays either in direct assaults on the compounds or against the numerous Spanish sorties. Thousands of archers and slingers filled the roofs of neighbouring buildings to keep up a constant, heavy rain of missiles on the defenders. So thick was the storm of arrows, darts, and stones into the compound that they littered its courtyard like chaff on a threshing floor. The Mexica were fully sure of victory and though they did not attack during the night, gave the defenders no peace. The lights of Mexica women and their laments searching among the slain in the dark conveyed eerie images of hell to the Spaniards. The Mexica shouted their sureness of victory through the night to unsettle those inside the compound, now half burned out from the fires shot inside. 'The gods have delivered you, at last, into our hands. Huitzilopochtli has long cried for his victims. Stones of sacrifice are ready. The knives are sharpened. The wild beasts in the palace are roaring for their offal.' They had special taunts for their old Tlaxcallan enemies, 'And the cages are waiting for the false sons of Anahuac, who are to be fattened for the festival!'[6]

One of the Spaniards inside the compound, Bernal Díaz de Castillo, whose body bore the scars of those days, wrote with glowing respect of the Mexica in battle.

'We noted their tenacity in fighting, but I declare that I do not know how to describe it, for neither cannon nor muskets nor crossbows

Mexica assaults on the Palace of Axayácatl repeatedly threatened to overwhelm the Spaniards and Tlaxcallans inside. (Drawing by Keith Henderson)

availed, nor hand-to-hand fighting, nor killing thirty or forty of them every time we charged, for they still fought on in as close ranks and with more energy than in the beginning. Sometimes when we were gaining a little ground or a part of the street, they pretended to retreat, but it was merely to induce us to follow them and cut us off from our fortress and quarters, so as to fall on us in greater safety to themselves, believing that we could not return to our quarters alive, for they did us much damage when we were retreating.

'Then, as to going out to burn their houses, I have already said that between one house and another they have wooden drawbridges, and these they raised so that we could only pass through deep water. Then we could not endure the rocks and stones hurled from the roofs, in such a way that they damaged and wounded many of our men. I do not know why I write thus, so lukewarmly, for some three or four soldiers who were there with us and who had served in Italy, swore to God many times that they had never seen such fierce fights, not even

Massed Mexica squadrons drove every sortie by the Spaniards and Tlaxcallans back into the palace compound.
(Drawing by Keith Henderson)

when they had taken part in such between Christians and against the artillery of the King of France, or of the Great Turk, nor had they seen men like those Indians with such courage in closing up their ranks.'[7]

Here Díaz was describing the type of combat in which the Spaniards and Mexica were locked. The Spaniards attempted repeated sorties to destroy the buildings from which the Mexica poured missiles into the palace and at the same time seize bridges that controlled movement throughout the city. Spanish weaponry and fighting skills usually meant they could capture these objectives, but because of their limited numbers the Mexica would swarm over their garrisons as soon as the Spanish main body left. Each Spanish sortie won a pyrrhic victory. Although many Mexica were killed, each engagement left a few more Spaniards killed and many more wounded. Casualties among the Tlaxcallans were extremely

heavy since the Mexica fought them on even terms. The Mexica and their allies easily replaced every man lost. Cuitláhuac understood that this equation was in his favour.

Still, it must have frustrated him that so much Mexica blood was required to pay for each Spanish life. It was not as if the Spanish had some innate superiority. Mexica warriors were every bit as courageous and skilful as the Spaniards, but their skills were 2,000 years out of date compared to the Spaniards. It has been said that Precolumbian Mexican civilisation was on the level of ancient Sumer and Old Kingdom Egypt. This was certainly so with military technology, and technology determines much of weapons and tactics, although technique and genius have often been a wild card. In this case, steel weapons allowed the Spanish to develop a swordsmanship that employed the thrust compared to the overhand swing required of the

Mexica obsidian-edged sword. The very act of reaching back for such a swing opened the warrior to a swift and deadly thrust, and two inches of steel will kill a man. Additionally the Spanish fought in disciplined ranks much like the Roman legion. In fact, Spanish armies in Europe were embarking on a hundred year reign of superiority by using a very Roman-like sword and buckler formation called the tercio. As with the legion, it was a lethal killing machine. The Gauls, whose metals technology was in no way inferior to the Romans and whose physical stature was indeed superior, succumbed to the same killing machine of sword thrusts. Added to their swordsmanship, the Spanish had a major firepower advantage with their cannon, arquebuses, and crossbows. These were very deadly weapons and seldom failed to kill. Mexica atlatl darts and arrows, on the other hand, were not powerful enough to penetrate Spanish steel or the quilted cotton armour of the Indians so favoured by the Spaniards for its lightness and strength.[8] However, the obsidian-edged sword made ferocious wounds against unarmoured flesh. Francisco de Aguilar wrote of the first battle with the Tlaxcallans, '. . . only two Indians were waiting for the horsemen, one on each side of the road. One Indian at a single stroke cut open the whole neck of Cristóbal de Olid's horse, killing the horse. The Indian on the other side slashed at the second horseman and the blow cut through the horse's pastern (lower leg), whereupon this horse also fell dead.'[9] Mexica missiles as well as edged weapons were more likely to cause the numerous wounds of which the Spanish complained. Only the sling stone was greatly feared for it could do more damage than any arrow as it cracked skulls or broke arms. Overall Spanish military skills were also of a high order; the centuries-long Reconquista of the Iberian Peninsula had bred the most efficiently martial race in Europe. Many of the Spaniards were veterans of wars in Italy or against the Turks. The Reconquista had also imbued the Spanish with an indomitable will to conquer and

Cuauhtémoc's name hieroglyph.

unshakeable belief in their Christian cause. Finally and not least of Cortés' advantages was the noble Spanish stallion, fit companion for a bold Conquistador, a major battlefield weapon in itself that trampled its way through the most stout-hearted band of Mexica. Nevertheless, Cuitláhuac's equation was checking Spanish skill, steel, and stallions. Time and numbers were on his side.

As the fighting raged, Cortés spied a group of resplendent Mexica directing the fighting from atop a neighbouring building. Their war costumes and shields glittered with gold and silver. One was treated with great deference. He thought he could identify Cuitláhuac and asked Motecuhzoma if that were so. Motecuhzoma's answer was vague; he thought they were relatives of whom one was the lord of Ixtlapalapan. He suggested that Cuitláhuac could not be elected tlatoani until he, Motecuhzoma, were dead. What Cortés said is not recorded, but he cannot have been pleased with himself to know that the warlord who was relentlessly dragging him to the edge of disaster had been the very man he had freed so offhandedly only days before. Neither does history record if Cuitláhuac and his party recognised Cortés across the havoc of war.

Shortly thereafter Cortés forced Motecuhzoma to order his people once more to cease their attacks. As the crowd hushed in habit from his imperial presence, four Mexica captains came to the base of the wall from which he spoke to tell him they had elected Cuitláhuac as the new tlatoani. That news may have been more crushing than the stone that struck him in the head as the crowd's reverence wore through and unleashed a hail of missiles on him.

THE BATTLE FOR THE GREAT TEMPLE

Motecuhzoma's stoning only momentarily caused a pause in the attacks. That same day

Cuitláhuac sent several captains to pry Cortés from the city by suggesting a golden bridge beckoned out of the city, a ruse whereby a trapped force will abandon its resolution and courage when an escape is offered. They brushed aside his words of conciliation and said they would continue to fight until the Spaniards had left. If the Spaniards would not leave, the Mexica would fight until they had killed them all. They recommended that the Spaniards leave the palace and depart their country. Cortés was wary, fearing the Mexica would trap his entire force on one of the causeways.

Cortés now saw that 'his life and authority depended upon his fists and stout heart,' and decided to make one more sortie to deliver such a beating to the Mexica that they would sue for peace on better terms. He led a major assault using four mobile wooden towers filled with arquebusmen and crossbowmen, four cannons pulled by Tlaxcallans, 500 Spaniards, and 3,000 more Tlaxcallan infantry. His aim was to assault by ladder the large buildings that controlled a major bridge leading out of the city. The attack collapsed as Cuitláhuac unleashed such a mass of squadrons which pressed their enemies so closely they could not even fire their weapons. The Mexica threw so many heavy stones on the towers that they broke apart. The Spanish were lucky to scurry back into the palace with only a few casualties; as usual they said nothing about Tlaxcallan losses.[10] Cuitláhuac had now hemmed Cortés in closely. From the surrounding building heights, missiles were taking an increasing toll of the defenders, especially the Tlaxcallans.

Cuitláhuac's equation, however, did not take into account the genius and valour of Cortés as a war leader. The Conquistador quickly recognised that the Templo Mayor was the key, at least temporarily, to their safety. Three times over three days he sent out strong sorties to seize it, but they all failed. Each time a major Spanish-Tlaxcallan force fought its way into the Sacred Square and assaulted up the Templo Mayor, fighting at every step and level. The Mexica had posted 500 picked men on the temple who resisted desperately, throwing their lives away to carry the Spaniards and Tlaxcallans down the stairs. Three times the Mexica repulsed the assaults. With each repulse, Mexica morale soared. Seeing that the moment called for personal leadership, Cortés led the fourth assault, a shield strapped to his wounded left hand. Preceded by the fire of crossbows and arquebuses, he led the attack against a storm of arrows, darts, stones, and even logs that carried away many of his men. Every step was contested, leaving it slippery with Mexica, Spanish, and Tlaxcallan blood. Men grappled and fell over the sides to their deaths, still clawing at each other. Finally the Spaniards and Tlaxcallans made their way to the top, killing most of the last of the garrison and throwing the priests over the side. Others threw themselves off the top rather than surrender. The idols of Huitzilopochtli and Tezcatlipoca were thrown down the steps and the temple houses set afire. The Tlaxcallans must have shouted in triumph as the temple burned, for that was the Mesoamerican symbol of a fallen city. The Mexica roared in rage, throwing away the tradition as they fell, squadron by squadron, on the Spaniards and Tlaxcallans who were trying to return to the safety of the compound. Cortés's secretary echoed the Conquistador, to gave a final salute to the fallen Mexica. 'Five hundred Indians died like brave men, and if their weapons had been equal [to ours] they would have killed more than they lost, so strong was the place and such was their courage.'[11]

Again Cortés made an offer of a truce, hoping that Mexica morale had taken a hard knock with the burning of the Great Temple. Cuitláhuac's emissaries threw it back in his teeth. They would never make peace with those who had burned their gods and killed so many of their men. They could bear their losses because they killed Spaniards while they died. They told Cortés to see the multitudes marshalled on every building and in every street. There were endless numbers to take their places, and they would gladly die twenty-five to one to rid the land of the Spaniards. If Cuitláhuac never appeared at these discus-

The battle for the Great Temple drawn by Keith Henderson captures its desperate nature.

sions with Cortés under truce, he possibly had taken to heart his late brother's unfortunate experience of Spanish good will.

Cuitláhuac's equation had to endure one more violent struggle as Cortés again sortied to drive a corridor to the Tlacopan causeway, the only one the Mexica had not broken down. The Spaniards destroyed a number of buildings to use the debris to fill in the canals, but as soon as the main body withdrew, the Mexica overran each outpost. Cuitláhuac's firm hand could be seen in the relentless application of numerical superiority. The Spaniards could seize an objective but not hold it as the Mexica swarmed around them in the open places or seeped among the buildings, throwing up barricades and walls to block Spanish cavalry and fire-power. Even in the open, he threw his squadrons at them, taking hard losses in order to wear them down. He gave them no rest as their deaths and wounds multiplied, their gun-powder ran low, and their food ran out.

Then Cortés pleaded to be allowed to depart the city within eight days and leave behind all the Mexica gold. The message was delivered by a high-ranking priest captured in one of the early forays into the Sacred Square. At the very least, it may have convinced Cuitláhuac that the Spaniards were at their last extremity. Now all he had to do was wait. Unfortunately, waiting was exactly what Cortés had decided not to do. He had been back in Tenochtitlan exactly one week. He had entered as master of the Mexica empire working through the puppet Motecuhzoma. Now all his plans were in ruins at the hands of a skilled and relentless warlord.

Upper, the Spaniards and Tlaxcallans tried to slip away at midnight during the rain. Lower, a Mexica woman sounds the alarm.

TWIN BATTLES: THE CAUSEWAY AND OTUMBA

The night of 30 June was deluged by a heavy thunderstorm followed by hail which extinguished the fires of the Mexica sentinels and dispersed them to the protection of their homes. The loss of so many experienced military leaders perhaps allowed discipline to weaken under the lash of the hail, a failure that Cuitláhuac was later to punish.[12] It was a dangerous lapse when faced with an opponent such as Cortés for whom the aphorism that 'fortune favours the bold' seems to have been coined. At midnight

under cover of the dark and rain, the Spaniards and Tlaxcallans slipped out of the ruined Palace of Axayácatl in silence. Certainly, Cuitláhuac did not consider at this point that the Spaniards would make a dash for safety. Perhaps he believed that the Spaniards could be lured out by his offer of a golden bridge. Given the Mexica love of the ruse, he may well have planned then to have trapped them on a causeway as the Spanish feared.

It was a portable wooden bridge, however, upon which the Spaniards had put their faith. The bridge, built from the palace ceiling beams and carried by Tlaxcallans, would be carried at the head of the column and placed across the first canal, allowing the entire force to cross. Then the bridge would be carried to the next canal and so on to repeat the process. Incredi-

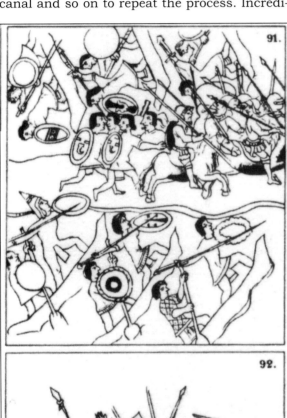

The Mexica attacked the enemy as they fled along the causeway to Tlacopan.

bly, the column was able to move unannounced through the city under the cloak of rain, crossing four intact bridges, until it reached the lake's edge where the causeway to Tlacopan began. Then a woman gathering water saw them shuffling along in the wet gloom and cried out, 'Mexica, come quickly, our enemies are leaving. Now that it is night, they are running away! As fugitives!' The alarm was then taken up by lakeside sentinels and priests keeping their vigils on their temple heights. On the pyramid of the burned-out Great Temple itself, a priest of Huitzilopochtli shouted, 'Mexican chiefs, your enemies are leaving, run to your canoes of war.'[13] The huge drums, left unmarred by the Spanish, now throbbed their alarm across the sleeping city.

The warriors were almost instantly in the streets, quickly organised, and sent to the Tlacopan causeway. Thousands filled canoes that sped through the canals and along the lake as other thousands rushed through the streets after the Spaniards. For the Spanish, it must have sounded like doom itself was upon them.

'A gathering sound was heard, like that of a mighty forest agitated by the winds. It grew louder and louder, while on the dark waters of the lake was heard a splashing noise, as of many oars. Then came a few stones and arrows striking at random among the hurrying troops. They fell every moment faster and more furious, till thickened into a terrible tempest, while the very heavens were rent with yells and war-cries of myriads of combatants, who seemed all at once to be swarming over the land and lake!'[14]

So eager were the Mexica to come to grips with the enemy that they rammed their canoes against the causeways, shattering them as they leapt onto the roadway. The column surged forward blindly as the arrow storm tormented them out of the blackness. Now they had no tactical advantage, no sword and buckler killing machine, no massed arquebus and crossbow fire. The Mexica now killed at advantage among the frightened mass, so filled with battle joy and anger that they slew instinctively. They struck them the death of criminals, blows on the back of the head.[15] The Spaniards were so desperate to escape that they fought 'only to save their own skins' when immediately threatened.

The horde of fugitives had rushed over the first break in the causeway and came to sudden halt at the second break at the Toltec Canal, the Bridge of the Massacre. The crush from behind pushed many into the water while their leaders screamed hopelessly for the portable bridge to be brought forward, but it was stuck fast in the walls of the first break.

The word spread quickly and triggered panic, well-named by Homer as 'brother to blood-stained rout.' All organisation and discipline broke down. Men jumped into the canal, only to be crushed by those falling on them. A few of the horsemen leapt in and climbed the other bank, others rolled back into the splashing mass of struggling men, animals, artillery,

The chaos and slaughter at the Toltec Canal as the crush of fugitives pushed those ahead into the water. It was here that the legendary Salto de Alvarado or Alvarado's Leap is supposed to have occurred. Trapped on the wrong side of the canal, Pedro Alvarado is reputed to have used his lance to pole vault over the writhing mass below to safety on the other side. (Drawing by Keith Henderson)

ammunition wagons, bales of loot and supplies, and the chests and straw boxes of gold. Many of the Spaniards who had loaded themselves down with gold sank to the bottom quickly. Gradually a pathway of human flesh and the debris of war substituted for the lost portable bridge, allowing survivors to cross. Dawn streaked the sky to illuminate

'The dark masses of combatants, stretching along the dike, . . . struggling for mastery, until the very causeway on which they stood appeared to tremble, and reel to and fro, as if shaken by an earthquake; while the bosom of the lake, as far as the eye could reach, was darkened by canoes crowded with warriors, whose spears and bludgeons, armed with

Above: The Mexica pursued the fleeing enemy around the lake.

Left: The aftermath of the Mexica victory on La Noche Triste. Upper, the bodies of the enemy are disposed of. Centre, the abandoned loot is carried off. Lower, the canals are searched for more treasure.

blades of "volcanic glass," gleamed in the morning light.'[16]

The Mexica had also pressed the rear of the horde on the causeway, but here the Spanish artillery had kept its nerve spewing hundreds of deaths into the Mexica ranks. But such was the determination of the Mexica that they rushed over the bodies of their dead and over the guns in a slashing tide. A knot of cavalry dashed at them to check them for only a moment, but was met by a wall of long flint-headed pikes that jabbed at them as the Mexica yelled, 'Oh! villains, are you still alive?' Now the tide surged forward again, engulfing horse and man, hacking and stabbing until the beasts and their cavaliers crashed into the roadway, spilled over into the water, or dashed to safety. Cortés himself had rushed back to the disaster from the van only to be thrown from his horse into the water. The Mexica, good swimmers, leapt in after him to seize the greatest prize of all, but again his luck held, and he was rescued by his companions.

The Battle of Otumba.

He led the survivors to the mainland and safety. To his amazement, there was no immediate pursuit of his few hundred survivors. The Mexica had lost themselves in an orgy of looting and taking prisoners of hundreds of despairing Spaniards and Tlaxcallans. Again the absence of so many experienced leaders allowed disci-

pline to break down at a critical moment. For the Mexica, the ruin of the Spanish host represented an incredible opportunity for wealth and trophies. Again the breakdown in discipline was revealed as everyone took what he pleased, instead of turning it in as the lot of the crown for redistribution by merit, a policy firmly adhered to in the past. The temptation must have been irresistible, for the wealth of empire was spilled along the causeway and in the water, as well as the steel weapons and accoutrements of perhaps a thousand Spaniards. As Cortés and his few hundred survivors panted in exhaustion and shock in Tlacopan, as many as several hundred Spaniards had made their way back to the Palace of Axayácatl where they were overwhelmed in a day or two and the survivors sacrificed to Huitzilopochtli.

The few hours that it took for Cuitláhuac to bring order out of the chaos of victory allowed the enemy to drag themselves into Tlacopan. For Cuitláhuac, now attempting to organise a pursuit, there must have been little time for satisfaction. There should have been. He had inflicted the single greatest defeat on European arms the conquest of the Americas was ever to witness. Capturing this tragedy, the Spanish named this disaster La Noche Triste (the Sad Night). The Spanish dead numbered nearly 1,000, while the Tlaxcallans perished in their thousands. Total losses for Cortés may have been as high as 5,000 Spaniards and Tlaxcallans.[17]

But the fruits of victory are gathered in the pursuit, and the Mexica were to be too slow by only hours. Warriors from surrounding towns converged on Tlacopan as the pursuit from the city began crossing the causeway. The enemy now reduced to fewer than 400 Spaniards and perhaps 2,000 Tlaxcallans limped northward around the lake harassed by Mexica and allied warriors. At the town of Otumba (Otompan) to the west of the lakes the Mexica pursuit army caught up with them. Cuitláhuac had accompanied the army, but for some reason gave command of the battle of Otumba to the Cihuacoatl. There is some evidence that the Mexica were not their usual well-ordered host.[18] Again the loss of so many leaders at the Toxcatl massacre and the fighting in the city was telling. Much of the host was also composed of Texcocan warriors and other local allies.

Now was the opportunity for the Mexica to put an end to the enemy, but they reverted to their custom of trying to take prisoners, and trying to take a resolute and skilled fighting man alive rather than killing him outright, is a far more difficult task. Mexica numbers, however, were telling as squadron after squadron crashed in relays into the tiring Spanish and Tlaxcallan ranks. From Cortés' admission as to how near the end of their tether they were, the prisoner-taking obsession of the Mexica was the thin margin upon which the Spaniards survived – that, and Cortés, legendary boldness. He charged on horseback with four companions through the Mexica ranks aiming straight at the Cihuacoatl. The Snake Woman was surveying the battle from his litter and wore the great Mexica national banner strapped to his back, unmistakable even in the rainbow of other bright costumes surrounding him. Cortés' horse struck him such a blow that he was thrown from the litter, and the standard was knocked loose. Then Juan de Salamanca drove a lance through him,

The Mexica national standard of gold and green quetzal feathers – Quetzalteopamitl.

reached down and retrieved the standard, and gave it to Cortés as his trophy. With the death of the Cihuacoatl, plainly shown by Cortés' triumphant display of the banner, the Mexica host lost heart and fled. More than a banner, in a European sense was lost; the banner in the Mesoamerican sense, housed the spirit of the divine patron of the Mexica. Cortés had not just seized a standard – he had seized the god!

PICKING UP THE PIECES

As the Spaniards disappeared towards Tlax-callan, Cuitláhuac returned to Tenochtitlan to repair the damage to his capital and restore to normalcy the world the strangers had disrupted. Despite the ominous defeat at Otumba, Cuitláhuac and the Mexica were convinced they had delivered an irretrievable blow to the Spaniards who would not return. Further campaigning was difficult because this was the height of the agricultural season, in which wars were rarely fought. Every hand was needed to till the earth and rebuild the extensive ruins Cortés had left. The Mexica were initially so amazed by their victory that they displayed the naked Spanish corpses in rows where they showed 'like white reed shoots, or white maguey shoots,' or 'white maize ears.' The Tlaxcallans they threw into the lake among the beds of reeds. The living prisoners were another matter. Several hundred Spaniards and a large number of Tlaxcallans were among those now dedicated to Huitzilopochtli and the other gods. After so much slight and insult, Huitzilopochtli was ravenous. These sacrifices and the ongoing round of festivals required the presence of the tlatoani. The formality of a coronation war was disregarded; surely the battle for Tenochtitlan had been proof enough of Cuitláhuac's fitness to rule. His coronation took place on 16 September, almost two months after the victory and perhaps an indication of the time necessary to restore the city to a minimum of normalcy for such an important event.

Despite his great victory, Cuitláhuac found himself in a much weaker position than any of his imperial forbears. Cortés had left a major wound in the Mexica imperial system that was not healing. He had struck at the foundation of the Mexica reputation for invincibility. In his months in Tenochtitlan he had worked to loosen the bonds of loyalty of the subjects of the empire. Their allegiance, for the most part, was fear-induced and was susceptible to dissolution when fear receded. Even on their retreat

The damage done to Tenochtitlan was repaired, the temples restored, and new images of the gods fashioned.

around the lake, some cities readily helped them.

Cuitláhuac quickly realised that the Spaniards were still a threat when they found refuge in Tlaxcallan. If the armies of Motecuhzoma could not defeat Tlaxcallan, Cuitláhuac's weakened forces could not do so to finish off Cortés. He tried diplomacy. His emissaries came bearing salt, cloth, and other treasures that years of Mexica blockade had deprived them of. They asked the Tlaxcallans to bury their animosity 'in oblivion' and to make common cause against those who had profaned the temples of their mutual gods. They cautioned them that they, the Mexica, had also offered the Spaniards friendship, and been given death and ashes in return. Cuitláhuac went so far as to offer the Tlaxcallans a place in the Triple Alliance on terms of equality, an unheard-of concession. They refused. It was the decision of old men, embittered by years of relentless Mexica hostility. Many of the young leaders had grown to detest and fear the Spaniards and were eager for the Mexica alliance, but the old men of Tlaxcallan could only remember the past, that the Mexica were ever 'fair in speech and false in heart.' They, who could only remember the past, refused the Mexica, and so threw away their children's future.

Cuitláhuac sought elsewhere for allies, sending emissaries to the Tarascans, the only other great power in Mexico. The Tarascan king was equally suspicious of the Mexica and recognised their extremity by the tlatoani's rich gifts. He sent out his own agents who reported that there had, indeed, been a great battle in Tenochtitlan which was filled with corpses and stank of death. His ambassador returned from Tenochtitlan and reported the fulsome reception he had received. Cuitláhuac was quick to review the situation with him, 'Look at that mountain range over there. Behind it are the people who have come from Taxcala.' He took the ambassador by canoe to Texcoco and led him to a mountain from which the entire region could be surveyed.

'You people from Mechuacán [Michoacán] will come from that way over there and we shall go this other way to catch them between us and thus kill them all. Why should we not be successful since everyone flees from you people of Mechuacán, who are such great archers? You have seen them, now take this information to your Master and tell him that we plead with him not to break our agreement. This is what we say to him, our gods have told us that Mexico City will never be destroyed, nor will our houses be burned. Two Kingdoms only are appointed, Mexico and Mechuacán. Take heed for there is much work.'[19]

They returned to Tenochtitlan where Cuitláhuac further pleaded for the Tarascans to come and fight it out in Anáhuac before the Spaniards came to them in Michoacán. But, the ruler of the Tarascans was as fearful and shortsighted as those in Tlaxcallan. No answer was set. Despite these disappoint-

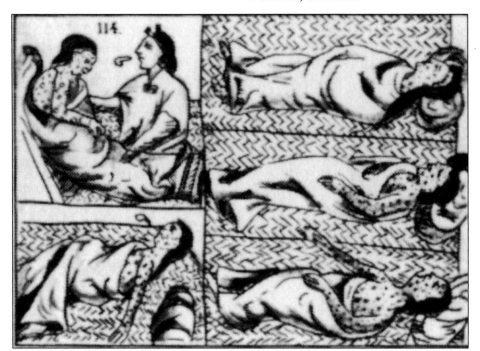

ments, Cuitláhuac worked to strengthen the defences of Tenochtitlan. Fortifications were expanded and improved; canals were widened and deepened. He also ordered more long, flint-tipped pikes made to keep off the horses of the Spanish.

A sign of the shrinking writ of Mexica authority at this time was Cuitláhuac's offer to his subject allies to remit one year's tribute if they would help hunt down and kill all Spaniards within reach. Some had done that as the fighting had raged in the city; Texcoco had overwhelmed the 40 Spaniards and 200 Tlaxcallans and sent most to Tenochtitlan for sacrifice; Tuxtepec had fallen on 77 Spaniards and 1,000 Tlaxcallans; Zultepec had killed 50 in an ambush in a ravine; Quecholac had slain 15 Spaniards in their quarters, and more died at Tépeaca; four more had been killed at Villa Rica on the coast and more at Catatami and Xalacinco.[20] Other vassals particularly outside Anáhuac, were now silent and paid their tribute late as they came to realise that Cortés had found a secure base in his Tlaxcallan alliance. These vassals were now in the gratifying position of hearing Mexica ambassadors address them in mild and conciliatory words, almost begging for help. That in itself reeked of weakness. More worrisome was the political paraly-

sis of the second pillar of the Triple Alliance, Texcoco, with its rival princes. There was little that Cuitláhuac could do to terrorise these defecting or temporising vassals. The campaign season (primarily the dry period from December to April) was still some months away.

Now in the Autumn, Cortés with some Spanish reinforcements and a large Indian army was actively subduing areas outside Tlaxcallan. To block further expansion, Cuitláhuac sent troops to block them at Tepeaca. With their vassals from Tepeaca, the Mexica issued from the city to offer battle in fields of corn and maguey. Despite a fierce initial resistance, their force was broken by a charge of a tight knot of 23 Spanish horsemen; into this confusion the Spanish and Tlaxcallan foot rushed in to rout them. The Tlaxcallans harried them from the field with great slaughter.

As this was happening smallpox was raging through Central Mexico. Brought to Mexico by one of Narváez's African slaves, Francisco de Eguía, it had already started in Cempoallan. He brought it to Tenochtitlan with him and must have been spewing its virus with every breath in the short week there before he died in the Palace of Axayácatl. The rapidity of its progress and its lethality brought public life to halt everywhere it touched. Cuitláhuac's ambassadors to the Tarascans may even had spread it there. From Sahagún's account, 'like a covering, covering-like, were the pustules,' it may have been one of the more severe forms described as confluent because the skin lesions run together and make one mass of purulent eruption. Never had the Mexicans encountered such a horror. 'There spread over people a great destruction of men.' Seemingly much of the population was stricken simultaneously and lay helpless in agony. Many died simply from hunger and the absence of basic nursing which would have pulled them through.[21] The plague killed upwards of 30 to 40 percent of the population of Anáhuac and did not subside in Tenochtitlan until 60 days had passed. The death toll in the capital may have been as high as 120,000, and in the millions in all of Central Mexico. One of the first to die, on 4 December, was the tenth tlatoani of the Mexica, Cuitláhuac, 'Keeper of the Kingdom,' the warlord and champion of his people.

An heroic and patriotic figure for any age, Cuitláhuac was fated to inherit a fatally weakened empire. A man of shrewd judgement and ability, he had opposed cooperation with Cortés from the start, regarding the Spanish band as nothing but a gang of criminals. He should be remembered for rising to the moment to strike off the chains Cortés had thought he had easily fitted on the Mexica. He had also earned a great distinction in the annals of war by inflicting the greatest single military disaster on European arms in their conquest of the Americas. Yet it was a pyrrhic victory; the implacable enemy escaped, and he could not repair the damage done to the fear-based empire both by his fate-besotted brother and the daring genius of the great Conquistador.

CUAUHTÉMOC – THE FALLING EAGLE (1520–1525)

Cuitláhuac's death left the Eagle Clan bereft of mature war leaders. His mantle fell upon a young nephew, Cuauhtémoc (Descending or Falling Eagle). He was in his early twenties, but what experience he lacked, he more than made up in spirit, determination and fighting skill. He had proved himself in the fighting after the Toxcatl massacre, leading the forces of Tlatelolco. That he had done so was not unusual; his mother was Tacapantzin, daughter of the last Tlatelolcan king, Moquihuix, slain by Axayácatl. His father was the Mexican Alexander, the tlatoani Ahuítzotl. From him he had inherited a talent for war. He had spent most of his life at Ixcateopan, in the modern state of Guerrero but appears to have moved to Tenochtitlan about 1515 where he became a leader of Tlatelolco.[22]

Apparently this young man had been picked out early by Motecuhzoma for great things. The tlatoani had given him two of his legitimate daughters in marriage, the older being Xuchimatzatzin by whom he had several children. The younger was Tecuichpo, Motecuhzoma's favourite child. Such was his position that he sat in the Eagle Council when Motecuhzoma asked for advice on what action to take regarding the strangers. Along with Cuitláhuac, he had taken a hard line. He had also not feared to criticise Motecuhzoma's moral surrender once the Spaniards had entered the city. Such a man would surely have been involved in the plot of Cacamatzin and only by sheer luck avoided arrest and imprisonment with the other lords. His luck continued to run clear when he did not attend the deadly Toxcatl Festival. He further burnished his reputation by leading the men of Tlatelolco

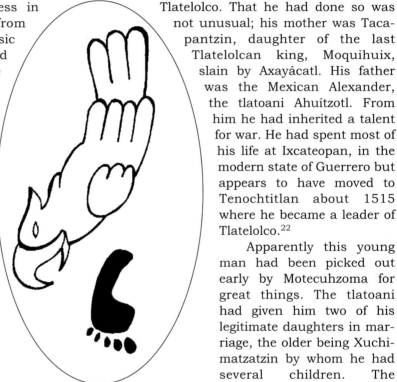

Cuauhtémoc's name hieroglyph.

in the fighting that gutted the centre of the city. He was the bold young man who denounced Motecuhzoma when he tried to order the Mexica to disperse.

'What is that which is being said by that scoundrel Motecuhzoma, whore of the Spaniards? Does he think that he can call to us, with his woman-like soul, to fight for the empire which he has abandoned out of fright. . . We did not want to obey him because already he is no longer our monarch and, indeed, we must give him the punishment which we give to a wicked man.'[23]

With that, while the Mexica captains were speaking to Motecuhzoma, the enraged young prince drew back his atlatl and loosed a dart at his uncle. The dart drew hundreds of other missiles after it from the mass of warriors, in a deluge that struck Motecuhzoma down.

In the fighting that followed over the next week, Cuauhtémoc was in the forefront, leading the men of Tlatelolco in the assaults on the Palace of Axayácatl and in the rout along the causeway. He was a symbol of implacable revenge. If Cuauhtémoc despised the Spaniards; however, they appeared to have been impressed by him. Díaz would write of him that he 'was a young man of about twenty-five years, very much of a gentleman for an Indian, and very valiant, and he made himself so feared that all his people trembled before him. . .'[24]

THE BATTLE FOR ANÁHUAC BEGINS. THE EMPIRE FRACTURES

Shortly after the Mexica defeat at Tepeaca, Cuauhtémoc was elected by the Eagle Council to succeed his uncle lately dead of smallpox. Although his coronation would not take place until February 1521, he moved quickly to secure his throne. He put to death Motecuhzoma's son, Axoacatzin, and others to crush the revival of any pro-Spanish element. He had inherited an empire in a state of convulsions. While a major expedition outside Anáhuac to hunt them down might have seemed attractive, it did not take into account the enormous political damage already done to the empire by Cortés, multiplied many times by the catastrophe of the smallpox epidemic. The deaths of so many people had winnowed the ranks of reliable and able men upon which he had to rely. Such was the need to maintain the political centre of the empire, that he did not campaign in person in any of the subsequent battles outside the city. He may also have felt that a major campaign outside Anáhuac would be highly risky. The Tlaxcallans and other allies provided Cortés with large numbers of first-rate fighting men who, in the past, had been more than a match for major Mexica armies. Moreover, such an expedition would be an enormous logistical effort at the very time when such support by his remaining vassals was not reliable. Conversely, an enemy attack on Anáhuac and Tenochtitlan in particular, would put all the logistical difficulties on the enemy's side. Cuauhtémoc thus had every reason to stay in Tenochtitlan.

Nevertheless, he now quickly moved to prevent further enemy forays by sending forces to Cuauhquecholon and Itzyocan, south of Cholollan, to block Spanish expansion through the main pass into Morelos and thereby into Anáhuac. The Mexica behaved with such wanton cruelty that four lords of Cuauhquecholon begged Cortés to drive them out. Never loath to take an opportunity to secure local allies, he first subdued a doubtful Huexotzinco on his route. He then sent a force which drove the Mexica out of Cuauhquecholon, with the help of its king, back onto their garrison at Itzyocan where they were again defeated by the pursuing Spanish. Cortés' objective in tearing away these vassals was to secure his lifeline to reinforcements coming inland from Veracruz.

These defeats dramatised Cuauhtémoc's dilemma. A major showdown outside of Anáhuac was too great a risk; however, by not actively defending the empire, its vassals would fall away or be broken one by one. Cortés was not one to let Cuauhtémoc worry too long over this dilemma. On 28 December he launched his campaign to reconquer

Opposite page: Cuauhtémoc is enthroned as the tenth tlatoani in February 1521. (Drawing by Keith Henderson)

Tenochtitlan with almost 600 Spaniards and more than 20,000 Tlaxcallans and other allies. Cuauhtémoc had had word of the expedition and had stationed a force in the mountains to ambush it, but Cortés brushed this aside at Coatepec. He marched first on Texcoco. Caca-matzin's successor, Coanacochtzin, sent a message of friendship, but he and most of the population fled across the lake to Tenochtitlan. Cortés then gave the city over to sack and massacre by the Tlaxcallans who burned its splendid palaces and the imperial libraries of the Triple Alliance. It was also here that he was joined by the disgruntled Texcocan prince, Ixtlilxochitl, and by the lords of many of the major Acolhua cities. Fully appraised of these shifts, Cuauhtémoc sent emissaries to per-suade the Acolhua lords to stay loyal, but they failed. The complete collapse of Texcoco was a major blow to Cuauhtémoc who badly mis-judged the consequences of Cortés' successful reentry into the Valley. In a few days, the sec-ond city of the Triple Alliance had been wrenched away and fought for its enemies who now controlled most of the eastern shore of the Valley of Mexico.

This reverse did not dishearten Cuauhté-moc but rather drove him to new efforts to resist the Spanish. Although, the defection of Texcoco had been a bitter blow, he fully mobilised the western half of the Valley. Smaller towns were emptied of their popula-tions which were concentrated in a few, larger, and more easily defended cities. Still loyal vassals were ordered to send warriors for the defence of Tenochtitlan, and large numbers arrived, some from as far away as the Hot Lands. It seems, though, that he did not make sufficient provision for standing siege in Tenochtitlan. This imperial city, one of the handful of great cities of the world, depended on all of Anáhuac and many provinces to keep it fed in times of peace. Sustaining such a city, now reinforced by thousands of warriors and swollen by refugees would be a near impossibility. Per-haps, Cuauhtémoc never considered that Tenochtitlan would be totally cut off from its hinterland. Its fleets of thousands of canoes would be able to circumvent any siege, he thought.

THE BATTLES OF IXTLAPALAPAN AND TLACOPAN

The canoe fleet was a weapon Cuauhtémoc now used vigorously to recapture the lakeside cities that had gone over to the Spanish. Neverthe-less, Cortés was able to counterattack and defeat each Mexica descent. Then Cortés marched on Ixtlapalapan which controlled the Chalca cities at the south-eastern end of the great lakes of the Valley and remained a staunch Mexica ally. If he could seize this city, the Chalca would shake off their allegiance to the Mexica and add their fine warriors to his host. Their allegiance would also secure his lifeline to Veracruz. But Cuauhtémoc was appraised of this march and struck at the Spanish and Tlaxcallans from land and lake at the same time. Eight thousand warriors landed to reinforce the fighting men of Ixtlapalapan and attacked the enemy two leagues outside the city while a canoe-born force landed to attack their rear. Finally the Spanish cavalry again broke the centre of the Mexica force, and their infantry poured through the shaken for-mation. The Mexica retired to the town which was half built on the water and slipped away on their canoes. The Spanish and Tlaxcallans became careless as they looted the town in an orgy of bloodshed, killing 6,000 of its inhabi-tants. They then camped in its buildings which rested on pilings in the lake. In the darkness, the Mexica broke the nearby Dike of Nezahual-coyotl which separated the salt and fresh waters of the lake. A wall of water washed through the town as terrified Spaniards, Texco-cans, and Tlaxcallans fled to dry land barely ahead of it to the jeers of the survivors of Ixtla-palapan and the Mexica. The water had spoiled the Spanish gunpowder, and now the Mexica were upon the enemy again with the dawn, their canoes emptying thousands of warriors in a major counterattack. The enemy were lucky to be able to fight their way off the peninsula and drag themselves dejectedly to Texcoco.

Despite his repulse of Cortés at Ixtlapalapan, Cuauhtémoc was essentially reacting to the Conquistador's initiatives. Next Cortés attacked from the north and drove down to Tla-copan with 30,000 Tlaxcallans and 300 Spaniards in early February. On the way he attacked the island city of Xaltocan in the northern arm of the lake system, which Cuauhtémoc had reinforced. Xaltocan was a Tenochtitlan in miniature, cut by canals attached to the mainland by a causeway. For Cortés it was a good opportunity to experiment with the assault methods he would need to reduce Tenochtitlan. The inhabitants cut the causeway which left him unable to even approach the city while being harassed by the canoe-borne enemy. Then Indians informed him the causeway had been dismantled only enough to let shallow water hide it. Cortés attacked across the sunken causeway, capturing the city, sacked it and left it in flames.

With the smoke from Xaltocan signalling Corté's approach Cuauhtémoc had emptied Cuauhtitlan, Tenanyocan (Tenayuce), and Azcapotzalco in his path and fortified Tlacopan with deep ditches and earthen ramparts. Tlacopan was the third city of the Triple Alliance, capital of the Tepaneca nation, and sat at the end of a causeway from Tenochtitlan itself. The Tepaneca remained loyal and with the Mexica

The Mexica could not withstand the charges of the Spanish horsemen in the open field. (Painting by Diego Rivera)

defended their city, but to no avail. The enemy broke them in the field under its walls and pursued them through the city as the population fled out of the opposite gates or into Tenochtitlan. While Cortés occupied the palace, the Tlaxcallans sacked and burned much of the city.

For six days he tested the strength of the causeway defences as the Mexica tested his methods as well. They taunted him, 'Do you think there is another Montezuma to let you do what you please?' Cuauhtémoc was surely an observer as the fighting coursed back and forth over the causeway, as Mexica and Tlaxcallan heroes challenged and fought each other with all the fury and style of Homer's heroes. His heart must have leapt as Cortés was once nearly overwhelmed by a Mexica ruse that sent him and his men fleeing back to their lines just ahead of capture. He also must have heard Cortés shout his offer to talk peace with him. Yet he remained silent, as his warriors replied for him that they were all lords fit to speak to Cortés. When he said they would die of hunger, they threw tortillas at him, telling him to eat if he were hungry. After six days, Cortés returned to Texcoco.

If, for the second time, Cuauhtémoc thought that he had repulsed an attack by Cortés on Tenochtitlan, he was badly mistaken. The attacks on Ixtlapalapan and Tlacopan had been grand raids and reconnaissances. Each had left a major loyal city in ashes on the outskirts of Tenochtitlan itself. Worse was to follow. The Chalca, seething for 50 years over their defeat, had been sending out numerous feelers to Cortés. Cuauhtémoc had been aware of this restiveness and had strongly garrisoned their cities. To his shock, Cortés returned eight of the captured Mexica lords he had taken when they had been driven out of those garrisons. He refused to reply to Cortés' demand for submission, recognizing that under its conciliatory words was the bitter taste of surrender. As the Spanish departed, he determined to strike quickly to reassert control over the Chalca. A 20,000-man army in 2,000 canoes darted across the lake. The Chalca called upon their old allies from Huexotzinco and together met the Mexica in battle at the end of February. This time, the Mexica met defeat solely at

Indian hands. With the loss of Chalco, the noose had tightened perceptibly around Tenochtitlan.

Cuauhtémoc watched with increasingly powerlessness as Cortés severed his communications with his remaining vassals to the south and east. The Mexica had been beaten everywhere they had met the enemy in open combat. Yet, they were adapting as best they could. They tried to engage the Spaniards on broken ground wherever possible to deny them the use of their horses and their tight fighting formations. They were also using long, flint-tipped pikes to ward off the horsemen, much as the Swiss pikemen were more successfully doing in Europe. In April Cuauhtémoc watched as Cortés cut a deeper swath through loyal vassals to the south, storming strong hilltop forts at Yauhtepec, and then seized Cuauhnáhuac, the home of the first Motecuhzoma's mother of fabled beauty. Then he struck back into the Valley of Mexico and attacked Xochimilco on 16 April. Cuauhtémoc was ready.

THE BATTLE OF XOCHIMILCO

Xochimilco was an island city like Tenochtitlan, connected to the mainland by a causeway. Cuauhtémoc had had breastworks built on the mainland covering the causeway entrance, and these were strengthened by water-filled canals. Cortés now found these defences manned by the levy of Xochimilco heavily reinforced by Mexica. More Mexica squadrons were assembled outside the defences to manoeuvre against the enemy. The Spaniards were taken aback by the hedge of Mexica spears tipped with Spanish swords captured on La Noche Triste.

Cortés attacked directly, but the Mexica repelled repeated assaults on the causeway entrance, despite the concentrated fire of his crossbows and arquebuses. The Mexica now pressed the enemy on the landward flanks of the causeway entrance. Their onset made the Spanish fight even harder, dashing through the shallow water to seize the main bridge into the city. The Xochimilca and Mexica were pressed back through the streets and over the canals of the city. Behind the Spaniards, the Indians had been breaking down the causeway to trap them. They were interrupted, run down, or lanced by Cortés and a detachment of horsemen and Tlaxcallans who were returning to the mainland to keep open their rear. Spanish horsemen on level ground were almost unbeatable, but Cortés would chivalrously give the Mexica their due, 'We found ourselves hard pressed, for they were courageous men, many of whom dared to face the horses with their shields and bucklers.'[25]

On the mainland, Cortés and his horsemen were suddenly on the receiving end of Spanish steel. The Mexica had met their charge with a hedge of pikes headed with Spanish swords. Four horses were brought down, and it was here that Cortés' own horse either foundered or was pulled to the ground by a swarm of Mexica hands. With a shout the Mexica swarmed over him. Not sharp steel, flint, or obsidian sought out his life, but countless hard hands to drag him off for sacrifice. At this moment, the Conquest hung in the balance. He could have been killed a dozen times, but Huitzilopochtli's hunger saved him from a sudden death. In that moment, a Tlaxcallan champion waded in among the Mexica with his obsidian sword and a rush of Spaniards followed to his rescue.

The Indians in Xochimilco had confused the Spanish by begging for peace in one place while continuing to fight in another. They were playing for time. Cuauhtémoc had dispatched a fleet of 2,000 canoes filled with 12,000 warriors to attack from the water while another 10,000 men attacked by land to join the large masses already hemming in the Spaniards.[26] This became evident when Cortés climbed the main temple and saw the movement of troops. By this time, the Mexica had hemmed in most of the enemy into the city's large courtyarded palaces. One determined attack broke into the compound with a hail of arrows and stones that wounded many of the enemy, but a determined counterattack wiped it out. In the night the canoe fleet landed its thousands to reinforce the defenders of the city. In the night Cortés hurried his Tlaxcallans to fill in all the breaches in the causeways with rubble and adobe from demolished buildings. La Noche Triste still haunted him, and he wanted a speedy exit out of what was more and more

clearly a trap. The next day the Mexica attacked again and again. On the mainland the Mexica reinforcements advanced, their captains waving Spanish swords and shouting, 'Spaniards, here we shall kill you with your own weapons! . . . Moctezuma is dead, and we have no one to fear when we eat you alive!' Then with a shout of 'Mexico, Mexico, Tenochtitlan, Tenochtitlan!' the host surged forward.[27] Into it crashed the Spanish horsemen with their lances couched, followed by their Tlaxcallan squadrons. The Mexica were broken and fled to the hills, suffering many dead, but they regrouped and followed after Cortés when he returned to the city.

Cuauhtémoc had been following the battle closely from Tenochtitlan. Four captive Spaniards were brought to him and revealed how few their numbers were and that most were wounded. He fed their hearts to Huitzilopochtli and sent their body parts around to the towns that had gone over to the enemy, boasting that not one of them would leave Xochimilco alive. Cuauhtémoc was clearly playing a game of attrition in a constricted combat zone. He dispatched more large contingents by canoe and land to Xochimilco, explaining to his captains that relentless attacks would so weary the Spaniards that they would eventually grow careless. Unfortunately for the Mexica, some of these captains had been captured and revealed this plan. Cortés recognised a losing hand, and ordered a retreat the next morning. First he burned the city, a conflagration that was easily seen in Tenochtitlan. The Mexica harried the retreating column, making sudden sorties from rough ground or from the canals and dikes, places where the horses could not go. The enemy entered an abandoned Coyohuacan and burned it on their way out. Along the road to Tlacopan, the Mexica lured Cortés into an ambush on rough ground, and only his swift flight saved him. Two of his pages were not so lucky and were dragged to Cuauhtémoc and sacrificed.

Although his prize had eluded him, Cuauhtémoc may have felt that his strategy of only fighting the enemy on home ground was successful. After all, he had now defeated another major attack. The battle of Xochimilco, however, had been only a tactical victory. It was very much a strategic defeat for the Mexica. Two more great loyal cities, Xochimilco and Coyohuacan, now were in ashes, joining Ixtlapalapan and Tlacopan. And Cortés had returned to his main base with his forces largely intact. For Cuauhtémoc there had been an omen in the fighting. Cortés had repeatedly escaped capture himself, chilling evidence of divine favour. Cuauhtémoc's priests were also telling him the horrifying news that the gods had become silent, and the rumours spread that they had died or abandoned their city.[28]

Cuauhtémoc had no choice but to continue to believe. He embodied the world of his nation which revolved around its gods. For good or ill the Mexica had struck their bargain long ago with Huitzilopochtli, and they would keep it. But the gods were many and multi-faceted, their attributes changing and exchanging with the moment, and all needing propitiation. In his anxiousness, he may have visited the workshop where the artists were chiselling the exquisite greenstone statuette of Quetzalcoatl he had commissioned. Quetzalcoatl was much in everyone's mind and not just because of Motecuhzoma's identification of him with Cortés. Around its base were carved glyph dates of disaster. There was 4-Wind, the date Quetzalcoatl had destroyed the previous world of the Fourth Sun, and 9-Wind, the symbol for the nine levels of hell and reeking of evil. Hugh Thomas speculates that the image 'intended to show Quetzalcoatl as a star of the night carrying the sun down to hell. The aim would presumably have been to prevent such things from occurring by a prior, ceremonial depiction of it, in stone.'[29]

THE SECOND BATTLE OF TENOCHTITLAN (1521)
BOLD HEARTS

Such propitiation had no effect on Cortés. In early May he set in motion the campaign that would settle the mastery of Anáhuac, reviewing his Spanish and Tlaxcallan host to thunderous shouts of 'Castilla Castilla, Tlaxcala Tlaxcala!' His force had grown to nine hundred Spaniards

of which almost 90 were horsemen, and about 120 were crossbowmen and arquebusiers. The rest were the deadly sword and buckler men. Each man was well-armoured to ward off Mexica weaponry. They were protected by either their own metal armour or the native quilted cotton armour. Arms, legs, and necks were also carefully protected. They had learned much. Cortés also had eighteen cannon. He had sent sample copper-headed crossbow bolts to each of the friendly cities asking for each to produce 8,000 and received 50,000 in five days. The Spanish marvelled that the craftsmanship was better than their own. At this moment, Cortés unleashed his secret weapon – thirteen flat-bottomed brigantines crewed with 300 Spaniards and each armed with a small cannon. He then summoned his Indian allies in large numbers. He divided the remaining Spaniards among three separate forces, each of approximately 150 sword and buckler men, 25-30 horsemen, artillery, and 20-30,000 Indian allies. Alvarado commanded the force which blocked the Tlacopan causeway; Gonzalo de Sandoval that which blocked the Ixtlapalapan causeway, and Cristóbal de Olid the Coyohuacan causeway. The northern causeway to Tepeyacac was ignored. Cortés had hoped that this golden bridge might tempt the Mexica out into the open where they would be more easily defeated.

Cuauhtémoc would not be tempted from his island fortress which he saw as the strength and substance of the Mexica now that his spies brought word of the attack. In fact, he had staked everything on breaking Cortés quickly on the defences of the city and the strength of his warriors. After all, he had driven Cortés away three times already. He relied entirely on this strategy; he was not prepared to withstand a lengthy siege, something exceedingly rare in Mesoamerican experience, which may explain the failure to properly provision the city. He may also have felt that the city's fleet of canoes which had free use of the lakes could easily supply the defenders. Although a young man with a young man's receptivity to new ideas, he was still a creature of a world ruled by its own strict etiquette of war and honour. Cuauhtémoc's misfortune was to be opposed by men ruled by a violent

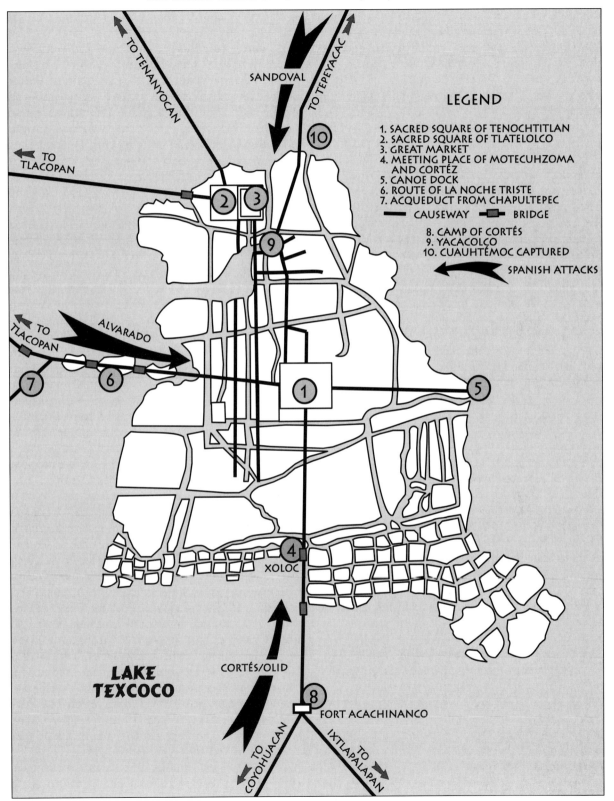

LEGEND

1. SACRED SQUARE OF TENOCHTITLAN
2. SACRED SQUARE OF TLATELOLCO
3. GREAT MARKET
4. MEETING PLACE OF MOTECUHZOMA
   AND CORTÉZ
5. CANOE DOCK
6. ROUTE OF LA NOCHE TRISTE
7. ACQUEDUCT FROM CHAPULTEPEC

CAUSEWAY —■— BRIDGE

8. CAMP OF CORTÉS
9. YACACOLCO
10. CUAUHTÉMOC CAPTURED

◀━ SPANISH ATTACKS

The Siege of Tenochtitlan

and adaptive expediency and a relentless drive. No Mesoamerican warlord with a nation to feed would have dreamt of campaigning in the midst of the intensive agricultural season, but not only was Cortés on the march but he had summoned his eager Indian allies in their scores of thousands from their own fields. This boldness would brutally intensify the problem of supplying Tenochtitlan.

Cuauhtémoc was under no illusions as to the mortal danger threatening the Mexica. Most of the empire had fallen away or been isolated. All the traditional nearby enemies of the Mexica had united with the Spaniards. The Acolhua, a pillar of the Triple Alliance, had even defected. The gods remained silent, and the end of the world of the Fifth Sun seemed to hover on the horizon. It was a time when morale can evaporate as men count the odds and sigh; many counselled peace and suggested that four captured Spaniards should not be sacrificed but given back as a gesture of accommodation. It was also a time for greatness. And to this greatness, the son of Ahuítzotl, the Lion of Anáhuac, rose. To the assembled Eagle Council, the lords, and the captains he spoke, hiding nothing of their danger. The whole land was marching upon them; their enemies had united, and their friends had deserted them. 'I charge you now to remember the bold hearts and spirits of the Aztec Chichimecs, our ancestors' who as a small tribe had descended into Anáhuac with its millions, subdued it and then the whole world. . . 'all fell into their hands.'

'They risked their lives in order to glorify our names. That is why the Aztec name has reached the renown and excellence that it now conveys and is feared throughout the world. Therefore, O valorous Aztecs, do not be dismayed, do not be cowardly. Strengthen your chests and hearts in order to succeed in the most important enterprise that has ever been presented to you. Behold, if you do not succeed, you, your wives, and children, will become slaves forever. And your possession will be stripped from you! . . .'

He had them. He could see it in their faces as he wrapped them into his will. 'Do not scorn me because of my extreme youth but consider that what I am telling you is the truth. It is your duty to defend your city and your homeland,

and I promise you that I will not yield until I give back its freedom or die.'[30]

Then he personally tore open the chests of the captured Spaniards and offered up their steaming hearts to Huitzilopochtli. With them, several thousand Indian captives were offered up as well. Now that blood spilled like rivulets down the steps of the temples again, Huitzilopochtli deigned to speak to Cuauhtémoc again, promising to help destroy his enemies. There would be no going back.

THE SIEGE BEGINS

Fortified with the assurances of his god, Cuauhtémoc was not dismayed when the forces of Olid and Alvarado promptly broke the Chapultepec aqueduct. Rather he taunted them from the city saying that their arrival only hastened the time of the sacrifice which would be pleasing to the gods, and their blood would delight the snakes, and their Christian flesh would please the tigers who had already acquired a taste for it. Then to the massed Tlaxcallans, he said:

'Ah, you cuckolds, slaves, and traitors to your gods and king! You will repent of what you are doing against your lords! For here you will die the evil death, either from hunger or our knives! Or we shall take and eat you in the greatest sacrifice and banquet ever celebrated in this country! And as a sign and reminder of it we are here tossing you the arms and legs of your own men, who were sacrificed for victory! Later we shall invade your country, raze your houses and leave not a trace of your people!'[31]

The forces of Olid and Alvarado quickly found that the causeways had been broken down in many places and barricades built. As they attempted to attack over these obstacles, the Mexica massed to oppose them and filled the lagoon on either side of the causeways with war canoes whose warriors hurled arrows, darts, and stones at them. 'The king, in his small canoe, armed with sword and shield, flew from one place to another to watch the activities of his men,' and encourage them to greater efforts. If he did not himself enter the fray, it was because 'his spirit and heart would be more useful than his hands. . .' He had demonstrated his personal prowess in the fighting in the First Battle for Tenochtitlan. As young as he was, he objectively realised that the Mexica needed a commander in chief, more than they needed another hero. The Mexica were a race of heroes.

The initial fighting on the causeways presaged much of the future combat. The Spaniards were tormented by missiles from the canoes, but pressed their assaults forward by wading through the shallow water in the causeway breaks to assault the barricades on the other side. In this they were given vital support by the crossbowmen, arquebusiers, and cannon which would decimate the Mexica defenders. Then the assault would push on against the Mexica on the causeway until another breach was encountered. The Spaniards did most of the fighting on the causeways; the space was too narrow to accommodate their numerous allies. In the fighting on the causeways, Mexica numbers were hampered by the narrow front as well. Although they could push replacements forward easily, they were vulnerable to the Spanish firepower and their deadly sword and buckler men. Nevertheless, at this point, Cuauhtémoc was fighting them to a draw.

Then Cortés upset the stalemate on 1 June. Cuauhtémoc had had word that the brigantines were about to be launched at this time, and dispatched a flotilla of 500 war canoes to intercept them. Rough weather hampered the canoes as Cortés attacked boldly. Many were wrecked as the brigantines pushed rapidly through them. The rest fled for the safety of the city's canals while Cortés sailed his ships through the breaks in the Dike of Nezahualcoyotl and straight to the fort at Acachinanco where the Coyohuacan and Ixtlapalan cause-

The fire stone at the base of the Great Temple. The Spaniards set a cannon on a similar stone before the Temple of Tetzcatlipoca, then lost it when the Mexica counter-attacked. (Drawing courtesy © Scott Gentling, photographed by David Wharton)

ways joined to form the main north-south causeway to Tenochtitlan. Cortés and 30 men leaped onto the causeway and cleared the fort of Mexica. Then he sent the brigantines to the aid of his struggling contingents on the causeways. They shot up the Mexica in the canoes forcing them off the lake or to the other side of the causeways. The Mexica causeway defenders now cut off by the fort's capture recoiled back to the city as the defenders jumped into their canoes and escaped.

On 10 June Cortés attacked down the causeway toward the city, overwhelming one breach and barricade after another. His brigantines fought along both sides of the causeway, now driving off the canoes and tormenting the Mexica in their turn. The combination of mobility and firepower represented by the brigantines accelerated the advance far beyond what Cuauhtémoc had thought possible. Finally the advance reached the last cut in the causeway and the barricade across the entrance to the city itself. The cannon shattered it, sending the warriors fleeing to the next barricade. The brigantines slid into the breach, and the Spaniards ran across their decks and through the ruined barricade.

Two more barricades were forced along the main thoroughfare down which Cortés had marched in triumph on that 8th of November so long ago in 1519. His Indian allies were in the city in large numbers as well. The Spaniards broke into the main square with such speed that the Mexica panicked, and many fled into the adjacent Sacred Square. The Tlaxcallans and Chalca pursued them with vengeful glee among the temples and calpulli buildings. Soon fire and smoke began swirling up into the sky. The Spaniards set up a cannon on the fire stone just inside the Eagle Gate and in front of the Temple of Tezcatlipoca to sweep the area all the way to the Coatlan, the House of the Eagle and Jaguar Warriors. The black-clad priests atop the nearby Great Temple did not flee. They beat a deep booming rhythm on

Right: The 10 June assault on Tenochtitlan. Upper, the Spaniards attack up the Ixtlapalapan causeway. Centre, the barricade at the city entrance is destroyed by cannon. Lower, The Spaniards attack through the Xolloco district.

Upper, the fighting on the first day raged from Xoloc to the Sacred Square. Lower, The Mexica captured the cannon the Spaniards had set up on the fire stone and threw it into a deep canal.

the great drum to summon the Mexica to defend Huitzilopochtli's shrine. The drummers watched two Spaniards come for them with drawn swords but kept drumming until they were cut down. Many of the best warriors had been fighting from their canoes when the drum's alarm summoned them. These quickly landed and rushed to the Sacred Square, shouting, 'Mexica, come find them!'

Cuauhtémoc appeared in the confusion at this moment, rallied those in flight, and organised the arriving warriors. He dressed down those captains who had allowed their men to flee, and threw the reinforced mass into a violent counterattack that drove the enemy from the Sacred Square. Now it was Cortés' turn to reproach his men for their conduct, but the Mexica attack was so fierce that they all retreated for their lives, even abandoning the cannon in the Sacred Square. The Mexica dragged it away and threw it into a deep canal. The arrival of horsemen again panicked the Mexica who retreated out of the main square. The Spanish again entered the Sacred Square where five Spaniards mounted the Great Temple and butchered twelve Mexica nobles who desperately tried to defend the house of Huitzilopochtli. The timely arrival of the horsemen had saved the day for the Spaniards. The Mexica could not stand up to their charges in such a large open area. Still, the horsemen were not enough, wrote the biographer of Cortés echoing his master's vivid memories, because the Mexica 'fought like mad dogs, with no fear whatsoever.' As soon as the horsemen withdrew, the Mexica rushed forward again sweeping up stragglers and forcing the rest back onto the causeway. 'In short, everyone ran away and everyone fought well. Such is war.'[32]

The fighting now settled down to a set pattern. Cortés maintained his camp at Acachinanco fearing that the Mexica would cut him off if he moved it to the city. Each day at the end of fighting, his forces returned to the camp. Each night the Mexica excavated all the causeway breaks Cortés' allies had filled in during the day and rebuilt all the barricades. Each morning the Spaniards found the breaks deeper than the day before and the barricades even more formidable. Much of this work was done by the women of the city; Cuauhtémoc had decreed total mobilisation and was directing a very effective series of countermeasures. 'In this work many fainted from fatigue, and very many perished from loss of sleep and hunger, but they could not do otherwise, for Cuauhtémoc was present.'[33] He relentlessly drove his people each night to repair the damage done to the city's defences.

Unfortunately, the Spanish attacks daily burnt a bigger hole in the brilliant fabric of the city. With each day's fighting the Spanish burned or pulled down more and more buildings. They greatly feared the deluge of stones thrown from the roof tops as they fought through the streets. Here Mexica women were as effective as their men. Now Cortés ordered the systematic destruction of each building in order to give the cavalry its level ground for action and to fill up the canals with the debris. The canals were natural barriers which the Spaniards had to wade across at their peril and natural avenues along which the Mexica could attack or escape. As June wore on, the mists of that season made the early morning conflagrations seem like lurid visions of hell.

This contest between the Indian allies and the Mexica women might have gone on indefinitely had not hunger begun to sap the vitality of the defenders. Weakened fingers and bodies could no longer match the pace of destruction. Cortés by now had come to the conclusion that he needed to take some dramatic action to shock the Mexica into surrender; otherwise the entire city would be destroyed. Therefore, he settled upon destroying part to save the rest and set fire to all the great buildings and palaces surrounding the great square, including the Palace of Axayácatl and Motecuhzoma's wondrous aviary. He also concluded that the golden bridge at Tepeyacac was only funnelling food into the city and transferred Sandoval's detachment to cut it off. Cuauhtémoc's resolve remained unshaken as did his grip on the obedience of the Mexica. But a greater danger than Cortés was hunger. Famine stalked the city as the granaries emptied. Every night hundreds of canoes slipped out of the canals and into the lake to harvest what lake products they could or to buy food from other towns. They bought at famine prices – a handful of golden jewels or precious stones for a handful of maize. The nobles of once vassal cities slipped into Tenochtitlan with canoe loads of food to leave with an equal weight of treasure. Tenochtitlan was spending the wealth of empire just to survive each day. Still, hunger was killing each day more of the people than the fighting. Ixtlilxochitl brought this lifeline to the attention of

The fighting for the city frequently took to the shallow waters of the canals and lake.
(Drawing by Keith Henderson)

Cortés who quickly severed it with patrols of his brigantines and allied canoes. Each morning his brigantines came back to base with numerous Indians dangling from the yardarms.

With the growing hunger, came treacherous allies. Sandoval had ravaged the cities on the Ixtlapalapan peninsula so cruelly that many fled to Tenochtitlan. The rest just changed sides. The leaders of Xochimilco, Ixtlapalapan, Cuitláhuac, Mizquic, and Mexicatzinco secretly informed Cuauhtémoc that they were sending a fleet of canoes filled with warriors to help the Mexica. He was overjoyed and showed his vassals much honour, presenting them with devices, shields, and to each man a gourd of frothing chocolate, a rich gift. He said to them, 'It is well. You have shown favour. You have suffered fatigue. You have wearied yourselves. Help the city; let it be attempted.' As the Mexica began to escort them to the battle, they suddenly broke away and began to loot the lakeside districts. They carried off many young women and heaped their canoes with loot. They had barely poled out of the canals when they were intercepted by a Mexica fleet whose warriors fell upon them in rage, killing most of them and rescuing all the women. The surviving 'allies' were dragged before Cuauhtémoc and the king of Cuitláhuac, Mayeuatzin, who had fled to the safety of Tenochtitlan before his city changed sides. Turning to Mayeuatzin, Cuauhtémoc said, 'O my beloved younger brother, perform thy office.' Whereupon, Mayeuatzin sacrificed four of his subjects on the spot and Cuauhtémoc another four. If anything brought home the complete isolation of the Mexica, it was this treachery. Over the 80 years that Xochimilco had been conquered by the Mexica, many had come to live in Tenochtitlan. They now paid for their kinsmen's betrayal. Every adult Xochimilca male in the city was killed.[34]

The presence of Mayeuatzin and other vassal kings in Tenochtitlan, as this episode indicates, had weakened the Mexica immeasurably. They had loyally joined Cuauhtémoc but had left their kingdoms essentially leaderless in their absence and easy prey, for Cortés was quick to appoint new kings who served him. Coanacochtzin of Texcoco and Tetlepanquetzatzin of Tlacopan, the two lesser kings of the Triple Alliance, had fled to Tenochtitlan with many warriors and civilian refugees. They would have served Cuauhtémoc better had they rallied the power of their kingdoms. Instead they lost their kingdoms and all their resources and provided Cuauhtémoc with only more mouths to feed.

Day after day, as June burned into July, Cuauhtémoc rallied his people to resist the attacks that were devouring the city. The war-

riors contested every enemy advance from behind barricades thrown across streets, from the rooftops with hails of stones, and from the canals with canoes full of archers. Again and again he threw vicious attacks at the enemy, often pushing them back in desperate flight, and often in turn was counterattacked by the horsemen who ran down or lanced the boldest of the Mexica as they raced ahead of the others.

Cuauhtémoc resorted to every ruse and trick in the experience of the Mexica and devised new ones to counter the enemy. He set an ambush for the brigantines that were tightening the noose of starvation around the city. Thirty of the largest war canoes with picked crews were hidden in the reeds of the lakes as other canoes decoyed two of the brigantines past them and onto a hedge of underwater sharpened stakes. The Mexica swarmed over them, killing one captain, mortally wounding the other, and wounding everyone else in both crews. They captured one brigantine, but the other with the survivors managed to break away. When again Cuauhtémoc tried this same trick, it was turned back on him. This time the brigantines fled with the canoes after them, right past six more brigantines lying in ambush in the reed beds. The ensuing ambush decimated the Mexica canoe force.

Another of Cuauhtémoc's ruses nearly dragged Alvarado to the stone of sacrifice. The Mexica had watched carefully how the enemy had filled in each breach in the causeways before advancing. Cortés had adamantly insisted on this precaution, but in his desire to be the first to seize the great market square of Tlatelolco, Alvarado was becoming careless. The Mexica noticed, and one night after he had returned to his camp, they removed the fill in the breach, widened it, and deepened the channel. They also dug pits in the water along either side of the breach and filled the water with hidden sharpened stakes. The next morning, on 23 June, they made a point to personally insult Alvarado himself, with all the gestures and body motions that seem to be international in their meaning. In his rage he quickly bridged the gap with two brigantines and charged across with his Spaniards and Tlaxcallans behind him, leaving the gap to be filled in behind them. They pushed on, driving the Mexica from one barricade to another until they passed a street of large buildings and temples. There a sentry waited and brandished his shield as conch shell trumpets blared. The shout went up, 'O Mexica, courage!' From behind the buildings, a large number of Mexica attacked with such fury that the enemy recoiled, fell back, then fled in rout back to the

The hero Tzilacatzin leads the attack that drove Alvarado's men into a canal.

gap which had not been filled in. They spilled into the water in their panic, pushed by the press of those behind. Others leaped for safety into the water and fell into the pits. The Mexica canoes darted back to fall upon them thrashing about in the water. The brigantines tried to rescue them but impaled themselves on the stakes. Mexica missiles converged on them so heavily that many of the crews were killed or wounded, forcing a withdrawal. Fifteen Spaniards and many Tlaxcallans were dragged from the water and rushed immediately to Cuauhtémoc and to death stretched over the stone. So fired were the Mexica that they pursued Alvarado's survivors and threw themselves upon his camp all through the night. Alvarado's force barely hung on.[35]

The crisis passed; it represented the trap Cuauhtémoc struggled within. His victories were of the minor, tactical sort while the totality of the siege was a growing strategic disaster. Cortés now employed his Indian allies more and more as he expanded the battlefield within the city. This caused great joy in the Mexica who had no fear of their ancient enemies, killing many and dragging more off to sacrifice. The Mexica would remember that they and their Indian enemies filled these battles with songs of war and death so eagerly did they fight each other. But Cortés had more willing allies than he could employ (he boasted of 200,000 men under his command), and each day saw more and more of the city disappear into rubble, thrown into the canals by seeming ant hills of these same Indian allies. Each day the brigantines reinforced with thousands of Indian canoes penetrated from the lake up the canals, burning houses and killing. And over each day throbbed the snakeskin drum from the Great Temple across the smouldering city and across the lake, to mix with the constant roar of fighting men, the shriek of whistles, the blare of conch trumpets, the rattle of musketry, and the roar of cannon. Cortés would remember the din for the rest of his life; it was 'as if the world were coming to an end.'

Cavalry was a vital advantage for the Spaniards. They rode down and lanced Mexica almost at will when they attacked in groups. Alone they could be dragged out of the saddle and killed.

In one day the Mexica of Tenochtitlan abandoned their ruined city to take refuge in Tlatelolco.

And so it was – for the Mexica. Cortés' destructive forays into Tenochtitlan had made the city uninhabitable. He himself recounted how his horsemen would ride the streets lancing any Mexica they came across. Cuauhtémoc's plans for defending the city were equally in shambles. It was time to strike a bargain with the other half of the Mexica nation, his own city of Tlatelolco, separated from Tenochtitlan by a wide, defensible canal. Already many Tenochca had fled there for safety. The Tlatelolcans had manfully participated in the defense of the island capital despite their subservient position. They were Mexica, as proud as their Tenochca neighbours, and their position as vassals rankled. Now they saw their chance to rearrange power within the Mexica nation. Cuauhtémoc had no choice but to agree to their terms which put the management of the empire in Tlatelolcan hands. This cannot have been too painful an agreement; after all he was the grandson of the last independent ruler of Tlatelolco, and his power base was there as well. All in one night and day the people of Tenochtitlan abandoned their ruined city and trudged across the canal into Tlatelolco, led by their priests carrying the statue of Huitzilopochtli to his new home. 'There was raised a cry of weeping; there was raised a shout. Many were the tears of the beloved women. And as for us men, each one took his woman; one or another carried his child upon his shoulders.' Cuauhtémoc himself relocated his headquarters to a building known as Yacacolco.

Cortés was quickly informed and tried unsuccessfully to win the Tlatelolca over.[36] He may well have known that a peace party existed. Cuauhtémoc had just executed two more sons of Motecuhzoma who had represented a faction wishing to begin negotiations with the enemy. In retaliation, the faction assassinated the high priests of Huitzilopochtli and Tezcatlipoca, who, as leaders of the priesthood, undoubtedly had advocated a hard war policy.[37]

THE LAST MEXICA TRIUMPH

Despite this refusal, Cortés smelled blood. He had already captured half the city and knew that hunger killed daily for him. His captains had demanded that a major coordinated attack be made with its objective the great market square of Tlatelolco. At first he had hesitated, but now he supported the idea. On 30 June, all the Spanish forces would attack at the same time towards the great market. Cortés reinforced his own contingent and divided it into three separate elements each of which had as many as 10,000 allies attached.

The attack ground forward relentlessly. The Indian allies swarmed through the city storming the buildings as the Spaniards blew through one barricade after another. Cortés still worried about filling in every canal his forces passed. He became instantly suspicious when one of his elements drove deeper into the city than they should have, had they stopped to fill in each breach. He rushed to the scene in time to find his men rushing wildly to the rear. Cuauhtémoc had sprung another trap and ambushed the overconfident column which now came flying back, Spaniards and allies, to crash through the loose fill in the canal and into the water. The Mexica were on them, hacking and stabbing at the panicked mass. They leaped into the water to kill or take prisoners. The enemy frantically clawed their way out of the water and onto the roadway, sloughing off so much mud that few could keep their feet in the slippery muck. Cuauhtémoc was everywhere among his squadrons inspiring their attack and issuing commands with the blare of hos conch-shell trumpet. The battle fury of the-Mexica surged each time it sounded.

Cortés himself rushed forward with a group of Spaniards to fight as rearguard but was engulfed in a tide of Mexica who had swum across the water. Five champions closed in on him. One leaped upon him and pinned his arms, but his body-guard severed the Mexica's hands, then himself fell hacked to death by obsidian swords. Cortés was pulled to safety to join the rout of the rest of his force along a narrow dirt street between two canals now full of Mexica canoes. The Mexica slaughtered the retreating enemies so packed on the narrow roadway that they could only shuffle along, shooting at them from their canoes or pulling them into the canoes as captives.

Cortés finally rallied the survivors on the Tlacopan causeway and held off the pursuing Mexica. The air filled with wild shouts of joy and songs of rejoicing as the Mexica realised the extent of their victory. 53 Spaniards were hurried along to Yacacolco along with thousands of Texcocans, Chalca, Xochimilca, and Tlaxcallans. As many as another 50 Spaniards and 2,000 allies lay dead in the streets or bobbing in the canals. The captives were gloried in. The Mexica would remember how the Spaniards bore themselves. 'One went weeping; one went singing; one went crying out while striking the mouth with the palm of the hand.' At Yacacolco, they were lined up before Cuauhtémoc to be counted and admired. Atop the temple the braziers were fired and fed with heaps of copal incense, and up the steps were dragged the naked Spaniards painted with the yellow streaks of sacrifice, feathers stuck in their hair. Even from a distance, their companions could discern their pale bodies ascending the narrow steps 'to the sound of trumpets. . . and also a drum, a most dismal sound indeed it was, like an instrument of demons, as it resounded so that one could hear it two leagues off, and with it many small tambourines and shell trumpets, horns and whistles.' The heads of the Spaniards as well as those of four horses were strung up on the temple skull rack. Those of the allies were not. The bodies now represented the only major addition to the food stores of the city, though the Mexica were careful to let the Spaniards know what they thought of it, 'To show how evil you are, even your flesh is bad to eat, for it is as bitter as gall, so bitter we can't swallow it.'

Cuauhtémoc did more than officiate at the sacrifices at this moment of triumph. He coordinated violent attacks on the columns of Sandoval and Alvarado driving them out of the city, back across the causeways, and into their camps where only the fire of cannon into their packed ranks saved the Spaniards that day. He had also ordered his men to throw the severed heads of Spaniards into the ranks of the retreating enemy. The allies were thoroughly demoralised by the extent of the Mexica victory, and the Mexica claimed that the bloody heads were those of Cortés, Alvarado, or Sandoval, depending on the column. The Mexica also quickly spread the rumour among them that in eight days the Spaniards would be completely destroyed. In hours, almost all of the allies had deserted, melting away by their tens of thousands until only a few committed kings and their personal retainers remained. Cuauhtémoc made the most of this moment, sending the heads of Spaniards and horses around the cities of Anáhuac to proclaim the imminent and utter defeat of the enemy. He also stepped up the assaults on the Spanish camps by night and day.

The hopes of the Mexica soared for those eight days as their courage strove to fulfill Huitzilopochtli's prophecy. Now it was they who attacked constantly, and it was the Spaniards who desperately defended their camps. All

Hope was kindled among the Mexica as the Spaniards were joyously dragged up the steps of the temple to be sacrificed to Huitzilopochtli. (Drawing by Keith Henderson)

Cortés could do was hold on. His allies were the crucial element that made his offensive strategy possible. In this crisis, Ixtlilxochitl, the Texcocan prince, whispered his advice – patience. When the eight days have passed without a Mexica victory, the allies will return. And when the eighth day had come and gone, and Huitzilopochtli had failed to reward his chosen people with victory, the allies felt that a divine sentence of doom had been passed on the Mexica. They returned as quickly as they had left.

THE QUETZAL-OWL AND THE FIRE SERPENT

The Mexica had been at pains to hide the effects of the growing hunger within the city, but every advance gave grim evidence. Tenochtitlan had been a city of gardens and trees. Now every field had been torn up for the roots and every tree stripped of its bark. A few desperate Mexica escaped to tell Cortés that each night a horde of people picked over the ruins for something to eat. He ambushed them in the early dawn, killing over 800 women and children, a stratagem in which he took much pride. Inside their shrunken city, the Mexica were dying daily of hunger by the thousands. The granaries were long since emptied. The people ate boiled leather and corn husks and even adobe bricks to fill their emptiness. Birds, lizards, and insects were delicacies and almost impossible to find. The lack of clean water was even worse; the brackish water was so foul that it killed many with a bloody flux. At first the dead had been carefully stacked in houses, but even that could not cope with the numbers of corpses that soon overwhelmed the Mexica tradition of care for the dead. Bodies soon began to litter the streets and fill the canals.

All this was evident as Cortés began his attacks that systematically ate away at the Mexica refuge. By the middle of July, the Mexica stopped opening up the breaches in the causeways and roadways the Spanish had filled in. Cuauhtémoc's rule now extended to barely one-eighth of the city. So many refugees had crowded into it that there was barely room to stand in the houses, and the streets were paved with corpses. Still, the Mexica would not entertain Cortés' repeated pleas to negotiate,

but now their despair was as evident as their courage. About this time, Alvarado captured the major well of brackish water upon which the Mexica had relied. The day after the slaughter of the scavengers (25 July), Cortés burned the palace of Cuauhtémoc. By now most of the city had fallen, and Cortés and Alvarado's forces had linked up. Behind them, thousands of Indian labourers demolished every structure in the captured part of the city. On 27 July

Cuauhtémoc surrenders to Cortés after being intercepted as he tried to flee across the lake in a canoe. 'Tell the captain I have done my duty,' he said in his despair, '... Now that I am his captive, let him take this dagger and kill me with it.' (Drawing by Keith Henderson)

Alvarado took the great temple of Tlatelolco and burned it. The Spaniards began to encounter starving people who wandered almost mindlessly towards them; even they took pity and protected them.

His Indian allies were completely untouched by such sentiments. Undeterred by Cortés' strict orders, they killed all the Mexica that fell into their hands. In early July Alvarado captured a district of the city with a thousand

Finally even the Mexica could fight no longer. Towards the end, each day's fighting was more and more a slaughter for the Mexica. (Drawing by Keith Henderson)

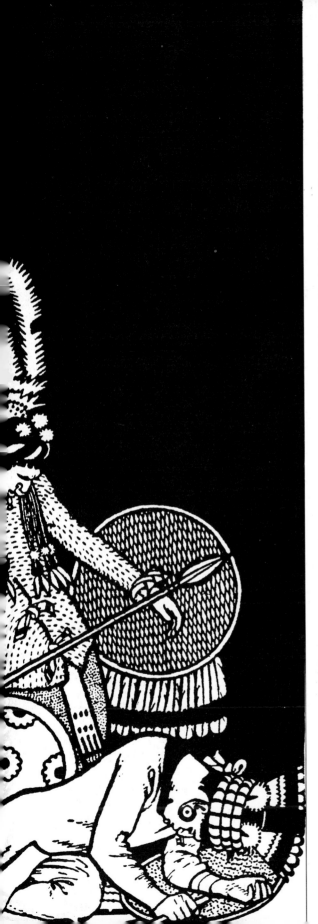

houses; the allies butchered the 12,000 inhabitants of the district against orders. As victory beckoned, Cortés found he had less and less control of his native allies who were determined to exterminate the Mexica. The city was resembling a vast slaughter house, and the actual perpetrators of the Mexica genocide were their own fellow Indians.

Cuauhtémoc was desperate. In the past he had firmly refused even to discuss peace with Cortés. Now he resorted to peace offers as ruses. He accepted offers to meet Cortés to discuss peace but invariably failed to show up while the Conquistador waited patiently for hours. Cuauhtémoc was probably milking each opportunity to trick the enemy into stopping his attacks, even if only for a few hours. It was apparent that Cortés was hungry for a surrender that would preserve even the remnant of the city and its population. But at the heart of these shadow shows was Cuauhtémoc's growing realisation that his cause was hopeless. His eyes could not evade the starving misery around him, but he had pledged to restore Mexica glory or die. The contradiction must have been eating him alive. The depth of his despair was evident as he explained to his council that he had tried endless countermeasures to thwart the enemy, but they had all failed. The council and especially the die-hard priesthood was adamant to continue fighting. They reminded him of all the treacheries of which Cortés was guilty – the seizure of Motecuhzoma and the Toxcatl massacre among them. His promises were worthless, they argued. This was echoed in excuses given Cortés for his failure to arrive as promised for negotiations – fear that he would be shot by a crossbow or arquebus.

In these last days, Cuauhtémoc saw every advantage fall away. Cortés' ally, Ixtlilxochitl, captured his own wounded brother, Coanacochtzin, the king of Texcoco. The Texcocan warriors fighting for the Mexica then deserted and joined the rest of their countrymen serving Cortés. It can have been of little satisfaction to Cuauhtémoc that the Conquistador, rewarded Ixtlilxochitl's loyalty by demanding a ransom for his brother that stripped Texcoco of its remaining gold.

In the final fighting Cuauhtémoc resorted to utterly desperate measures. So many warriors had fallen that he dressed women in their weapons and armour and had them appear suddenly on the roofs of buildings in the path of the oncoming enemy. It worked - momentarily - causing the enemy, especially the Indian allies to recoil at the sudden appearance of unexpected strength. Then keener eyes discerned the truth, and the allies attacked, mocking the Mexica. As the last of his earthly expedients failed, he grasped at a final appeal to the spirit of his father and to heaven. He had taken with him from his now ruined palace the great quetzal owl war costume of his father, the great Ahuítzotl. The costume was a shimmering mass of rich quetzal feathers, a fortune in themselves. Apparently it was famous, for it was instantly recognised in battle by the Indian allies. It was customarily donned and worn into battle as the last act in a victorious war. He chose a great warrior, Tlapaltecatl, to wear it. 'This device was the device of my governor, my beloved father Ahuítzotl. Let this man wear it. May he die with it. May he display himself with it proudly before [our foes]; may he make himself seen with it by them. May our foes behold it; may they marvel at it.' He was given four flint-tipped atlatl darts, sacred to Huitzilopochtli, which represented the fire serpent, the fire drill, the weapons with which he was armed when he emerged from the womb.[38]

The Cihuacoatl, Tlacotzin, addressed the warriors, telling them that the power of Huitzilopochtli, which had conquered the empire, resided in these darts. If only one or two of the Spaniards were killed or wounded with them, then the Mexica would have one last chance at victory. Cuauhtémoc, the Eagle Council, and thousands of Mexica watched the Quetzal-Owl rush forward, with his four bodyguards, into the fighting. The costume flared wide as he ran, like some terrifying apparition of iridescent green and gold. Even the Spaniards blanched at the sight of this otherworldly figure. The Indian allies panicked, and the Quetzal-Owl took three prisoners from among them. He was last seen leaping from a rooftop into the battle and was lost to sight.

Then nothing. He had disappeared. With him the last Mexica hope had also disappeared. Sahagún's Indian informants remembered how the world had become an empty husk for the Mexica at that moment; they were utterly numbed.

'Finally the battle just stopped; thus silence reigned; nothing took place. Then our foes departed. All was quiet and nothing more took place. Thus night fell. And upon the next day nothing at all took place. There was no one who spoke aloud. The common folk only lay destroyed. . .'[39]

The second week of August saw the end come. The final defences crumbled. Cortés ordered the brigantines to enter the city and hem the Mexica in against his landward attack. He noted that they were entirely out of arrows, darts, and stones. His allies slaughtered or captured 40,000 Mexica in an orgy of slaughter that horrified Cortés who wrote:

'So loud was the wailing of the women and children that there was not one man amongst us whose heart did not bleed at the sound; and indeed we had more trouble in preventing our allies from killing with such cruelty than we had in fighting the enemy. For no race, however savage, has ever practised such fierce and unnatural cruelty as the natives of these parts.'[40]

His letter to the king of Spain still echoes his horror of the last days as he found the shrunken city stacked with corpses; he estimated 50,000 had died from hunger and bad water alone.

Cuauhtémoc had completely lost control; the people were already fleeing across the shallow lake or streaming over the causeways when they could. As the tlatoani saw his world collapse in chaos, Cortés planned for the final attack the next day. That night of 12 August, the sky intermittently drizzled. Late at night a fiery object swirled out of heaven like a whirlwind trailing sparks and fiery debris, making a noise of cracking, until it crashed into the lake. The Mexica watched in terrified silence.

The next day none of them stirred to arms as they waited for death. Cuauhtémoc and the Eagle Council bowed to the inevitable and discussed among themselves what tribute to offer the Spaniards and how to surrender. That would soon be irrelevant. The city, as an organised entity, simply disintegrated into a mass of desperate refugees. Cortés pushed in with only his Spaniards against minor resistance. The greatest problem was the horde of terrified people trying to escape the city. He had strictly ordered the allies to harm no one, but even so they killed another 15,000 that day. By now the Cihuacoatl and the Eagle Council had surrendered, but Cortés was eager to capture Cuauhtémoc alive. Cuauhtémoc could not bring himself to surrender and made one last attempt to evade his fate, hoping to slip across the lake to safety. As he climbed into a great twenty-man canoe, the cry went up through the city, audible even to Cortés, that the tlatoani was fleeing. His large canoe with its king's men was quickly intercepted by a brigantine, specially alerted to his escape. Cut off, Cuauhtémoc rose with sword and shield to defend his family. When the cannon was trained on the canoe, he threw down his weapons and surrendered. The brigantine's captain treated Cuauhtémoc with great respect and escorted him to the deck, laying mats before him and offering him and his family the best food he had. The captain asked Cuauhtémoc to order the rest of the canoes to cease fighting. He answered 'It is not necessary. They will fight no longer, when they see that their prince is taken.' Already the Mexica in the canoes had put down their weapons.[41]

Cuauhtémoc was escorted to Cortés by three Spanish captains holding tightly to his mantle determined to not let him loose. Cuauhtémoc's bearing had not deserted him even at this moment. Cortés asked him through Marina, his interpreter, 'Ask Cuauhtémoc why he permitted the destruction of the city with such loss of lives of his own people and of ours? Many were the times that I begged him for peace.' Cuauhtémoc answered, 'Tell the captain that I have done my duty; I have defended my city, my kingdom just as he would have defended his had I attempted to take it from him. But I have failed!' He then put his hand on Cortés' dagger at his belt. 'Now that I am his captive, let him take this dagger and kill me with it!'[42]

Cortés, the admirer of chivalrous legends, was much affected by this act of heroic nobility and assured Cuauhtémoc of his safety and that he esteemed him all the more for his courage. He had Cuauhtémoc's family brought and provided with the best food in the camp. He also assured him that he would confirm him in his own authority. Then he escorted him to a rooftop, pointing at the scene of desolation and turmoil, before them and begged him to order the last of his warriors, still huddled on rooftops, to surrender. Cuauhtémoc raised his arms, and the war was over.

'I KNEW WHAT IT WAS TO TRUST TO YOUR FALSE PROMISES, MALINCHE.'

That day he and the other surviving lords were escorted to Coyohuacan under careful guard. That night the heavens opened in a great deluge that rocked the valley and pounded the ruins of Tenochtitlan to their foundations. 'It seemed as if the deities of Anáhuac, scared from their ancient abodes, were borne along shrieking and howling in the blast, as they abandoned the fallen capital to its fate.'[43] His thoughts were still with the tormented survivors, and he quickly begged Cortés to allow them to flee the charnel house of ruins and find refuge around the lakeshore. The Conquistador quickly assented. His Indian allies still ignored his orders to spare the survivors, so he thanked them and encouraged them to go home which they happily did, laden with loot. Then for three days through the continuing downpour, the last of the Mexica, emaciated and haggard, trudged out of the corpse-stuffed rubble heap that once was one of the glittering jewels of the planet. Some of them were seen from time to time to stop and gaze back upon the bones of their city. Now instead of Tlaxcallan barbarities, they suffered the gauntlet of Spanish greed. Women were stripped to find any gold hidden on them. Young men were branded for slavery, and the comely, light-skinned young women carried off. Spanish mastiffs were set upon the priests to tear them to pieces.

Cortés' chivalry, however, had its limits, and Cuauhtémoc and the other lords were summoned back into his presence to discuss the matter of gold. Cuauhtémoc arrived in a royal costume of dirty quetzal feathers to signify his defeat. 'What of the gold?' Marina asked for

Cortés. Then Cuauhtémoc ordered all that had been saved by the Mexica to be laid before Cortés. Thinking of the vast pile that he had accumulated before La Noche Triste, he could only ask, 'Is that all?' The Cihuacoatl, Tlacotzin, disingenuously asked what had the Spaniards done with all the gold that Motecuhzoma had given them. Cortés said it had all been lost in the retreat, and now tersely said, 'You will produce it all.' Tlacotzin again dissembled by saying that the Tlatelolca had stolen it since it was they who had fought the Spanish on the retreat. Only the Tlatelolca, but not the Tenochca, had been expert at fighting by canoe. Now Cuauhtémoc broke in angrily at the insult to the city of his ancestors, 'What art thou saying, O Cihuacoatl?' He pointed to the gold and made it clear that whatever had been recovered now lay before Cortés. 'Is this quite all,' Cortés asked in growing distress.

His anxiety was justified. No sooner did his army learn of the meagre amount of gold squeezed from the Mexica that they began to accuse Cortés of stealing the difference between it and their expectations. The royal treasurer, Alderete, demanded that Cuauhtémoc be tortured to extract the missing gold. At first Cortés resisted for he had extended his protection to Cuauhtémoc. But in the end he more feared angering the king's treasurer than standing by his honour. After all, Alderete was in a position to denounce him for stealing the missing gold himself. Informed of the torture proposed for him, Cuauhtémoc tried to hang himself. He and Tetlepanquetzatzin, king of Tlacopan, were tied to poles, their feet covered with oil and set alight. As the agony played over Tetlepanquetzatzin's face, he looked plaintively for a sign from the impassive Cuauhtémoc that he would say something that would stop the torture. But Cuauhtémoc only glared at him, calling him weak and cowardly, and said, 'And do you think, I, then, am taking my pleasure in my bath?'

The only thing Cuauhtémoc would say is that ten days before the surrender the gods had signalled his defeat. He then ordered all the remaining treasure thrown into the lake. Perhaps this or the upbraiding by the Texcocan prince, Ixtlilxochitl, prompted Cortés to order the torture stopped. The lake was then

'And do you think, I, then, am taking pleasure in my bath?' Cuauhtémoc heroically withstood torture when the Spaniards forced Cortés to put the tlatoani to the question to reveal where all the gold lost on La Noche Triste had gone. (Drawing by Keith Henderson)

Thus died Cuauhtémoc, the tenth and last tlatoani of the Mexica, murdered by Cortés who feared him above all other men. (Drawing by Keith Henderson)

searched but only a few small items were found. More likely, the treasure was thrown into the sacred whirlpool at the deepest spot in the lake. The torture left Cuauhtémoc crippled; he walked with a limp thereafter, but he had bought a victory with his pain – the victory of denying from his enemies that which they valued most.

For the next four years, Cuauhtémoc remained the titular king of Tenochtitlan, but it was to the Cihuacoatl that Cortés entrusted the government of the city he was charged with rebuilding. It was this Tlacotzin who expressed to Cortés the matter-of-fact attitude with which the Mexica had accepted the Conquest. It was the way of the world – 'The Mexica had no lands when we first came here; the Tepaneca, the Acolhua, the Chalca, and the Xochimilca, all had lands. We took their lands. But what we did was no different from what you have done, our lord, for you came with arrows and shields to take our lands and cities from us.' Cortés still so feared Cuauhtémoc might hatch a plot that he arranged to have him within calling distance at all times. Cuauhtémoc may even have accepted baptism. Even some of the surviving Mexica clergy believed that Huitzilopochtli had died and asked the newly arrived Franciscan missionaries simply to be left alone to die. These years for Cuauhtémoc are largely unrecorded except that he approved the dispatch of 15,000 Mexica warriors on Spanish expeditions to subdue new provinces.

Cuauhtémoc and Tetlepanquetzatzin accompanied him on another such expedition to Honduras in 1525, because, as Gómara wrote, they 'might disturb the country and rebel during his absence.'[44] It was an epic march through towering jungles and swamps which brought the Spaniards themselves to mutiny. It was the Mexica whose fortitude and energy shamed the Spaniards back to their duty.

At the beginning of Lent, they emerged from the wilderness into the fruitful Maya province of Acalan where they halted. Cortés was to claim that a member of Cuauhtémoc's entourage came to him to reveal his master's plan to fall upon the Spaniards and massacre them in difficult country such as that through which they had just passed. He arrested the two kings and a number of their lords. These latter he questioned separately, stating that Cuauhtémoc had admitted his guilt. They all implicated Cuauhtémoc as the leader of the plot but denied being part of it themselves. Through all this, the two kings, according to Cortés, remained silent. His account is directly contradicted by Díaz, who was there. He maintained that the two kings flatly declared their innocence. They admitted to discussing the suffering they had undergone (walking on crippled feet for hundreds of miles, perhaps) and watching so many of their vassals die on the march. Death was preferable. Cuauhtémoc even stated that there had been a number of nobles who had wanted to rise in revolt, but that he had forbidden it, and without his consent, such a thing was impossible.[45]

Cortés swiftly pronounced a sentence of death. As Cuauhtémoc was led to the ceiba tree from which he was to be hanged, he said to Cortés, 'I knew what it was to trust to your false promises, Malinche; I knew that you had destined me to this fate, since I did not fall by my own hand when you entered my city of Tenochtitlan. Why do you slay me so unjustly? God will demand it of you!'[46]

And surely He has done so. The bones of Cortés lie ignored in a small church in Mexico City, his name despised in the land he conquered. A mighty bronze statue of Cuauhtémoc towers in a square in Mexico City, and his name is borne by countless Mexican boys in whom the brave blood of Anáhuac and Castille mingles. And deep within the bustle of modern Mexico City, above the ghostly noise of battle still rings the paean, 'O Mexica, courage!'

1. Cuitláhuac's name has been translated as 'Lord of Cuitláhuac, Keeper of the Kingdom" by Doris Heden and Fernando Horcasitas, translated s in Fray Diego Durán, *The Aztecs: The History of the Indies and of New Spain* (New York: Orion Press, 1964) p. 357. Alternately, the name is translated as 'Excrement Owner' by Ross Hassig, *Mexico and the Spanish Con quest* (Norman and London: University of Oklahoma Press, 1994) p. 162.

2. Fernando de Alva Ixtlilxochitl, *Obras Históricas*, ed. O'Gormon (Mexico, 1975) 12, cited in Thomas, p. 732, n. 67. Ixtlilxochitl credits Cuitláhuac's son, Don Alonso Axayácatl, as the source of the information that Cacamatzin was murdered by the Spaniards

y el otro q̄ suçedio en el dho señorio yguaue temncin y ços tubo la
dha rrebelio hasta q̄ bos le bençistes y prendistes y en la otra meytad
del dho medio escudo de la mano yzq̄erda a la parte de abaxo po
dais traher la cibdad de tenustitan armada sobre agua en memo
ria q̄ por fuerça de armas la ganastes y sujetastes a nr̄o señorio y por
orla del dho escudo en campo amarillo siete capitanes y señores
de siete probincias y poblaciones q̄ estauen en la laguna y entorno
della q̄ se rebelaron contra os y los bençistes y prendistes en la
dha cibdad de tenustitan apresionados y atados con vna caçe
na que se venga açerrar con vn candado Debaxo del dicho es
cudo venga vn yel mo çerrado con su tinble en vn escudo
a tal como está la g...   q̄ nales dhas
armas vos damos   por bras ar
mas conoadas y se   ualadas de
mas de las armas   q̄ ne as i tene
ys de bros predeçe   çores y q̄ e
mos yes nr̄a merçe   d voluntad
que vos y bros hijos   delçendien
tes y dellos y deça   da b nollos
las ayais i tengais   por bras ar
mas conocidas y   çenaladas
y como tales las po   dais y pue
dan traher en bros   y posteros
y ca las y ca los deça   da b nollos
dhos bros hijos y   delçendien
tes y en las otras   partes q̄ bos
y ellos q̄ nisieredes   y bien tobie
redes y por esta nuestra   carta o por su tras
lado sinado de escribano ph   blico mandamos a
los ylustrisimos ynfantes nuestros muy caros y amados hi
jos y hermanos y a los ynfantes Duques marq̄ses condes rri
cos homes mae stres de las hordenes priores Comendadores y
cub comendadores alcaides delos castillos y casas fuertes
yllanas E a los del nr̄o conselo oydores de las nras abdienci
as y a todos los corregidores asistentes ygovernadores y alcal
des yalguaziles de la nra casa y corte y chancelleria y a todos
los concelos rregidores alcaldes y alguaziles de la nra casa
y corte y chancelleria y a todos los concelos rregidores alcaldes
y alguaziles merinos prebostes yotras justicias E juezes qua

The coat of arms presented to Cortés by Carlos V for the conquest of Mexico. In the upper right quarter of the shield are three crowns, signifying that Cortés had conquered three kings: Motecuhzoma II, Cuitláhuac, and Cuauhtémoc.

either at the death of Motecuhzoma or a few days before. The latter would support the contention that Alvarado had had him and most of the other lords arrested with him in January 1520 killed during the Toxcatl massacre.

3. Hugh Thomas, *Conquest: Montezuma, Cortés, and the Fall of Old Mexico* (New York: Simon and Schuster, 1993) pp. 390-391. Thomas states that the murder of most of the Mexica lords, including Cacamatzin, and the slaughter in the Toxcatl festival were simultane ously executed. Anthony Pagden, editor of *Hernan Cortés: Five Letters from Mexico* (New Haven and Lon don: Yale University Press, 1986) pp. 477-478, sug gests that the murder of the lords, including Caca matzin, took place when the Spaniards fled Tenochti tlan on La Noche Triste, citing a number of Indian sources. It seems likely that Alvarado, obsessed with visions of a Mexica plot to murder the Spaniards dur ing the Toxcatl would have ensured that the Indian who had instigated the major plot nipped in the bud by Cortés, would have been one of the first to die.
4. Cortés, ibid., p. 82.
5. Francisco López de Gómara, *Cortés: The Life of the Conqueror by His Secretary*, ed. and tr. Lesley Byrd Simpson (Berkeley, Los Angeles, London: University of California Press, 1964) pp. 137-138.
6. William H. Prescott, *The Conquest of Mexico*, Vol. II, (Philadelphia: J. P. Lippincott, 1908) p. 303.
7. Bernal Díaz del Castillo, *The Discovery and Conquest of New Spain* (New York: Ferrar, Straus, and Cudahy, 1956) pp. 303-304.
8. Mexican cotton armour was quilted and soaked in salt brine to make it dense and very effective. Most of the Spanish rank and file eagerly adopted it. It was reputed to stop a stout crossbow bolt at relatively close ranges.
9. Francisco de Aguilar, 'The Chronicle of Fray Fran cisco de Aguilar,' ed. and tr. Patricia de Fuentes, *The Conquistadors: First-person Accounts of the Conquest of Mexico* (Norman and London: University of Okla homa Press, 1993) p. 140
10. Gómara, ibid., pp. 214-215.
11. Gómara, ibid., p. 216.
12. Durán, ibid., pp. 304-305.
13. Thomas, ibid., pp. 409-410.
14. Prescott, Vol. II, ibid., p. 350.
15. Thomas, ibid., p. 410.
16. Prescott, Vol. II, ibid., p. 355.
17. Díaz, ibid., p. 320. Díaz cites the number of more than 860 Spanish and 1,000 Tlaxcallan dead. Thomas, ibid., pp. 734-735; Juan de Cano who was also present cites 1,170 dead. Gómara, ibid., p. 221; Gómara gives a figure of 450, probably based on Cortés' testimony. Most of the rest of the Spanish accounts give figures that vary around 300. Gómara also claims 4,000 Tlaxcallans died as well.
    Considering that Cortés returned with 1,300 Spaniards to Tenochtitlan, according to Díaz, to join the perhaps 120 men under Alvarado, he had at least 1420 Spaniards when the severest fighting began. Apparently he returned to Tlaxcallan with fewer than 400 men. The figure of at least 1,000 Spaniards killed on La Noche Triste is likely. As many as 200 more Spaniards and over 1,200 Tlaxcallans may have been killed in other places at the order of Cuitláhuac.
18. Thomas, ibid., pp. 425, 736 n. 28.
19. *The Chronicles of Michoacán*, eds. and trs. Eugene R. Craine and Reginald C. Reindorp (Norman: Univer sity of Oklahoma Press, 1970) p. 65.
20. Díaz, ibid., pp. 321, 328 ; Cortés, pp. 184, n. 14 p. 484.
21. Fray Bernadino de Sahagún, *General History of the Things of New Spain (The Florentine Codex)* Book 12, *The Conquest of Mexico* (Santa Fe, NM: The School of American Research and the University of Utah, 1975) p. 83.
22. Thomas, ibid., p. 451.
23. Codex Ramírez, *Relación del origen de los Indios habi tan esta Nueva España según sus historias*, 145, cited in Thomas, ibid., p. 401.
24. Díaz, ibid., p. 328.
25. Cortés, ibid., p. 199.
26. Cortés, ibid., p. 200; Díaz, ibid., p. 381.
27. Gómara, ibid., p. 260.
28. Durán, ibid., p. 310.
29. Thomas, ibid., p. 486.
30. Durán, ibid., p. 312. It is interesting that Durán paints such a picture of 'invincible determination' while Spanish sources such as Gómara, ibid., p. 265, and Díaz, ibid., give exactly the opposite pic ture. They portray Cuauhtémoc, as preferring peace at the onset of the siege and pressured into resis tance by his ferocious councillors and captains. I find Durán's account to be much more in character with the Cuauhtémoc who led his men in the

assaults on the Palace of Axayácatl, who taunted Motecuhzoma for his foolish cowardice in being duped by the Spaniards, and who refused even to respond to every one of Cortés' offers of negotiation. The Spanish accounts seem more an after the fact justification of their own conduct.

31. Gómara, ibid., p. 266.

32. Gómara, ibid., p. 272.

33. Gómara, ibid., p. 275.

34. Sahagún, Book 12, ibid., pp. 95-97.

35. Sahagún, Book 12, ibid., p. 99; Durán, ibid., pp. 313-314; Cortés, ibid., pp. 233-234; Díaz, ibid., pp. 419-421. The accounts of this action vary consider ably. Sahagún claims 15 captured Spaniards, Durán 40, Cortés three to four, and Díaz five. Interestingly Durán states that the Mexica had carefully con structed a false bridge to resemble the fill the enemy had left the day before in the causeway breach and pulled it apart as the rear of the enemy column charged across. However, Durán's informants hope lessly confuse this engagement with the later disas ter that claimed more than 50 Spanish lives and even places here Alvarado's leap which actually took place a year before on La Noche Triste!

36. Sahagún, Book 12, ibid., p. 91; *Anales de Tlatelolco*, in Leon-Portilla, *The Broken Spears* (Boston: Beacon Press, 1992) p. 134; Thomas, ibid., p. 509.

37. Tezozomoc, *Crónica Mexicana*; in Thomas, ibid., p. 506.

38. Sahagún, Book 12, ibid., p. 117.

39. Sahagún, Book 12, ibid., p. 118.

40. Cortés, ibid., pp. 261-262.

41. Prescott, Vol III, ibid., p. 189.

42. Durán, ibid., p. 316.

43. Prescott, Vol. III, ibid., p. 195.

44. Gómara, ibid., p. 339.

45. Prescott, Vol. III, ibid., p. 272. Díaz was no friend of Cortés and could be expected to give the version that did not necessarily flatter the great Conquistador. Miguel León-Portilla, *Pre-Columbian Literatures of Mexico* (Norman and London: University of Oklahoma Press, 1986) pp. 168-169. A Mayan account of the conquest specifically states that Cuauhtémoc actively encouraged the local Maya king, Paxbolon-achá, to join with him to wipe out the Spaniards, but he promptly reported this to Cortés.

46. Prescott, Vol. III, ibid., pp. 272-273. Gómara, ibid., p. 356. Gómara largely repeats Cortés' story but does not fail to condemn his actions, arguing that 'Cortés, indeed, should have preserved his life as a precious jewel, for Cuauhtémoc was the triumph and glory of his victories'; but Cortés did not want to keep him alive in such a troubled land and time.

BIBLIOGRAPHY

Anawalt, Patricia Rieff, 'Riddle of the Emperor's Cloak', *Archaeology*, May/June 1993.

Berrin, Kathleen and Esther Pasztory, eds, *Teotihuacan: Art From the City of the Gods*, Thames and Hudson, London, 1993.

Carlson, John B., 'Rise and Fall of the City of the Gods', *Archaeology*, November/December 1993.

Clendinnen, Inga, *Aztec: An Interpretation*, Cambridge: Cambridge University Press, 1991.

Coe, Michael D., *The Maya*, 5th ed. London: Thames and Hudson, 1993.

——, *Mexico: From the Olmecs to the Aztecs*, London: Thames and Hudson, 1994.

Conrad, Geoffrey W. and Arthur A. Demerest, *Religion and Empire: The Dynamics of Aztec and Inca Expansion,* Cambridge: Cambridge University Press, 1984.

Cortés, Hernan, *Letters From Mexico*, tr. Anthony Pagden, New Haven and London: Yale University Press, 1986.

Craine, Eugene R. and Reginald, Reindorp, eds and trs. *The Chronicles of Michoacán*, Norman: University of Oklahoma Press, 1970.

Day, Jane S., *Aztec: The World of Moctezuma*, Denver: Denver Museum of Natural History and Roberts Rinehart Publishers, 1992.

Davies, Nigel, *The Ancient Kingdoms of Mexico*, New York: Penguin Books, 1982.

——, *The Aztecs*, Norman and London: Oklahoma University Press, 1989.

——, *The Toltec Heritage*, Norman and London: Oklahoma University Press, 1980.

——, *The Toltecs Until the Fall of Tula*, Norman and London: Oklahoma University Press, 1987.

Demarest, Arthur A. 'Violent Saga of a Maya Kingdom', *National Geographic*, Vol. 183, No. 2, February 1993.

Díaz del Castillo, Bernal, *The Discovery and Conquest of Mexico*, New York: Farrar, Straus and Cudahy, 1956.

Durán, Fray Diego, *The Aztecs: The History of the Indies and of New Spain*, tr. Doris Heyden and Fernando Horcasitas, New York: Orion Press, 1964.

Fagan, Brian M., *Kingdoms of Gold, Kindgoms of Jade: The Americas Before Columbus*, London: Thames and Hudson, 1991.

Freidel, David, Linda Schele, Joy Parker. *The Maya Cosmos: Three Thousand Years on the Shaman's Path*, New York: William Morrow and Company, 1993.

Fuentes, Patricia de, ed. *The Conquistadors: First-Person Accounts of the Conquest of Mexico*, Norman and London: University of Oklahoma Press, 1993.

Gillmor, Frances, *Flute of the Smoking Mirror: A Portrait of Nezahualcoyotl Poet-King of the Aztecs*, Tuscon: University of Arizona Press, 1968.

——, *The King Danced in the Marketplace*, Tuscon: University of Arizona Press, 1964.

Gruzinski, Serge, *Painting the Conquest: The Mexican Indians and the European Renaissance*, Paris: Flammarion, 1992.

Hassig, Ron, *Aztec Warfare: Imperial Expansion and Political Control*, Norman and London: University of Oklahoma Press, 1988.

——, *Mexico and the Spanish Conquest*, London and New York: Longman, 1994.

Klandell, Jonathan, *La Capital: The Biography of Mexico City*, New York: Henry Holt and Company, 1988.

Landa, Fray Diego de, *Yucatan Before and After the Conquest*, tr. William Gates, New York: Dover Publications, Inc., 1978.

León-Portilla, Miguel, *Aztec Thought and Culture*, tr. Jack Emory Davis, Norman and London: University of Oklahoma Press, 1990.

——, *The Broken Spears: The Aztec Account of*

the Conquest of Mexico, Boston: Beacon Press, 1992.

—-, *Pre-Columbian Literatures of Mexico*, Norman and London: University of Oklahoma Press, 1986.

López de Gómara, Francisco, *Cortés: The Life of the Conqueror by His Secretary*, tr. Lesley Byrd Simpson, Berkeley: University of California Press, 1964.

Matos Moctezuma, Eduardo, *The Great Temple of the Aztecs: Treasures of Tenochtitlan*, London: Thames and Hudson, 1988.

—-, *Life and Death in the Templo Mayor*, tr. Bernard R. Ortiz de Montellano, Niwot, CO: University of Colorado Press, 1995.

Markman, Roberta H. and Peter T. Markman, *The Flayed God: The Mythology of Mesoamerica*, San Francisco: Harpers, 1992.

Michel, Genevieve, *The Rulers of Tikal: A Historical Reconstruction and Field Guide to the Stelae*, Guatemala: Publicaciones Vista, 1991.

Miller, Mary, 'Maya Masterpiece Revealed at Bonampak', *National Geographic*, February 1995.

Nicholson, H. B., *The Art of Ancient Mexico: Treasures of Tenochtitlan*, Washington: National Gallery of Art, 1983.

Nicholson, Irene, *Mexican and Central American Mythology*, London: Paul Hamlyn Ltd, 1967.

Pohl, John M. D. and Angus McBride, *Aztec, Mixtec and Sapotec Armies*, London: Osprey Publishing Ltd., 1991

Prescott, William H., *The History of the Conquest of Mexico*, 3 vols, Philadelphia: J. B. Lippincott, 1873.

—-, *The Conquest of Mexico*, 2 vols., Illustrations by Keith Henderson, London: Chatto and Windus, 1922.

Sabloff, Jeremy A., *The Cities of Ancient Mexico: Reconstructing a Lost World*, London: Thames and Hudson, 1994.

Sahagún, Fray Bernadine de, *A General History of the Things of New Spain (The Florentine Codex)*, Santa Fe, NM: The School of American Research and The University of Utah, 1979.

Schele, Linda and David Freidel, *The Blood of Kings: Dynasty and Ritual in Maya Art*, London: Sotheby's Publications, 1986.

—-, *A Forest of Kings*, New York: William Morrow, 1990.

Soustelle, Jacques, *Daily Life of the Aztecs On the Eve of the Spanish Conquest*, Stanford: Stanford University Press, 1970.

Stuart, George E., 'Maya Heartland Under Siege', *National Geographic*, Vol. 182, No. 5, November 1992.

—-, 'Mural Masterpieces of Ancient Cacaxtla', *National Geographic*, Vol. 182, No. 3, September 1992.

Stuart, Gene S., *The Mighty Aztecs*, Washington, DC: The National Geographic Society, 1981.

Thomas, Hugh, *Conquest: Montezuma, Cortés, and the Fall of Mexico*, New York: Simon and Schuster, 1993.

Townsend, Richard, *The Aztecs*, London: Thames and Hudson, 1993.

Wilkerson, S. Jeffery K., 'Following the Route of Cortés', *National Geographic*, Vol. 166, No. 4, October 1984.

Wise, Terrence and Angus McBride, *The Conquistadores*, London: Osprey Publishing Ltd, 1992.

INDEX

ILLUSTRATION CREDITS

Patricia F. Tsouras, for her patient, good advice and the superb execution of the maps on pages: 16, 25, 53, 64, 99, 114, 123, 152, 164, 171, 205.

The estate of the late Keith Henderson and his publisher, Chatto & Windus, for their assistance in providing the illustrations on pages: 16, 21, 65, 91, 93 (upper left and upper right), 105, 112–113, 125 (upper/lower), 130, 132, 140, 141, 146, 148, 151, 155 (upper/lower), 156, 157, 160, 161, 162–163, 165, 166, 168, 174–175, 181, 183, 184, 187, 190–191, 199, 210–211, 216–217, 218–219, 220–221, 224–225, 226.

Mr. Scott Gentling, for his generous donation of the illustrations on pages: 28 (upper), 36, 37, 40, 41, 42–43, 44–45, 46, 47, 48 (upper/lower), 55, 78, 116, 126, 129, 150, 207.

Mr. Stuart Gentling for the kind use of his drawing of the map of the city plan of Mexico-Tenochtitlan from which the illustrations on pages 164 and 205 were made.

Peabody Museum, Harvard University, pages: 23, 27, 33 (upper and lower – watercolour copies by Antonio Tejeda, 1948), 34 and 35 (watercolour copy by Adela C. Breton, 1904-6).

The University Museum, University of Pennsylvania, pages: 10 (upper), 14, 68.

From the *Florentine Codex* published by the School of American Research and the University of Utah Press, pages: 86, 87, 100, 109, 167, 170, 172, 188, 189, 192, 193, 195, 196, 208, 209, 212, 213, 214.

The National Geographic Society, pages: 38–39 (Felipe Davalos / National Geographic Society Collection).

The Library of Congress, pages: 10–11 (upper), 12, 26, 27 (right), 28, 29 (lower), 31, 50, 58, 63, 75, 110, 135, 139, 158, 173, 186, 201, 228.

Author, pages: 9 (after Freidel and Schele), 13 (after Graham), 18, 24 (after Lothrop), 49 (after Franco), 57 (after Franco), 77, 84 (after Gillmor), 85 (after Franco), 90, 92 (after *Codex Mendoza*), 93 (lower – after *Codex Mendoza*), 94 (after Franco), 102 (after *Codex Mendoza*), 107 (after Franco), 108 (after Franco), 118 (after Franco), 121 (after Franco), 179, 185 (after Franco), 194 (after Pohl and *Lienzo de Tlaxcalla*), 197 (after Franco).